WISDOM AS
A WAY OF LIFE

WISDOM AS A WAY OF LIFE

THERAVĀDA BUDDHISM REIMAGINED

STEVEN COLLINS

EDITED BY JUSTIN MCDANIEL

PREFACE BY DAN ARNOLD

AFTERWORD BY CHARLES HALLISEY

Columbia University Press *New York*

COLUMBIA
UNIVERSITY
PRESS

Columbia University Press gratefully acknowledges the generous support for this book provided by a Publisher's Circle member.

Columbia University Press
Publishers Since 1893
New York Chichester, West Sussex
cup.columbia.edu

Library of Congress Cataloging-in-Publication Data
Names: Collins, Steven, 1951–2018, author. | McDaniel, Justin, editor.
Title: Wisdom as a way of life : Theravāda Buddhism reimagined / Steven Collins ; edited by Justin McDaniel ; preface by Dan Arnold ; afterword by Charles Hallisey.
Description: New York : Columbia University Press, 2020. | Includes index.
Identifiers: LCCN 2019049701 (print) | LCCN 2019049702 (ebook) | ISBN 9780231197205 (cloth) | ISBN 9780231197212 (paperback) | ISBN 9780231552042 (ebook)
Subjects: LCSH: Buddhist philosophy. | Theravāda Buddhism. | Anātman. | Self (Philosophy)
Classification: LCC B162 .C65 2020 (print) | LCC B162 (ebook) | DDC 294.3/91—dc23
LC record available at https://lccn.loc.gov/2019049701
LC ebook record available at https://lccn.loc.gov/2019049702

Cover design: Milenda Nan Ok Lee
Cover image: Photo by Justin McDaniel

CONTENTS

PREFACE

DAN ARNOLD

This book represents the last contribution to Buddhist studies and to the intellectual histories of civilizations by Steven Collins (1951–2018). Steve had finished a complete first draft only a few months before his untimely death in February 2018 and had gone as far as to circulate the manuscript among a number of close colleagues and friends. Among those who would have first seen the complete draft was this book's editor, Justin McDaniel, who had already started profusely commenting on the manuscript before it fell to him to facilitate its posthumous publication. Steve knew his manuscript needed revision, but he was already confident in thinking it would be generatively provocative, and also in announcing it as his last scholarly contribution. (Steve's untimely death is all the more poignant given how greatly he was looking forward to a retirement spent reading novels and rereading Western philosophers, not to mention spending time with his grandchildren.)

A world-renowned scholar of the Pāli Buddhist traditions of South and Southeast Asia, Steven Collins was at the time of his death the Chester D. Tripp Professor in the Humanities in the Department of South Asian Languages and Civilizations and in the Divinity School at the University of Chicago, where he spent almost three decades of his influential career. As suggested by Charles Hallisey's afterword to the present book, the distinctive scholarly contributions Steve made over the course of his career find their fullest expression in a triptych of books, of which this is the third. The first, rewritten from a 1979 Oxford doctoral thesis, was published by Cambridge University Press as *Selfless Persons: Imagery and Thought in* Theravāda *Buddhism* in 1982, almost a decade before Steve's 1991 appointment at the University of Chicago. (Prior to coming to Chicago, he had taught at Indiana University and Concordia University.) Given the particular importance that *Selfless Persons* had for me, I am inclined to begin situating the present volume by saying a few words about Steve's first book, and about the history of my acquaintance with its highly accomplished author.

Selfless Persons first came across my radar screen some ten years after its publication, at around the same time that Daniel Dennett's *Consciousness Explained* was published (1991). For me, that was toward the end of a desultory and ultimately abortive stint as a graduate student at Columbia University, and my simultaneous discovery of these two books was galvanizing; taken together, they helped me realize that it was not history but *philosophy* that really interested me. I left Columbia and spent some five years working at Denver's Tattered Cover Bookstore, where I had the mental space to do some significant intellectual retooling; an inordinate percentage of my pay went for books in Buddhist and modern Western philosophy. My early karmic connection with Steve's work was maintained in those years by part-time work toward a master's degree at the Iliff School of Theology, where I worked not only with José Cabézon (whom I knew from his teaching at Carleton College my junior year) but also with Paul Griffiths, who taught a course at Iliff during the summer of 1993. Paul, it turned out, had among his colleagues at the University of Chicago none other than Steven Collins, and it was therefore natural that my intellectual retooling should unfold in tandem with the thought that I ought perhaps to study in the University of Chicago Divinity School's program in Philosophy of Religions.

So when I came to scout Chicago's program a year before my matriculation there in 1997, I was particularly eager to meet Steve, whose *Selfless Persons* had played so central a role in facilitating my recent process of intellectual discernment. I'll never forget our first meeting. By then resolved to undertake doctoral studies in Buddhist philosophy, I was of course eager to talk about the philosophical aspects of *Selfless Persons* and how its august author might figure in my studies at Chicago; I was thus rather taken aback when, early in our interview, Steve emphatically disavowed any philosophical interests. *Selfless Persons*, he allowed, had some philosophical dimensions, but he said he had decided that studying Indian Buddhist philosophy was just too hard. Doing a good job of it, he said, required knowing the Brahmanical Mīmāṃsā school of thought *backward and forward.* It required knowing Nyāya *backward and forward.* It required knowing Vedānta *backward and forward.* As he continued thus enumerating Indian traditions of thought integral to the understanding of Buddhist philosophy, each emphatic repetition of the adverbial phrase seemed a lash that flayed my fledgling philosophical aspirations.

While I felt rather reduced by the experience, my first meeting with Steve was much redeemed by the fact that the eminent English scholar positively lit up when, in concluding our conversation, I admired the spiffy Miles Davis T-shirt he was sporting. In the many subsequent years of our relationship—especially 2004–2018, the years we were colleagues at the University of Chicago—I would come to know Steve well, and to understand that his initially disheartening emphasis on how much work my proposed course of study demanded would not at all have been meant to dominate or intimidate me, or in any other way to exercise teacherly power. Steve's emphatic enumeration of the requirements for doing a good job of studying Indian Buddhist philosophy reflected, rather, his own uncompromising rigor in pursuing intellectually serious questions, which he always approached with humility.

These, surely, were among the intellectual virtues evident to all who had the chance to experience Steve's attentively engaged presence at lectures and seminars and the like, where he was almost invariably the one who asked the most incisive questions—questions that cut to the heart of the matter and brought sharply into focus for everyone present the intellectual stakes of whatever was at issue. Humility and incisiveness alike were evident in Steve's uncommon willingness to allow, for example, that he just didn't understand what someone was saying; as often as not, this brought into view that the speaker hadn't really understood what he or she really meant, either.

Although I thus came to appreciate that it was mostly his own exacting standards that led Steve to disavow having any philosophical acumen, I have persisted in believing that he was, nonetheless, every bit a philosophical thinker. Steve's work in the intellectual history of Theravāda civilizations invariably exhibits a rigorous concern for conceptual clarity and precision, and to identify something intellectually basic in connection with whatever is the topic. His work thus exemplifies not only intellectual history but also, more fundamentally, an interest in theorizing the ways something like *civilizational knowledge* circulates. This is evident in Steve's own characterization (in 1982) of the project *Selfless Persons*: "my main interest," he wrote then, "is philosophical."

Selfless Persons was pitched largely as an intervention in philosophy—"contemporary," to be precise, and "particularly in the English-language tradition." The problem with philosophy, Steve thought, is that it "suffers from a lack of historical and social self-awareness," so *Selfless Persons* aimed to show that philosophy "should not proceed in abstraction from intellectual history and anthropology, from the investigation and comparison of cultures."[1] From the beginning, one could say, Steve was concerned to make the understanding of civilizations somehow basic for the study of philosophy.

This is evident in the precise significance of the subtitle of *Selfless Persons*, which announces two analytic categories that it is the business of the book to theorize: *imagery* and *thought* in Theravāda Buddhism. Thought is here paradigmatically exemplified by the Abhidhamma literature's scholastic systematization and analyses of all the many categories mentioned in teachings attributed to the Buddha. All these categories arguably relate, directly or indirectly, to the Buddhist tradition's orienting claim, expressed in the title *Selfless Persons*—the "no-self doctrine" (*anattavāda*), which can be understood as the doctrine that persons are not individuated by anything worth the name "selves." To the extent, then, that thought is epitomized by the Abhidhamma literature's systematic exposition, we can say that "thought," for Theravāda Buddhists, constitutively involves a synchronic conception of the selflessness of persons: a snapshot, as it were, of all the kinds of impersonal factors that can enter into the occurrence or description of any action or event—a snapshot, that is, of *the truths discovered by the Buddha*—considered in an instant.

As against Abhidhamma's synchronic conception of the complete Buddhist account of the no-self doctrine, "imagery" here particularly means narrative imagery, and so mostly refers to what all of Steve's work really engages: texts—stories or plays derived from the *Jātaka* literature, for example, that dramatize and aestheticize the truths theorized in "thought," variously narrating the difference it makes that persons do not have selves. It is thus a chief aim of *Selfless Persons* to theorize "thought" and "imagery" as conceptually distinct analytic categories—as Steve would later emphasize, as modes of discourse most significantly distinguished by their essentially different temporalities. Thus, while thought represents Buddhist doctrine as a timelessly complete system of mutually relating truths, imagery, as narrative, is constitutively diachronic in its relations—essentially concerned with the narrative sequence in which the narrated events make sense as the kinds of events they are.

In addition to presenting what is widely acknowledged as a definitive treatment of the no-self doctrine as understood in the world of Pāli Buddhism, *Selfless Persons* is thus animated by a concern to theorize these differing discursive modalities as both necessary for the circulation of "Theravāda Buddhism." The latter here serves as an instance of civilizational knowledge, and it is a conceptually basic concern to theorize the chief unifying feature of the triptych now completed by the present book. The second of these—*Nirvana and Other Buddhist Felicities* (Cambridge University Press, 1998)—eschews the 1982 book's reference to philosophy, explicitly theorizing systematic and narrative modes of thought as both integral to civilizational thought worlds. Now the basic unit of analysis is akin to what some historians of the *Annales* school of thought refer to as *mentalités*: "mental outlooks as expressed in discourse and artifacts," according to Steve's own gloss of the concept, comprising all manner of things (fables, songs, statuary, philosophy, etiquette) that, as *Annales* historian Marc LeGoff emphasizes, "were not produced to serve as historical documents, but are a historical reality unto themselves."[2] Adopting the comparable idea of an *imaginaire* (another term favored by *Annales* historians), Steve's second book proposes an alternate conception of what he had earlier called "Theravāda Buddhism"; *Nirvana and Other Buddhist Felicities* are now to be understood, the book's subtitle tells us, as "*Utopias*," rather, of "*the Pali Imaginaire*."

Considering an *imaginaire* as necessarily comprising both systematic and narrative modes of thought, Steve's second book correlates the Abhidhamma literature's synchronic conception of doctrine with the kind of closure and ultimate felicity thought to result from the ideal renunciant's quest. Examining Nirvana (to quote the title of part I) "in and out of time," Steve can then theorize narrative thought as essentially concerned somehow to resolve tensions between that ideal and the ongoing demands of life and society. By variously performing that dramatic conflict, narrative thought can at once valorize a Buddhist ideal and acknowledge the virtual impossibility of its achievement. According to Steve, such distinct representations of Nirvana and other Buddhist felicities are both integral to the Pāli imaginaire. The fact that the trope of nirvana is often narrated in ways seemingly at odds with the tradition's systematic conceptions of it can be understood not as a contradiction to be explained, but rather as reflecting the many and various ways in which an idea central to the whole Pali imaginaire is (to be sure) *theorized* therein, but also *reckoned with*—performed, wondered at, venerated, exalted, exemplified, etc.

Here in *Wisdom as a Way of Life*, the basic distinction between systematic and narrative thought remains central. Narrative thought is theorized not only as involving a temporality distinct from that of synchronic conceptions of doctrine but also as necessarily involving what narrative theorists call "actants"—any of various narrative roles or functions that might be filled by one or more characters or other entities in a story. (The enumeration of a narrative event's actants might be thought analogous to the Sanskrit grammatical tradition's enumeration of *kārakas*, which are proposed as indicating all the ways any number of nouns can be related to a verb; actants, like *kārakas*, might thus be taken as variously denoting things like the agents, means, and locations of actions.) The generative tension that Steve sees at the heart of the Pāli imaginaire can thus be expressed in terms of the fact that according to the ultimate truth (*paramattha sacca*) as systematically theorized in Buddhist traditions, there *are* no real actants—but insofar as actants must nonetheless figure in any *story* of Buddhist achievements, an intractable tension between systematic and narrative conceptions of the tradition's ideals is, inexorably, integral.

In addition, the present book introduces new conceptual tools that had figured prominently in Steve's thought and conversations over the last decade or so. By the untimely end of his life, Steve had for many years been interested in what he calls "practices of the self," an idea informed by Michel Foucault's theorization of "technologies of the self" and by Pierre Hadot on philosophy as "a way of life." Consistently with the overarching concerns of the first two books in his triptych, Steve had become interested in the difference it makes to appreciate that the traditionally disciplined study of Buddhist philosophy was itself a practice, ultimately aimed at fundamentally transforming the practitioners thereof. Insofar as the ideal subjects of Theravāda Buddhist practice thus aim to constitute themselves as particular kinds of persons, the tradition's systematic conceptions of ultimate truth are never fully intelligible apart from narrations of the renunciant lifestyle that structures the whole tradition.

Among Steve's thoughts, surely, was not only that the Pāli Buddhist imaginaire thus readily admits of analysis in terms suggested by Foucault and Hadot but also that attention to the Pāli imaginaire's own presentations of its practices of the self might enrich other analyses deriving from Foucault and Hadot. Toward that end, Steve had for several years been planning to co-teach a seminar on practices of the self with two University of Chicago colleagues uniquely qualified to join him in this: Arnold Davidson, who has for years been lecturing to full houses on Foucault's *Hermeneutics of the Subject* (not to mention having edited and introduced Hadot's *Philosophy as a Way of Life*), and Margaret Mitchell, a scholar of the New Testament and early Christianity interested in the cenobitic communities of third- and fourth-century Egypt. Unfortunately, the seminar Steve and his colleagues envisaged will never be taught, at least not with Steve's involvement.

It is fortunate that Steve had before his death completed a manuscript of what he already took to be his last contribution to scholarship. The present book represents an edition of that work by Justin McDaniel, whose editor's introduction explains the kinds of judgments that remained to be made about the manuscript, as well as other aspects of his approach to the project. Justin was long a favorite interlocutor of Steve's, and his own work on Theravāda traditions of Thailand gives him a unique perspective on the agenda and presuppositions of this book, his edition of which was a labor of love that is worthy of thanks and praise. Justin consulted with Steve's wife, Claude Grangier, who had read Steve's manuscript and discussed it with him much. Publication of this book could not, of course, have gone forward without Claude's blessing, and she is to be thanked for her commitment to seeing the project through to the end. Thanks are due, as well, to Charles Hallisey, whose friendship Steve long appreciated for (among other things) all the ways it challenged him to clarify his thinking; Charlie's afterword is an invaluable guide to reading this book as consistent with the two major books that preceded it.

That *Wisdom as a Way of Life* exists, then, is thanks to the efforts and good will of all three of these people, who were in various ways among those dearest to Steve. Thanks are due, as well, to Columbia University Press's Wendy Lochner, who was enthusiastic about this book from the time she first read Steve's manuscript. Given the outstanding list of titles in Buddhist studies that Wendy has seen to publication over the years, it is fitting that Steven Collins's last contribution to the field should be published with the imprimatur of her editorial judgment. To invoke a gesture typical not of Theravāda but of Mahāyāna Buddhist traditions, it would be a good thing for a world badly in need of it if all the merit accrued in bringing this book to publication were dedicated to the welfare of all sentient beings.

EDITOR'S INTRODUCTION

JUSTIN THOMAS MCDANIEL

Steve Collins and I were sitting at a bar in Chiang Mai, Thailand, in 2015. We had stolen away for a few moments from a group of fifteen scholars from Europe, Asia, and North America who had come to Chiang Mai to participate in a workshop called the "Theravāda Civilizations Project." Steve had launched this project about eight years earlier with Juliane Schober (Arizona State University). This was Steve's late-in-life inspiration. He wanted to create an intellectual organization that had a small core of members engaged in historical, anthropological, linguistic, material cultural, and philosophical research on Theravāda Buddhism. These few members would provide free online resources, organize conferences and roundtables, publish articles, and reach out to a wide variety of younger or more highly specialized scholars who were working on related projects. He wanted to build a community, a resource, and systematize the study of Theravāda. He rightly saw that the study of Theravāda was less prominent in the academy and in classrooms than the study of Tibetan, Japanese, and Chinese Buddhism.[1] He wanted our scholars of Buddhist studies to have a seat at the table.

In that bar, we discussed all and sundry, as we often did over gin or bourbon. We laughed about our children, lamented our relationships with our fathers, and congratulated ourselves for having spouses who put up with us. This conversation was the first time I had heard about his writing of the book I am editing now. Steve had published many articles and four books in his career. However, like most scholars, he had also abandoned a number of projects started over the years. In previous conversations I had heard about books he had planned on "Mania and Buddhism," "Time in a Theravāda Monastery," and the ascetic motivation of nuns ("professional female monastics" as he liked to say), among many others. I should have taken his description of this present book more seriously while he was explaining it, but unfortunately, I forgot most of that conversation. I remember thinking, though, *Well, that seems interesting, but do we really need a book on Foucault and Buddhism?* What saddens me now is that I might have missed an opportunity to ask tougher questions, to hear more details about his plans, to learn something valuable. What I do remember is that he was troubled by this project. He saw it as his last major book and wanted to provide more guidance on how to study Theravāda Buddhism (and Buddhism more broadly) and less new research or new translations. He was sixty, starting to think about retirement, a little concerned about his health, and wanted to offer future students and younger scholars something to help them find their place in the field and reflect upon why we should study Buddhism.

A little less than four years later, I regret not asking more questions about his plans for this book, as I am now the editor of it, and Steve is sadly one of the departed. I miss him. It fills me with great sadness that he can't be the one here today introducing his last book. The task of editing it has been unsettling; I feel like I am sitting in stale repose at the end of a slow divorce. The process has been both liberating and devastating. I fear that all attempts to provide Steve's last book with architecture and a vocabulary will be effete. What I most want to get across is that Steve, as he states in the second section, was concerned ultimately with writing about "ordinary Buddhists going about their business with care." Steve cared about people, and he deeply respected those who took deep care in how they conducted their lives. I want to care for his words and his intentions in this book, as I believe he was a true gift to our time and our field. I will attempt to explain my process and my choices below and in the endnotes.

Steve Collins was (and will continue to be) an unsettling force in my life. Surprisingly, we were not personally very close. I wish now that I knew more about Steve's favorite albums (Steve was a huge jazz fan, and he talked about it with my son, also a jazz fan), his favorite philosophers (I don't know the difference between Hume and Spinoza), or his favorite foods (I don't even know if he was a tea or a coffee guy, or a scotch or a bourbon guy, really). I realize now how little I knew about his daily life. We talked about children a good amount (he wanted me to have three, and I wondered why I stopped at two) and horse racing occasionally (we both had fathers who liked to gamble), but usually the chitchat didn't last long—he wanted to get back to work and push me. Although never my official advisor, he was like a thief in the attic of my mind, moving boxes around, rifling through old memories, looking for heirlooms, and uncovering thoughts long neglected. He made me think about things I wanted to avoid, whether my childhood or big questions about culture, gender, and identity. I liked to stick to the facts, the texts, field notes, and he pushed me into the realms of reflection, interpretation, speculation, and theory. When I wanted to remain Irish and low to the ground, fingernails dirty with dark soil, only asking questions that started with "how" or "what," he forced me to be a little more French—regard the macrocosm—to ask why, where to, what next? He was never my friend; I had friends; friends agreed with me, friends were impressed I could pay my rent, friends let me drink too much. He was that person you didn't want to see, because he forced you to sober up and take difficult concepts and uncomfortable emotions seriously. He provided me with a sense of urgency, a sense that writing, students, and books were to be treasured and taught. Steve was unsettling, unnerving to me, because he was unpredictable; he threw me off balance with biting criticism that seemed to be unfair, but that I would later realize was totally right. He seemed at times to have the diligence born of desperation and other times the effortless wisdom born of a life of quiet repose. He had the patience of a sage and the rash temperament of a teenager. There was no fixed hierarchy of his interests and no desire to make those around him comfortable. He was like a living koan with a smile that was both warm and ironic. I could never quite tell if he was laughing at me or with me.

I remember one time, we were in Bangkok interviewing a prominent scholar nun. He was asking questions and I was translating them into Thai. He kept pushing me to ask questions that I thought would make her uncomfortable. I tried to be subtle and to soften the tenor of his directness. He couldn't understand what the nun and I were saying, but he seemed to know that I was avoiding the questions about power and gender that he was raising. He glared at me, and I realized that he was teaching me something about the difference between learning and research—the difference between reading and digging. I was happy to keep everyone smiling and friendly; he was there to wake us up and remind us that life wasn't something to be accepted, but interrogated. I respectfully asked the nun if I could ask her some perhaps impolite and improper questions, and she smiled and said in Thai—"It's about time; now let's get real. That is why I am a nun, after all—to get to the real" ("Chai laeo, wela ni, rao kuan put gaeo gup sing thi samkhan. Ni ben chiwit lae . . . chiwit kong maechi ben chiwit tae tae"). I went from being in control to being caught between not one, but two disapproving teachers. Steve couldn't just make me uncomfortable, he could make me uncomfortable by proxy. This is perhaps why his death has struck a blow to me of a kind I haven't felt in a long while: it touched in me something that I thought I had lost. I feel unsure about everything now—what I am doing, where I am going. I just know that I feel more than ever that life is not something to be accepted or gotten through, but cherished and spoken back to—something questioned, insulted, and wrestled to the ground. Steve didn't make my life easy, but he made it seem worth something. I miss Steve. I miss being pushed, I miss being rebuked and driven. I miss being inspired and unsettled. Steve was a presence that haunted me in life. Now, more than ever, I am glad I believe in ghosts.[2]

This book is in many ways a ghost that has haunted me since he passed in February 2018. He sent me and several other members of the aforementioned Theravāda Civilizations Project the draft of the book and two email messages about a month before he passed away while giving lectures in New Zealand. Steve's closest colleagues were excited by this email on January 16, 2018, twenty-nine days before he passed away suddenly:

Friends,

I am writing (to lots of people) to ask if you would be interested in reading the ms. of a book I have just finished, in draft form, and sending me your comments, major or minor. I have attached a title page and Contents, which will give you an idea of what it's about. It is very ambitious and wide-ranging—perhaps too much so. I like to think it's also original. I imagine that, if published, it will shake a lot of people up, for good or for ill.

I know everyone is busy, and I won't be in any way offended if you don't have time or interest to do this. If you don't just don't bother to answer this email.

Best wishes for 2018,
Steve

I wrote him back immediately, stating that I was excited to read the full manuscript. I had been drifting in the horse latitudes of my mid-career period—an unhealthy mixture of post-tenure self-satisfaction and existential despair, looking at possibly three decades in front of me without scholarly motivation and intellectual inspiration. I was happy to have Steve's ideas come and kick me in my self-contemptuous ass. He sent it and simply said, "Thank you! There's no hurry. Steve" on January 17, 2018. Little did I know then that there was indeed a great hurry.

Fortunately, that wasn't the last time I communicated with him. We also chatted over email about the "Life of the Buddha" volume of articles reflecting on the impact of the various biographies of the historical Buddha historically and literarily. He was heavily involved in that edited volume, and since he passed, Anne Hansen of the University of Wisconsin at Madison and I have taken over editing the project under the guidance of Steven Berkwitz of the University of Southern Missouri. I also was in discussions with Steve about another volume he was editing on critical terms in the study of Theravāda Buddhism. That project is currently in limbo, as the contributors are still recovering from Steve's passing and unsure about which direction we want to guide the field.

I add these details to reveal the range of projects both big and small that Steve was working on in his last month, and the care he had for the community of scholars in Theravāda Buddhist studies. In that month he also announced that he was planning on retiring a couple of years early, when he turned sixty-seven, so that he could finish these last projects.

What he left behind, besides all of his family, friends, students, and colleagues, was a lifetime of thoughts on music, philosophy, and Buddhist studies. A few months after the devastating news, I traveled to Chicago to visit his wife, Claude, and his close friend and colleague, Professor Dan Arnold. Claude let me examine his notes for the book, look through the articles and books he had been consulting while writing it, and talk about all and sundry. Dan's son, Benjamin, kindly helped pack and ship many of the books to my office in Philadelphia, and besides the books by and on Foucault, Hadot, and Buddhist notions of the self, I was honored to give a few of Steve's books on the history and craft of jazz to my own son. Steve always said that a scholar should have interests far outside their field, and his was jazz. It fills me with joy to see my son read Steve's books on Wayne Shorter, Sonny Rollins, John Coltrane, Dextor Gordon, and Sun Ra.

What I could gather from Steve's notes and the draft he sent was that he was struggling a bit with the structure of the book but was very confident about the content, especially emphasizing the importance of comparative intellectual approaches to the problem of the self. The book originally had three chapters, along with a preface and a few introductory notes. I allowed myself a heavy hand with the structure, reducing the three chapters to two larger sections, but a very light hand with the tone and language. I wanted Steve's unique and often acerbic wit and style to be fully present. Steve and I are stylistically very different writers, and over the years he was often quite critical of my overly American and very colloquial and familiar approach to writing. He was a proponent of "less is more" and wrote in a very precise and deliberate way. He was fond of quoting Blaise Pascal's famous line: "I have only made this letter longer because I have not had the time to make it shorter." I am a fan of the architect Robert Venturi's motto "less is a bore." However, here I defer to my mentor. Not only did Steve want to write a short and direct book about ideas, but he also insisted that there be no footnotes to clutter the argument and distract the reader. He would have added the scholarly citations in endnotes and provided a bibliography had he not left us so suddenly. Therefore, I had to add the references for the sake of scholarly accuracy and integrity. There are endnotes to avoid clutter, and to ensure that the reader can check the primary and secondary sources. I also note in the endnotes when I made editorial choices. I tried to keep these to an absolute minimum. I largely excised the first chapter, and two sections he originally entitled "preliminary comments" and "preface," because many of the topics he brought up in them were repeated in the second and third chapters. Steve did not like repetition for emphasis. He believed that scholars should trust their readers and write things clearly once. If he had had a chance to edit his own first draft, I fully believe that he would have removed the repetitions that I did. As for the content in the first chapter, preface, and preliminary comments that is not repeated later, I will use the lion's share of this editorial introduction to discuss these points instead of providing the sections in full.

This book has two main positive, even revolutionary, contributions to the field of Buddhist studies. I say "positive" because it also has a few highly critical comments about the field that were voiced in a rather negative tone. They are not the main arguments, but I will discuss them in this introduction and include a few in the endnotes. On the positive side, Steve is here largely organizing his thoughts around what I see as the *ganthadhura* (burden of the books) and *vipassanādhura* (burden of introspection)—distinctions in the study of Theravāda Buddhism. Steve did not classify them this way in the manuscript, but he and I had conversations about this topic, and I surmise he might have organized the book loosely in this way. Basically, *ganthadhura* is book learning. It means that a person can approach the study (burden) of Buddhism through studying texts and commentaries, listening to homilies, studying with teachers directly, and the like. They also should approach it though *vipassanādhura*, meditation, practice of rituals, performing acts of empathy and compassion, contemplating ethical conundrums, and caring for the lonely, poor, and sick. There is sometimes an inaccurate understanding that a person can choose one or the other; however, traditionally, each practitioner should focus on both.

In the two major sections of this book, Steve was trying to articulate why Theravāda mattered in much larger questions in the study of Buddhism and religion more broadly. He argued that the humanities need a Buddhist perspective on how to learn (narrative wisdom) and how to act (meditation/asceticism). He saw Theravāda Buddhists as providing thousands of examples from texts and practices that promote the idea of active and engaged learning for students of philosophy and history, as well as social and ethical actors. Steve didn't value Theravāda Buddhist knowledge over knowledge coming from any other religious or wisdom tradition, but he did argue that it has a unique perspective that should be part of humanistic studies. Humanistic studies is more than just studying intellectual, social, and cultural history for the sake of knowing more. It should make you reflect about the nature of a life well lived for yourself and for others. Steve himself struggled between being a historian and a philosopher, an archivist versus an instructor, a linguist in the library and a wordsmith in the classroom, a preserver of the past or a guide for the future. This book was his struggle with his role as a scholar of Buddhism and his role as a teacher and father and mentor. He was uncomfortable with himself, and he provided a wonderful example to his students, that personal emotional and intellectual struggle meant that a person cared deeply about what they did for and with others.

Specifically, he used this distinction between engaged textual study and engaged practice to structure his book by titling one chapter "Wisdom" and the other "Practices of the Self." I will summarize both here, drawing extensively from Steve's own summaries in his original preface and preliminary remarks.

Steve's first section, entitled "Wisdom," is largely about the study of Theravāda texts and how a student should approach this study. It includes topics such as narrative literature (focused primarily on the *Jātaka* stories in Pali) versus systematic literature (direct instruction on ways of being wise), the importance of comedy and romance in Pali literature, and why there are so many animal stories in Pali (a topic close to my heart). It is, I believe, the single best guide to how to read Pali literature for students and scholars I have encountered and will become the sine qua non for my students from this point forward. As Steve so succinctly writes: "As a collection they [*Jātaka*] give voice to, and indeed I would go so far as to say they celebrate, the diversity and complexity of everyday life and its values." He explores the ways this practice of the self actually works in textual study, expression, and performance. In his 1998 magnum opus, *Nirvana and Other Buddhist Felicities* (Cambridge University Press), he first mentioned what he saw as the two ways Theravāda Buddhists express themselves in texts: through narrative and through didactic systematization. In the present book he fully explains what he means. He was dismayed by the way scholars and students often separate the study of systematic explanation of the workings of the mind, the elements of the universe, and the process of time found in texts like the seven volumes of the Abhidhamma and its commentaries from the narrative literature found in the *Jātaka* stories, many of the suttas, and the commentaries on the *Dhammapada*. He insisted that they be studied in tandem, as long as one understood their differences in style, purpose, and performance. In the preface he writes:

> There are (at least) two ways in which Narrative Thought is fundamentally different from Systematic Thought which I want to emphasize: temporality and the need in the former for what Narrative theorists call actants. Narrative theory can become extremely complex (and often unreadable). The Oxford English Dictionary (hereafter OED) defines actant simply as "Any of various narrative roles or functions which may be fulfilled by one or more characters or other entities in a text." Originally in narrative theory the word was only applied to recognizable types—hero, villain, etc.—who often appear as opposed dualities. This kind of duality appears often in the Jātakas, where wise or compassionate actants are contrasted with the foolish and malevolent. . . . Systematic Thought is expressed in static, non-temporal forms of thought and textuality. . . . That is, "Buddhism" is equated with "Buddhist Doctrine" (also, alas, as "Early Buddhist Ideas"), presented as a timeless, abstract system centered around "The Four Noble Truths" (in fact "The Four Truths of Noble Ones"), the "Five Aggregates," "Dependent Origination," and all that. Yes, that is indeed Systematic Thought worked out in simple and complex ways by some Buddhist intellectuals, and indeed connected with Practices of Self, in some forms but by no means all.
>
> Systematic thought has often been thought to be the most basic form of mental functioning, indeed in the past seen as the only form of Intelligence, the one which is tested, for example, by traditional IQ tests, which assess various cognitive skills. This

entirely ignores the more recent field of Emotional Intelligence, which is said (by Psychology Today) to refer to forms of mental capacity such as the ability to identify and manage your own emotions and the emotions of others. It is generally said to include three skills: "emotional awareness; the ability to harness emotions and apply them to tasks like thinking and problem solving; and the ability to manage emotions, which includes regulating your own emotions and cheering up or calming down other people."[3] I think that both forms of intelligence are required from the readers or the audience of the Birth Stories to make sense of what Pali texts describe as paññā and paṇḍita, translatable in a preliminary way as "wisdom" and "wise person." The capacity to understand and empathize with characters within a narrative, to see the psychological and moral complexity of their actions and relations, to feel (and I do mean feel) the kinds of ethical and practical difficulties which they face, certainly requires a significant capacity for Emotional Intelligence. . . .

This is true of the great Vessantara Jātaka, for example. Like the Rāmāyaṇa, the Odyssey, King Lear, War and Peace, and countless other examples of Literature, one can read/listen to the Vessantara Jātaka and other, especially long Birth Stories, repeatedly without ever coming to definitive interpretative conclusions to them. . . . Narrative is based on a story which necessarily involves a single temporal sequencing, and at least one actant, in a way systematic thought does not. . . . Narrative theorists often call this a distinction between the narrative discourse and the story. You can tell a story in many different narrative ways, but it remains the same story, necessarily extended in sequential time, which must remain the same. In Aristotle's syllogism, nothing happens; there are no actants, no events. But these three are essential to Narratives.

Steve saw the very idea of the person who had cultivated wisdom in Buddhism as possessing systematic knowledge and emotional intelligence through reading/listening to and reflection on narrative. That wise person had a "capacity of judging rightly in matters relating to life and conduct; soundness of judgment in the choice of means and ends; sometimes, less strictly, sound sense, esp. in practical affairs: opp. to folly." Steve wanted this distinction to be not merely definitional, but an invitation to teachers to present Buddhist primary sources in a new and dynamic way, not to excise narrative in favor of systematic teachings or see narrative as merely popular or entertaining literature. He believed that both were essential to comprehending the way Buddhists came to understand their own textual heritage. He also found that

> a robust conceptual analysis of Narrative and Systematic Thought: they are, I hope, in my usage more precise than the vague "Stories" and "Doctrines." This is especially important if one wants to avoid, as I certainly do, the common assumption that Stories merely "express" or "illustrate" Doctrines, or give voice to some simplistic moral, as do (though only apparently) folklore and "didactic" (children's) literature (lower-case l). Many of the Birth Stories recounted in [this book] will be seen to be very much more sophisticated, in both Literary (capital L) and ethical senses than Systematic Thought, requiring emotional as well as cognitive intelligence to appreciate . . . [these stories were not the content of] "popular Buddhism," still less "morality tales" for children, as is so often alleged. . . . Even educated and sophisticated people like stories. And many of the Birth Stories are very complex and sophisticated, as I shall try to show. They are often, and clearly intentionally so, entertaining rather than uplifting.

In this book he gives dozens of wonderful examples of how these ways of approaching Buddhist textuality can work to create wise and emotionally intelligent people. This, combined with ascetic and meditative practices explicated in the first section, forms the basis of what Steve saw as the Buddhist educational project.

The second section is called "Practices of the Self." It is an expansive and almost lyrical reflection on why Theravāda approaches to meditation, asceticism, and physical training are such an important contribution to the modern condition. Steve by no means promoted commercialized trends of "mindfulness" in the workplace or daily "insight" meditation exercises. He was the least "new age" or urban guru-type person you could ever meet. He was a serious scholar and could come off as quite curmudgeonly, old-fashioned, and *very* Oxford-trained British. But you could also tell if you spent any time with him that he had earned his Oxford training; it was not given. He did not come from an old family with old money. He was English through and through, but like his last name suggests, he had just a bit of Irish class consciousness and a charming resentment of high tables and robed dons. He mixed his Lord Byron and John Galsworthy with a healthy dose of Oscar Wilde and Philip Larkin. He was subdued in his dress (largely black button-down shirts and black pants), in his music, and in his drink. However, despite not going in for spiritual obsessions or self-help fads, he firmly believed that Theravāda Buddhists had something important to offer intellectually to the project that modern historians and philosophers like Pierre Hadot, Michel Foucault, and Derek Parfit spent their lives investigating. He saw these Western philosophers as attempting to articulate what Theravāda Buddhists had been arguing for over two millennia—that the study of philosophy and ethics is largely "practices of the self," and therefore has to involve both textual study and an ascetic lifestyle. This is why Steve was particularly interested in writers and scholars like Max Weber and Leo Tolstoy, who voluntarily adopted ascetic practices in eating, celibacy, and silent contemplation. He often liked to compare Benedictine, Franciscan, Augustinian, and other practices in Catholic Europe, North Africa, and the Middle East to Buddhist practice in South and Southeast Asia.

In his preface and "preliminary remarks," as he labeled them in this draft, he explained his desire to put Hadot and Foucault in conversation with Pali Buddhist writers. His explanation is helpful and worth quoting extensively.

> The fruitfulness of this attempt [at comparison] will be, I hope, on both sides: for students of Buddhism, and of Hadot and Foucault.[4] . . . So, first, what did Hadot mean by Spiritual Exercises (Exercices spirituels)? In the essay of that title, he gives two lists . . . the first list is: research, thorough investigation, reading, listening, attention, self-mastery (la maitrise de soi, Greek enkrateia—an important word with a long history), and indifference to indifferent things (money, for example, and also health, even though this is to be preferred). The second is reading, meditations (meletai), therapies of the passions, remembrance of good things, self-mastery, and the accomplishment of good things. . . . The crucial point here, as it was for Foucault, is that those Ancient systems of thought and practice were not, or not merely undertaken in order to know the world better, but to know oneself and one's own subjectivity better, indeed to effect, as Hadot just said, "a transformation of our vision of the world, and . . . a metamorphosis of our personality."
>
> Hadot does not make any significant or programmatic distinction, as far as I am aware, between "spirituality" and "philosophy," but Foucault does. At the outset of his 1981–82 Lectures, The

Hermeneutics of the Subject, he writes: "We will call 'philosophy' the form of thought that asks what it is that allows the subject to have access to the truth and which attempts to determine the conditions and limits of the subject's access to the truth. If we call this 'philosophy,' then I think we could call 'spirituality' the pursuit, practice and experience through which the subject carries out the necessary transformations on himself in order to have access to the truth. We will call this 'spirituality' the set of these pursuits, practices, and experiences, which may be purifications, ascetic exercises, renunciations, conversions of looking, modifications of existence, etcetera, which are not for knowledge but for the subject, for the subject's very being, the price to be paid for access to the truth." . . . Neither of them was familiar, or so I hope, with the cheapening of the word "spiritual" in New Age nonsense, and occasionally, it must be said, in the "Religious Studies Industry."[5] . . . Hadot's and Foucault's use of "philosophy" and "spirituality" (separately or together), in the precise senses they gave them, are a much more fruitful means of analysis and comparison, at least in intellectual and textual history as opposed to anthropology, sociology, history and other such kinds of discipline not primarily concerned with ideas in texts. . . . Hadot . . . intends, first, as has just been said, that the practice of philosophy should be aimed, as a continual, life-style practice, at a transformation of the knowing subject rather than simply an increased knowledge of the world. . . . He refers, second, to the experience of, rather than discourse about, such things as the "existential choice of a certain way of life, the experience of certain inner states and dispositions' concentration on oneself and the examination of conscience, trying to maintain 'the view from above' as a form of physical imagination and ethical perspective. . . .

'Philosophy' here was part of a wider askēsis."[6] This has obvious resonances both with Hadot's Philosophy as a Way of Life

> and with Buddhist monasticism, at least certain aspirations ascribed to it in texts. For Foucault, Practices of Self were also, sometimes, called "technologies of Self. These are: techniques which permit individuals to effect, by themselves, a certain number of operations on their own bodies, on their own souls, on their own thoughts, on their own conduct, and this as a way to transform themselves, to modify themselves, and to attain a certain state of perfection, of happiness, of purity, of supernatural power, and so on. Let's call this kind of techniques a 'technique' or 'technology of self.'"

Steve didn't study meditation or ascetic practices in a narrow sense or separate those practices from textual study, philosophical or existential reflection, or even everyday learning of manners/etiquette. Indeed, what he learned from Hadot and Foucault especially was that "practices of the self" (or perhaps "practices of the non-self") fit very well with what the Theravāda Buddhist project entails. He writes:

> The phrase "Exercises and Practices of Self" could be taken very widely indeed, so widely that they would become useless as an instrument of comparison. Those of my readers who have had children, or have seen younger siblings grow up, will know that all parents, and obviously all societies, have to teach children everything, in Foucault's terms they have to be taught how to behave (se conduire, se comporter) in any and every domain: how to walk, eat, deal with waste matter, speak—and in what language(s)—how to dress, interact with others (physically and mentally), etc. The entire process of acculturation in this sense, in all societies, all civilizations, all cultures, is the cultivation of a certain kind of self, a certain kind of subject of experience and action, restricted to each communities' mores.

> One might say: acculturation is a universal necessity but there is no universal culture; selves are always constructed in specific times and places, in specific ways. The results differ widely but the process is the same. This learning of specific forms of physical and mental self-control, this askēsis, from childhood on, and the introjection of culturally specific ideals, is part of what constitutes sanity in any given social context . . . the introjection and performance of certain basic components of human sociality (so-called Morality) can be seen as a kind of wisdom, promulgated at length in Buddhist texts. It is helpful in this context to remember that the French word sage, when used of children, can mean both "wise" and "well-behaved" (sois sage! means "behave yourself"!) and formation which refers both to school and University education, the inculcation of a certain kind of subjectivity, of forming a certain kind of character.

Later he continues with a more specific explanation:

> A slightly less general and less comparison-useless form of self-construction consists in more specific vocations, each of which has its own construction of physical and mental subjectivity, its own askēsis. Examples are: training in the many different arts and crafts; in the production and capacity to appreciate high-status Literature (capital "L"); in athletics and sports, in military training; in alchemy and magic, etc., all of which require one formation, a training which produces a certain kind of individual who possesses certain skills, physical and mental, which others do not. One might say that vocational training produces certain kinds of skills achieved by certain kinds of person; I think one should rather say: the skills produce the persons. . . . [Hadot and Foucault] are referring not simply, or not at all, to the mere acquisition of new knowledges or skills, but to a transformation of the

individual's entire persona, internal and external—a change in subjectivity, in the subject of knowledge and not, or not merely, in the domain of knowledge which the knowing subject knows.

This transformational process Foucault called spiritualité, as opposed to philosophie. In his and Hadot's view ancient philosophers were led, ideally, by means of such Exercises to what they saw (of course to Foucault wrongly) as the discovery of a universal Truth. Foucault's work, drawing on Ancient and Medieval sources not to study them as historical documents comprehensible to the study of their own times, but to draw on them to help produce a certain kind of modern philosophy. In the Buddhist case . . . Practices of Self are not in every case connected with Truth, but sometimes simply with the transformation of consciousness in certain ways. But their pinnacle is certainly knowledge of the Truth of things, what the Pali calls "Seeing Things As They Really Are" (yathābhūta-dassana). Seeing this Truth is not only an epistemological matter, or one of spiritualité in Foucault's sense. It was ontological as well: during life it constituted Enlightenment (bodhi) and at death gave rise to final nirvana (better, nirvanizing), the transcendence of time, space, rebirth, and suffering. A change of subjectivity and "spiritual status" indeed!

From there Steve compares this approach to spirituality and/or philosophy to Theravāda Buddhist approaches to knowledge:

There are two kinds of Truth in Buddhism, which I translate as the Consensual and Ultimately Referential. Both of these indeed "function, circulate, have the weight of truth and are accepted as such." The "subject" is different in each: in Consensual Truth it is a continuing person with a serial identity who can refer to himself as "I," see himself as subject to the discourses of moral norms

> and ethical constraints and—to me importantly—function as an actant in narratives. In Ultimately Referential Truth, which is not a "higher" kind of Truth but just a different one, that person, that "I" is deconstructed into its constituent parts, both textually and as a matter of experience. This is not a matter of non-judgmental, non-evaluative "bare awareness," as contemporary psychotherapists and Modernist Buddhists like to say, but an active focusing of the mind on its contents in a Buddhistic way, that is without the assumption that there is a self which is the agent in these activities. There is, one might say, agency but no agent intentionality but no intender, attention but no attender. There is no subject but certainly the fact of subjectivity: thoughts, emotions present themselves to consciousness. Both the thoughts and emotions, and the consciousness to which they are presented, are impermanent events. These activities take place in the protected environment of monastic askēsis.

The purpose of the study of philosophy for Hadot, Foucault, and the Theravāda Buddhist writers was to investigate and interrogate the very idea of the self, and in doing so, there needed to be a concomitant ascetic practice.

Steve felt that Theravāda Buddhists (and Buddhists more broadly) had a considerable amount to add to the Catholic tradition of monastic practices that Hadot and Foucault were referencing. However, he didn't want to equate asceticism with meditation or see monasticism as simply a group of people meditating together, which he saw students do often in Buddhist studies. On meditation and monasticism more broadly he had strong opinions. On the latter, he wrote a very helpful summary of why "monk," "nun," and "monasticism" don't necessarily fit the Buddhist context without serious reflection on the misleading nature of these terms:

There is, I think, no alternative now than to accept the use of the words "monk" and "nun," in relation to Buddhism. But they are misleading. It used to be said that the English word "monk" was derived from Greek, monos, "alone," a definition which was then followed by the myth of Christian monasticism starting with Saint Anthony, who lived alone in the desert. It was only afterwards, so the myth goes, that Saint Pachomius organized communities of such ascetics, living the coenobitic life (from Greek koinos, common, and bios, life). In fact, as has been definitively shown by specialists over the last four decades, the word "monk" is derived from Greek monachos, meaning "single," in the sense of being unmarried. One influential theory is that the word was originally used of communities of such single women living together in Syrian cities. As to the myth of Saint Anthony, first promulgated by Saint Athanasius in his Life of Saint Anthony, which was to have a very great influence on future centuries of Christians, and Christian monks, one merely has to ask, from a simple, existential and ideology-free perspective: how did he survive? Athanasius says that he was provided with bread by angels, which you can believe if you wish. Common sense suggests that he must have lived near to sources of food and water. Specialists have now shown that the standard form of so-called desert monasticism in Egypt was for men and sometimes women to live in caves or small huts near human settlements, often indeed alone, living a life of prayer and contemplation while plaiting reeds into baskets, which they would take to villages on market days and sell for money and thence food. Not "outside" of society but inside it (as everyone is) albeit on the margins of it physically.

The Pali words for monk and nun are bhikkhu and bhikkhuṇī. These are desiderative nouns derived from the root √ bhaj, "to have a share." Thus, with a sociological insight typical of many Sanskrit and Pali technical terms, Buddhist monks and nuns are those who do not engage directly in production or reproduction, but who "desire to share" in the products of it. This is why it is often said that bhikkhu means "beggar," which is wildly misleading. . . . The word "celibacy" points in the same direction as monachos: single, unmarried. The French célibataire, as does Latin caelebs, refers simply to someone who is, from a legal and social-status point of view, unmarried. In English one can speak of a married couple "practicing celibacy" for shorter or longer periods, but this would be an oxymoron in French: you can't practice being unmarried if you are legally married. Likewise, to use one of my favorite examples from a French dictionary explaining the word, one reads there of an old widower, with children, as un vieux célibataire coureur, "an old celibate womanizer," which is nonsensical in English. It is true that in both languages the words can have, as a minor meaning, the other sense: French célibataire might be used to describe someone practicing chastity, and in English, at least in older English, the word celibate could mean unmarried. I want here to focus on the meaning "unmarried," "being single," as a temporary or permanent social status.

For my purposes we are not dealing here with people who happen to be, for one reason or another, unmarried, but rather with people who are, one might say, professionally unmarried, i.e. people who have taken some sort of vow, made some sort of promise, to live as a single person, for a number of months, years, or indeed for a lifetime. The word professional is not meant here ironically: OED has proper to, or connected with a profession or calling. Before giving the modern sense of the word as doing something as a livelihood for money rather than as an amateur, it has: pertaining to or marking entrance into a religious order. An ascetic professional has a vocation. The groups they participate in are, in sociological terminology, formal organizations: that is, not groups coming into being through the mostly involuntary, unplanned processes of kinship or other social relations, but formal organizations consciously constructed, with their own systems of (usually) written rules, intended to attain some overtly articulated goal.

I like to call such monastic organizations homosocial institutions, usually housed in physical institutions. The word homosocial comes from feminist writing, where it can have various specific uses, such as a preference for the company of members of one's own gender, aside from anything to do with sexual preference. I think this sense is, to some extent, applicable to Buddhism. I also find it helpful as a term of macro-sociological, civilizational analysis, and I shall return to it in a moment, when offering a comparative generalization about askēsis, institutions and Truth. . . .

It is often said that monks and nuns "leave" or "renounce" the world, and indeed the phrase "world renunciation" has been standard since Weber. I think that this concept of "the world" is in a sociological context irremediably imprecise, and should be abandoned. It was typical of Weber's oeuvre—of which I am a great admirer—to take Christian theological terms and use them as instruments of sociological cross-cultural analysis, as in the rightly famous essay "Religious Rejections of the World and their Directions." He did so with great acumen, and almost always with beneficially thought-provoking results. But he also got a number of things, especially about Buddhism, terribly wrong. About it he wrote: "Concentration upon the actual pursuit of salvation may entail a formal withdrawal from the 'world' [in English at least in scare quotes]: from social and psychological ties with the family, from the possession of worldly goods, and from political, economic, artistic, and erotic activities—in short, from all creaturely interests." "Withdrawal from the world" in this sense may or may not be adequate for Weber's interests, but it tends almost

> always to be used by others as equivalent to "leaving society," which is of course impossible. All monastics depend on others in society and are always and everywhere parts of it, often important parts. "Leaving the world" (fuga mundi) had, and has specific meanings in Christian monasticism, which is mental and not social, and which is not appropriate to Buddhism. . . .
>
> There is in Pali a dichotomy between the "worldly" (lokiya) and the "super-worldly" (lokuttara), which is sometimes used to justify the use of the word "world" in Buddhism. But lokiya/lokuttara never have a social-spatial meaning. They are terms only used to designate individual (so called) spiritual achievement or status. So, after all these linguistic divagations, here is a cross-cultural generalization and a possible comparative project: in many, but not of course all civilizations, the search for Truth—not just any truth or truths, but an overarching and universal Truth with ontological as well as epistemological dimensions—is pursued by a tiny minority of the population, specifically in very many though not in all cases by celibate professionals (usually males) living in homosocial institutions. This is a sufficiently widespread phenomenon, in a sufficiently large number of civilizations, as to warrant attention and comparative analysis. It is not, in my view, an issue to be approached individualistically. Individuals may want to live a life of chastity and behavioral restriction, to wear always a particular uniform, and so on.

He ends this section with an important question:

> What I like to call the civilizational enigma of asceticism is not why some individuals do this kind of thing but why other people pay for it. Why do some civilizations cherish and support materially as the embodiment of their highest values (at least rhetorically) a way of life which, if followed by everyone, would lead to

the extinction of humanity after a generation? Students in Introductory Buddhism classes often ask, as they should if they are paying attention: if being a monk or nun is the highest vocation in Buddhism, what would happen if everyone became a monk or nun?

On meditation, or supposedly, what most Buddhist nuns and monks do, he wrote:

> [Meditation] The word is found everywhere these days, not only in academic works but also in popular Self-help books, magazines, Apps for use on cell phones, and more besides, to help their users reduce stress and achieve some measure of calm. I have no quarrel with such things. If they help people, as they certainly do in many cases, well and good. But I think that in academic studies it has become a word which prevents thinking from being lucid, open-ended and exploratory. It constrains thought rather than enabling it. . . .
>
> A common modern stereotype about "meditation" is that personal experience, sometimes mental sometimes physical, is opposed to and superior to verbal, textual thinking. There are indeed Practices of Self in Buddhism which are non-verbal and sometimes physical. But the majority are not, and discourse, textuality are everywhere important components of them. Practices called "meditation" are forms of inner ritual, for which there is often, as with outer rituals, a prescribed series of words, a libretto, what Christians call a liturgy.

Clearly, for Steve the practice of *ganthadhura* and *vipassanādhura* were intertwined, and textual study and textual expression/performance was as much a part of meditation as the study of texts was a form of "practice of the self."

OTHER THOUGHTS . . .

There are several parts of Steve's preface and preliminary remarks that I have left on the editor's floor, not because they are not important, but because they speak largely to members of the aforementioned Theravāda Civilizations Project and are only understood in the context of that group's meetings and ongoing conversations. They would have been most likely removed at a later stage of editing by Steve himself. However, there are a few rather important points that should be mentioned. Steve admitted that these remarks didn't fit within the structure and purpose of this book rhetorically. At the end of the preface he wrote: "This chapter, I admit, has been rather heterogeneous and has raised a large number of disparate issues," and he notes that it is quite different in style and purpose from the other two chapters I introduced above. In his typical humorous way, he stated that the chapter was "as Monty Python used to say . . . something completely different." It *is* completely different and for the purposes of this present book not necessary, but it does merit some explanation. Indeed, I plan to edit it as a separate article and publish it under Steve's name. To summarize here, the chapter is about how to study Buddhism "civilizationally."

Along with Juliane Schober, Steve started the Theravāda Civilizations group because he wanted to show how Theravāda Buddhists contributed to world wisdom. He wanted Buddhist thought, practices, and literature to be a fundamental part of a humanistic education for undergraduates in the West as much as it is in Asia. He believed strongly that the classics of Buddhist literature are on par with those of Shakespeare, Dante, Milton, Chaucer, Rabelais, Goethe, Ovid, Cervantes, Homer, etc. He also believed that Buddhist approaches to the self are as valuable as those of Lacan, Freud, Montaigne, Ricouer, Aquinas,

Augustine, and Plato. He saw Buddhists as part of a civilization that has contributed equally to the humanistic endeavor.[7] He felt so strongly about this that he formed a scholarly society, earned a six-year grant to fund discussions and publications on this topic from the Henry Luce Foundation, and included in this draft an entire chapter on the topic. I think it is worth taking a little time to cite from it to hear Steve in his own voice. While it does not necessarily add to the two major arguments presented in this book, it does offer some foundation for his motivation behind writing it. I include two short reflections Steve wrote on the subject of "Early Buddhism" and its connection to the study of Buddhism civilizationally, and finally a passage on the subject of the very possibility of translation and comparison in the study of Buddhism in the West.

On the Civilizational Approach to the Study of Buddhism

Steve asked, "What does it mean to study the tradition of Pali texts civilizationally?" and then offered eight characteristics of a civilization, even though he admitted that

> in the last few decades it has become, according to some, politically incorrect to use a singular concept of civilization. This is because, so it is alleged, such a usage necessarily implies acceptance of a Western-European and American grand narrative of progress, where we stand at the summit of human social and cultural evolution. I think this is nonsense. Of course some western triumphalists may do that, but as academics we can, soberly and carefully, use the concept non-evaluatively. To have civilization, to be civilized, in my sense is not in itself an achievement and

> certainly not a moral achievement. . . . All human beings engage in various forms of representation and exchange, both linguistic and material. All human beings can pose themselves the questions—where does the world come from, what happens to individuals after death, why do bad people often enjoy success while good people don't?—and so on and so on, questions to which what I will call civilizational transcendentalist ideologies, which are phenomena of civilization, claim to give answers, answers which are preserved and guarded by a specific class (often called "clerics").

The eight characteristics include:

> 1. The fact that civilization introduces into previously non-agrarian societies a differentiation into two classes, those who give and those who take tribute, that is, part of the wealth created by an agricultural surplus, and to varying extents in due course by trade. . . . 2. The existence of different forms of power, each with its own elite. They might be identified differently: one attempt has been to to divide ideology and its power into the ideological, economic, military, and political forms. One might add, and in Burma, for example, the jurisprudential. For other purposes, certainly, one could choose different classificatory schemas. But whatever schema one adopts, the point is that there is in civilization more than one kind of power, and more than one kind of elite, who could and did both co-operate and conflict with each other. It is naïve to think of a simple binary opposition between the elite and the non-elite. 3. The presence in civilization of self-conscious and self-descriptive institutions, in both the senses of (usually but not always) physical buildings, and of their human curators, whose vocation it is to preserve in entextualized form (a word I will explain in the next section) what are seen as a

valuable multi-generational traditions, for example history and the evidence which allows it. It is wrong to ask, of any civilization, whether or not it has a sense of history, a historical consciousness. Of course it does, because it is a civilization. What kind of historical consciousness is another matter. Herodotus and the Mahāvaṃsa are quite different projects. 4. The production and multi-generational transmission of an elite Literature, both oral and written, in prestige languages, and conceived as having a special value as high-status Literature. I am not talking of folk-lore. Pali texts and the Practices of Self they describe and prescribe, offer both an ideology—that is, texts which co-operate with and celebrate other forms of power, notably the political and military—and an imaginaire—that is, texts whose main object is artistic, whether this be tragedy, comedy, satire, and much else besides, which may both support and contest other forms of power. . . . 5. Extensive vocational differentiation at all levels of society (I am thinking here of Max Weber's notion of Beruf, a specific vocation or calling), with the possibility, however rarely met with in fact in the premodern world, of upward (or downward) social movement. One such vocation, important to Pali texts but of course the direct concern only of an infinitesimally small number of people, is that of grammar, albeit that the existence of such a small grammatical class is of much wider civilizational significance. One cannot have a prestige language without grammarians to codify it, and, in so far as is possible, legislate its forms of expression, and be valued for doing so. 6. The explicit championing, debating and defending of certain ideas and certain values by differing groups, in conflict with identified others. This is important. Civilizations are as much arenas of lively and sometimes bitter conflict as of bland unanimity. Pali texts themselves contain values which conflict with each other. The Religious Studies Industry, seeing all Pali texts as those of a

> "religion," always think they have something to sell, some simple and unified set of values to advertise and promulgate. Often they don't: they provide autonomous spheres of art, entertainment, beauty, and at least in one case (Vinaya rules against sex with female corpses) pornography, for their own sake. 7. The inculcation in many cases of a court culture, surrounding a king, which often requires a very demanding form of what the French call formation. This is a useful term: it implies both education and the kinds of person such an education produces. We don't, alas, have any concept in modern English which corresponds to the Sanskrit śi ṣṭ a, one who is trained, formed, and thus unlike others qualified to understand and appreciate certain forms of art and other linguistic sophistication. No word in Pali seems to correspond exactly to this, though there are various lists of sippa -s, forms of training and knowledge. . . . An often-overlooked part of such culture, ignored by "legitimation" writing, is that of court jesters and others in similar structural positions as part of instead of opposed to, military-political power, that is to say those who are permitted, even encouraged to contest and satirize mainstream values. . . . 8. The existence of bureaucratized jurisprudential institutions, separate professions and forms of power not entirely equivalent to those of kings, albeit that the relation between these two traditional forms of life is, to say the least, variable.

Then Steve goes on to explain why he thinks the study of Buddhism civilizationally is necessary—it shows the importance of studying literature that was admittedly read, studied, and understood by a small class of elite readers, as he says theoretical physics and James Joyce are by a small class of Europeans. That certain knowledges are not widely shared doesn't mean that they are not valuable to study as a contribution to human civilization. Therefore, he writes:

> "Civilization" is thus a descriptive and analytical tool which, though like all such tools not perfect, helps to understand certain social formations, certain domains of textuality and also—though this is all-too-often not emphasized enough—certain entextualized aspirations, of which the realization, ideal or actual, may be held to be accessible to everyone or just to one or more kinds of elite. In Buddhist Studies in the last few decades it has become fashionable to say that while texts may talk of Meditation, the Path to Nirvana and other such high-falutin' things, in fact Buddhism "on the ground" consists for the most part in the revering ("worshipping" here is a dangerous word, one whose genealogy must be uncovered) of Buddha-images and relics, the wearing of amulets, and the like. To put it crudely (it cannot be put otherwise) while texts may say one thing, what Buddhists actually do is another. In my view, the empirical study of what Buddhists, in the past and now, actually do and how they live is obviously fascinating and vital. I very much enjoy spending time, in Thailand especially, watching Buddhists, and often participating with them in doing all those things. But to dismiss textual ideals as irrelevant to Buddhist history, especially to its intellectual history, is to miss a vitally important point: it is precisely the preservation of such ideals as ideals, whether or not they are actualized, which constitutes, in part, Theravāda civilization.

This motivation drove him to study the texts in the two major sections of this book:

> The texts we are dealing with, being written in the prestige and learned language of Pali, are accessible only to what is, demographically, a tiny minority of any population where Theravāda civilization can be said to exist: that is, for the most part, to an elite of educated monks and lay connoisseurs in royal courts. This

> fact in itself shows that Pali Narrative texts, for example, cannot be, or at least cannot all be conveying, as is so often assumed, "popular" or "folk" tales adapted to offer Buddhist "spiritual" (a horrible word) Teachings (sic) in simplified form. They are sophisticated Literature (capital L) written by adults for adults, who had the same conceptual, emotional and moral sensitivities that we moderns do. They convey and explore moral complexity, and they are entertainment, both serious and light, as much as they teach simple lessons (often for children, as is also often assumed). They are not contained within the straitjacket of "Buddhist Doctrine" assumed by the Religious Studies Industry to be the content of Pali literature. Practices of Self likewise I assume were enjoyed as admirable ideals in Pali texts, including stories, by at least as many people as those who actually practiced them. They are of a discursive and practical heterogeneity far more complex, and in my view far more interesting, than the narrow range of ideas and practices which have come to be called "Buddhist Meditation" in modernity.

Despite this argument, Steve did acknowledge that Pali literature coexisted with oral and written literature in other languages, as well as other ideologies and responses to the human condition. Moreover, Pali literature, while understood by a small elite, had influence far beyond this coterie of scholars in South and Southeast Asia. He wrote:

> A rhetorical orientation to the literature of the Pali Canon (the tipiṭaka) as a regulatory idea/ideal—though rarely entirety of the actual texts so designated. The entire tipiṭaka would not, indeed, or at least very infrequently, be found together in any one time and place. Even nowadays people donate versions of the whole tipiṭaka, wrapped in transparent foil or some valuable cloth, to

be left like that and venerated rather than read. . . . Among elites, what I have called the Pali imaginaire . . . a potential data bank; but note that there were rarely many texts outside specialist libraries, and Pali texts always co-existed with other texts, in Sanskrit and in vernaculars. It seems to me common sense to assume that these would first and always mainly have been Narrative texts, stories being more accessible and more attractive, before Buddhist Modernism, than texts of Systematic Thought. . . .

The availability of a heterogeneous set of Practices of Self, forms of askēsis, "Spiritual Exercises," in texts as ideals, and in practices rhetorically oriented by (though not uniquely aimed at) the goal of nirvana, as both an alleged individual achievement and as the (more easily verified) social status of someone, dead or alive, designated by social acclaim as Enlightened. More often than not, I think, such Celebrities, like Pali texts, were regarded more highly in practice for their performatively efficacious value. . . . It is important that Pali (the language, the Canon, the imaginaire, practices of self, etc.) never existed alone: they always co-existed with vernaculars, often with Sanskrit: there has never been a civilization in which only Pali was valued as a prestige language.

The spread of both language and literature was empirically varied: for example, in Cambodia between the 14th and 19th centuries it is, I think, a still open question whether at any time we are looking at a "Theravāda civilization" rather than at a civilization with some Theravāda components. In thinking of the spread of Theravāda we might think of the spread of both sounds and silences: the sounds of texts read out loud (performed), of chanting, protection and other mantras, sermons, etc.; and the silences of texts as mute objects, lighting incense and candles, venerating Buddha-images (usually done in silence), Practices of Self, etc. (almost all but not quite all of these are silent practices of the mind, "Mental-Spiritual Exercises").

On Early Buddhism and Buddhaghosa's Fantasy

I was considering leaving this section of Steve's draft completely out of this edition because, unlike all of his positive and forward-thinking contributions, this seemed more vindictive. Steve developed as a young scholar under the influence of Richard Gombrich, a legendary scholar of Theravāda Buddhism. Like Steve, Gombrich is first and foremost a scholar of Indic philology. Some of the other luminaries of Steve's generation of Buddhist studies scholars are Oskar von Hinüber, Lance Cousins, Nalini Balbir, Johannes Bronkhorst, Charles Hallisey, Collette Cox, Jens Braarvig, Richard Solomon, Peter Skilling, and others. Even though all of them have been board members of or active participants in the International Association of Buddhist Studies, these are mostly men, mostly white (like me) who consider themselves mostly linguists, translators, and textual scholars concerned with uncovering the content of early Buddhist texts, translating them into German, English, or French in different ways. I was trained in this way as well. What differentiated Steve was that he was one of the only Pali-Sanskrit specialists in Buddhist studies of his generation who was seriously trained in philosophy, and as his career developed he became more and more interested in the work of anthropologists and vernacular language specialists like Ashley Thompson, Craig Reynolds, Nicola Tannenbaum, Sarah Shaw, Jeffrey Samuels, Stanley Tambiah, Michael Carruthers, Anne Blackburn, Louis Gabaude, Nancy Eberhardt, Juliane Schober, Anne Hansen, Pasuk Phongpaichit, Chris Baker, Daniel Arnold, and John Holt, and started mentoring emerging scholars like Julia Cassaniti, Joanna Cook, Naomi Appleton, Thomas Borchert, Jake Carbine, Kelly Meister, Thomas Patton, and Benjamin

Schonthal, and many others. He also started working with me along with Thai scholars like Suchitra Chongstitvana, Anil Sakya, Pattaratorn Chirapravati, Maechi Vimuttiya, and Prapod Assavavirulhakarn, among others. He developed a great admiration for the creative textual-anthropological work of Kate Crosby. He became more social, engaged, and diverse in his scholarship and friendships. I remember him telling me when I was a PhD student that he never went to conferences and had stopped giving conference talks of any sort. Less than a decade later he was cofounding the Theravāda Civilizations Project, traveling often to Thailand, and leading conference roundtables and workshops. When I applied to the University of Chicago to work with him for my master's degree, he said I would be welcome, but that he had no interest in vernacular literature and wasn't planning to work on Thai, Lao, or Burmese material. Fifteen years later we were in the field together in Thailand interviewing nuns, he was studying the Thai language, and we were watching Thai films together. Steve's growing interest in the world of Buddhist studies beyond the close study of Pali and Sanskrit texts in the last twenty years of his short life led him to lash out at times at his former self and his early training. It seemed almost to me like a type of reckoning, a settling of scores with youthful indulgences and hesitations. His growing interest in the anthropological and vernacular literary messiness of Buddhist practice, the hybridities and the inconsistencies of quotidian Buddhist practices and expressions, made him question the linear historical, rational, and integrated view of Buddhist thought in which he had been trained. His reaction was unforgiving and fierce.

Richard Gombrich, a scholar with diverse interests, skills, and ideas, for Steve became more of a symbol of that view than a living and growing scholar himself. While Gombrich, like many other scholars of Steve's generation, believed that scholars could and should use limited textual evidence to help speculate on and reconstruct the ideas, practices, and even daily lives of early Buddhists (loosely 500 BCE to 1200 CE), Steve found this project increasingly useless and even intellectually dangerous. For him there was little compromise on this issue, and he spoke about it as if it was a vendetta and not a scholarly leaning. In his draft, he wrote:

> What can we know of "Early Buddhism"? The short answer is: nothing. The jazz pianist Herbie Hancock, as a young man in the early 1960s, joined Miles Davis's prestigious band. The music was complex and difficult, and at first, he says,
>
>> I was trying too hard . . . I kept filling up the space. . . . But there were some moments when I wasn't sure how to do that, or what was expected of me. So after a show one night I decided to ask Miles about it. "Miles, sometimes I don't know what to play," I told him. "Then don't play nothin'," he replied, not even looking up. Simple as that.
>
> An excellent principle, and an excellent attitude to take towards those who try to fill the spaces in our knowledge of Buddhism in its earliest phase by reading backwards things found in texts written and redacted many centuries, indeed in some cases a millennium or more after the Buddha's life (whenever that was, and assuming there was such a person as "the Buddha," which is by no means certain). The results are always wish-fulfilling, make-believe fantasies. Many of these later texts are what are called Buddhist histories, vaṃsa-s, which are quite unreliable historiographically. Honesty here is our best policy. Don't try to fill up the spaces. In his popular and influential book, *Theravada*

Buddhism: A Social History from Benares to Colombo, Richard Gombrich writes, from on high:

> I consider extreme scepticism to be a faulty method. If we are too rigorous we can doubt most of our knowledge of the past, certainly about ancient India, where the evidence is sparse and rarely dated. I am not urging that we should claim certainty when we do not have it, but that we should provisionally accept tradition till we have something to put in its place—all the while preserving a modest awareness of our uncertainty.

It is not clear to me what "certainty" might mean in most, if indeed any areas of human life, nor why skepticism should be regarded as a "method." It is an attitude, in my view close to integrity. Imagine that one is serving on a jury in a murder trial. Does one "provisionally" accept what people say just because they say it, and there is nothing else to go on? Convict someone just because one has no more convincing story to tell, regardless of the question of evidence? Buddhist history, obviously, is entirely unserious and unimportant compared to a murder trial, but in doing it one should proceed with the same rigor, the same principle as the legal one that something must be "beyond a reasonable doubt" (not certain) if one is to accept it. In a murder trial one does not come to a decision when "the evidence is sparse." Ignorance is not bliss, but admitting that that is our condition is more "modest" than making up stories. The story Gombrich tells is charming and narratively strong, but while telling it he forgets completely about "preserving a modest awareness of our uncertainty." It is a free country and he is free to make up what stories he likes, as are people to believe them. I am more concerned with the truth. If we can't have it, we should renounce stories which are without evidence to make them "beyond a reasonable doubt."

He further explained his strong opinions on this subject by questioning the very source of most of the knowledge we have as scholars of early Buddhist texts and history—the legendary fifth-century CE scholar-monk Buddhaghosa:

> The usual date given for Buddhaghosa—4th–5th centuries AD—is based on Pali and Sinhala texts which use two different names which have to be interpreted as referring to one and the same king, whose dating is itself, of course, debatable. Why believe it? But let us be generous: Buddhaghosa, or rather what the English monk and prolific translator Ñāṇamoli referred to as "the committee called Buddhaghosa," can "provisionally" be dated to sometime in the middle of the first millennium AD. Given that it is about that time that archeological remains of what seems to be, or to be like, the Pali language as we now know it, and some fragmentary parts of its tradition of texts, start to appear in Southeast Asia, we can only say that Theravāda civilization as we know it began sometime in the mid-first millennium AD. Theravāda Buddhism as a civilizational phenomenon begins in the earliest Chronicles, the Dīpavaṃsa, "The Chronicle of the Island" (i.e. Sri Lanka), and the Mahāvaṃsa, "The Great Chronicle," which are mythology rather than empirical history, despite their constant "dating" of kings. Most people reading these texts apply Gombrich's principle: "we should provisionally accept tradition till we have something to put in its place." Why? More important than these texts is the figure now known as "Buddhaghosa." A vast number of texts are attributed to him: commentaries on the Pali Canon—the Three Baskets of Sutta-s, Discourses, Vinaya, Monastic Discipline, and Abhidhamma, Further Doctrine(s)—as well as the stunningly comprehensive work of synthesis, the Visuddhimagga, "The Path of Purification." . . .

Ñāṇamoli's remark about "the committee" is appropriate, partly because of the sheer volume of the texts attributed to "Buddhaghosa," which it is difficult to believe were the work of a single person, and also because of various inconsistencies in them . . . which are more comprehensible from a committee not always working together than from a single person. But for the sake of ease of reading I shall henceforth use the singular name "Buddhaghosa" as a shorthand way of referring to this committee.

What did Buddhaghosa do, apart from writing commentaries and The Path of Purification? He created, or better put together, no doubt at least from some earlier materials, a make-believe world of the time of the Buddha, when the Great Man walked the earth and Enlightenment was readily available, sometimes after a single sermon, sometimes even after he uttered a single telling phrase. Bliss was it in that dawn to be alive. Although some pre-Buddaghosan textual sources in languages other than Pali do exist—all of them from the first five centuries AD—almost all modern scholarly accounts of Early Buddhism, with only a very few exceptions, rely on the Pali Canon (usually translations of it, of course). I call this "Buddhaghosa's fantasy" not because I wish to criticize it or be supercilious about it, but simply as a phrase depicting the Pali Canon as a roseate textual world of the imagination collected and constructed by Buddhaghosa, as "The Early Days." But how much earlier? The evidence, as opposed to over-optimistic and self-deluding guess-work, says that it was at the very least 500 years, a very long time then as now. I use the word "fantasy" in sense given in the Oxford English Dictionary as "Imagination; the process or faculty of forming mental representations of things not actually present." Perhaps what Buddhaghosa collected and constructed as the Canon was historically accurate, perhaps it wasn't. We don't and will never know.

This approach was not entirely agnostic and negative. It did not lead Steve into a world of complete hopelessness about the value of Pali texts. Instead, it led to this book. Steve wanted to get away from the idea that we could use Pali texts to reconstruct a Buddhist past and to value it instead as beautiful and complex literature to wander in and wonder with. This book is a product of not dismissing Buddhist literature written in classical languages; indeed, he draws from Buddhaghosa's oeuvre often, but appreciating it as a historical body of thought and human achievement. For Steve, literature was like music—something to delight in and be inspired by, not historicize or use as evidence of something else. Miles and Herbie were timeless for Steve.

On Translation and the Possibility of Comparison

Steve considered himself first and foremost a translator and close reader of Pali and Sanskrit. He was a wizard at etymology and philology, and I often joked that he was as interested in grammar as he was in jazz and that he actually had four children, the fourth being the *Oxford English Dictionary* (*OED*). He even published his own Pali grammar guide (in the original draft I reviewed, it was also a "reader" for students to use for practice, but that section was dropped by the publisher because of its length). He was a master of English and Latin grammar as well and showed that a student needed to know the terms and basis of English grammar (most native speakers of English don't) in order to seriously study the syntax, morphology, and lexicography of Indic and other Indo-European languages.

He also was a master translator and always translated his own Pali instead of relying on previous editions and translations.

Indeed, he often did the field a service by retranslating Pali texts. He considered it the first principle of a scholar of Theravāda Buddhist literature to master Pali, to avoid using foreign terms to understand Buddhist concepts. In an uncharacteristically obtuse passage, he wrote:

> In relation [to the need] . . . to avoid terminology taken from Christian theology, and on the contrary to search for existential, ideology-free categories, it is important to say that this is not something derived from one or other writer or tradition designated as Existentialist in Western philosophical tradition. I mean a vocabulary purged from ideological assumptions, one which sees only human beings, their bodies, their languages and history, their imaginations, their discourses, their self-consistencies and inconsistencies as existing. (People who say that academic writing is itself an ideology are beyond redemption.) For this book, Enlightenment, nirvana, rebirth, karma, the heavens, etc. do not exist. Only the human beings who imagined them into being have ever existed. The products of human imagination and action are what is to be described, not what is to be used in analysis. This often takes hard work, an askēsis of its own. It is not enough to say something like "I am presenting this in Buddhist terms . . ." or some such, and then carry on as if those categories were adequate for external analysis.

Basically, Steve argued that students and scholars should not be lazy and use English terms (often with Christian cultural baggage) to gloss Pali Buddhist terms. They should understand the Pali and explain it clearly, not just replace the word *samadhi* with "meditation" or *dharma* with "law," and the like. He called for care in writing and communicating, not efficiency. He provided examples of how quick and thoughtless glosses could obscure important differences in cultural context. Here is an illuminating example:

> What of the words "monk," "nun," and "monastery" (sometimes "temple") in the Buddhist case? Here I don't think academic discourse can avoid implicit comparison with the Christian uses of the words, from which of course, the words derive . . . "monks" and "nuns" can be defined as professional celibates (these two words being also used in precise, non-popular senses). But this would be too unwieldy to use in English prose. "Monk" and "nun" have become so entrenched in the study of Buddhism as to be, I suppose, harmless. At one point I considered using the Pali words bhikkhu and bhikkhuṇī (pronounced bikku and bikkunee) in this book as an act of deliberate de-familiarization and distantiation (Verfremdung), especially for non-specialist readers, but thought better of it.
>
> According to OED the word "monastery" means a "place of residence for a community living under religious vows, esp. the residence of a community of monks," which is, I suppose, acceptable in the Buddhist case. The Pali word usually translated as "monastery" is vihāra, from the verb √ vi-hṛ → viharati, which means, amongst many other things, just to live or pass time. The term vihāra is known in modern Buddhist vernaculars, but it is seldom used outside academic contexts. The most widely used word in Thai for the Residences of monks (there are others) is wat . . . always translated as either "monastery" or "temple." "Temple" is profoundly inappropriate. In OED it is said to mean an "edifice or place regarded primarily as the dwelling-place or 'house' of a deity or deities; hence, an edifice devoted to divine worship. . . . Historically applied to the sacred buildings of the Egyptians, Greeks, Romans, and other ancient nations; now, to those of Hinduism, Buddhism, Confucianism, Taoism,

> Shintoism, and the ethnic religions generally." I don't know what "sacred" means . . . still less "ethnic religions." But clearly "the dwelling-place or 'house' of a deity or deities" is inappropriate. The Residences of modern "nuns" are called in Thai samnak. In Burma, kyaung means "school," and phon-gyi, one term for a monk, refers to a person with great phon/puñña/merit. Hence a Residence is phon-gyi kyaung, since Residences for monks have almost always also been schools. In Sri Lanka there is Sinhala pansala from Pali paṇṇasālā, an ascetic's hut, itself from Sanskrit parṇaśālā a forest dwelling, from parṇa, "leaf" and śālā, "abode." There is also ārāmaya—in Thai ārām or phra ārām (phra being a marker of distinction, used for monks, residences, kings, and others)—from Pali and Sanskrit ārāma, originally an outdoor park used by monks and nuns, but soon coming to mean a Residence for them.
>
> Each of these indigenous terms has its own meanings and uses, its own genealogy, which in a more detailed study than this would need its own investigation. "Monastery" (still more "temple") is inadequate as either description or analysis. But what to do? One can't get rid of them.

Steve then goes on to show that awareness of the cultural and linguistic origins and changing usages of words is not just scholarly muscle flexing, but important as the very foundation of comparative work:

> But insistence on ideology-free vocabulary, and specifically one free from the Christian presuppositions . . . does not at all mean that projects of comparison—as long as they are conscious—are impossible. "Monasteries" are examples of what I will call "omo-social institutions," a category which, while not universal, does, I think, capture something essential to the comparative study of askēsis as a social phenomenon. Likewise "Wisdom Literature,"

> it can . . . be used as a comparative category, once freed from the association with some books of the Old Testament and Ancient Near Eastern texts with which it is now universally associated. (Google for "Wisdom Literature" to confirm this.) The analytical, etic study of Buddhism, as opposed to the emic re-description of what its texts and adherents say, must also be free from the ideological concepts of Buddhism itself. Thus, for example, it is common to translate the category of the Enlightened Persons (Buddhas and others) as "saints." But it is better to see both kinds of person as examples of the wider category "Celebrities," tokens of the same type.
>
> "Celebrity" is a word often thought only appropriate to the world of modern media, but it can be more widely useful. OED defines "celebrity" as the "state or fact of being well known, widely discussed, or publicly esteemed. Later usually: personal fame or renown as manifested in (and determined by) public interest and media attention." Premodern Buddhist media were oral and written texts, usually stories, Buddha-images (which often had their own biographies), amulets, specific (often unusual) styles of architecture, and so on. "Enlightened" celebrities only occur within them. "Saint" is a term from the Christian lexicon, where it has a specific meaning: someone who, after death, has been officially granted by the Church that status, attributed some specific position in heaven (whatever that means), and who is officially permitted to be the object of worship, another word whose genealogy needs to be sought. This word too has, to some extent, become an English word without theological connotations.

Steve provided a few other illuminating examples, and the two main sections of his book are an excellent guide for comparative work in religious studies in general. However, these sections of his original draft were the least polished and often jumped in a single paragraph to many different asides, examples, and points. He was often like this in conversation, just offering hidden gems buried in comments on football, music, gossip, career advice, and family. He was a delight to listen to, and I hope this last book of his is a delight to read.

In 2006, Claude and Steve were considering changing cities and positions to move to Riverside, California, where I was teaching in the University of California system. They had been living in cold and windy Chicago for over twenty years, their three children were now living as adults, and they were looking for a change of scenery and intellectual inspiration. Steve visited UC Riverside three times and Claude came once. Besides their formal interviews and scholarly talks, my wife and I laughed, drank, ate, and talked with them about raising children, writing books, and our goals as teachers. Although they ended up staying in Chicago (old libraries always were more of a draw than palm trees for them) and my wife and I ended up moving to Philadelphia three years later, I will always fondly remember those joyous encounters. One I remember quite distinctly, and upon reflection over the past few months I can see that the seeds for this present book were being planted by Steve back then. He and I got into a spirited argument at an outdoor café over margaritas. He commented that I seemed to imbibe too many sad books and movies. It seemed to him that I "danced in graveyards." I agreed, I was one of those kids who only wore black, wrote bad poetry, listened to Bauhaus and the Damned, and liked talking about the macabre. I said that I liked to test myself emotionally and psychologically. I liked to confront my own mortality. I tend to wear my emotions as scarves and hats instead of underwear and socks. I am quick to cry, quick to be angry, etc. He warned me to take life a little easier, as I had young children and should attend to joy and celebrate inspiring literature and sappy romantic movies (Steve surprisingly loved these, it seems!), and be positive in the classroom with my students and on the playground with my kids. I should listen to more Dizzy Gillespie and less Joy Division. I should go to exhibitions of Warhol instead of Kay Sage. He said that he used to be overly negative, basked in sadness, and focused on what was wrong with the world, but for self-preservation and peace of mind, he was making more effort to be kind to himself and others. He argued, in an anti-Freudian way, that repression/suppression of negative emotions was good, almost healthy—we should choose to be gentle, kind, and empathetic instead of always "informing" or "raising awareness" about all the sadness in the world and in our own condition.

I didn't really appreciate what he was saying then. I was a "realist" and gave my students the hard facts regarding our collective slow march to death. I focused on the nihilistic tendencies of Buddhist teachings on suffering, impermanence, and nonattachment. What Steve said to me then is expressed in many ways in this book. He wanted to celebrate the civilizational contributions of Buddhists to the problem and the complex grandeur of the self. He wanted to emphasize that Buddhists simply told really good stories about overcoming suffering and cultivating compassion. While Steve was a tough critic, demanding teacher, and acerbic wit publicly, he was gentle, kind, and funny in small conversations. This book, I hope, reveals what a powerful intellect with decades of dedication to the study of a complex body of literature written in an infuriatingly difficult language can offer to a reader when they want to make peace, make connections, and warmly touch upon our shared humanity across time.

WISDOM AS A WAY OF LIFE

Part One

WISDOM

1.1 INTRODUCTION

This chapter explores Pali narratives, taking as an example the collection of *Jātakas*, *Birth Stories*. This is a collection in which the stories are told in a standard form but have very heterogeneous content. I want to explore them as a world of the Pali imagination in general, but I will be specifically concerned with the concept(s) of "wisdom" and "excellence in wisdom," and the kinds of behavior thought to embody them. In Mahāyāna texts there is frequently a list of six such "forms of excellence," as I prefer to translate the word (it is usually "perfection"), culminating in "excellence in wisdom" (prajñā-pāramitā), which is, of course, a profound and sometimes nondiscursive understanding of "emptiness" (śunyatā), whatever that means.[1] In Theravāda there is a list of ten such forms of excellence, of which wisdom is the fourth: generosity, virtue (or morality, sīla), renunciation, wisdom, energy, patience, truthfulness, determination, loving-kindness (friendliness, mettā), and equanimity.[2] There is no ordering, and wisdom is not the culmination of them as a list. The forms of excellence are practiced—by celebrities in texts—together. My discussion of Pali Buddhist wisdom in *The Birth*

Stories will use two distinctions: explicitly between the quotidian and the supererogatory; and for the most part implicitly between forms of wisdom and wisdom seeking that are matters of practice, or might be, or are textual tropes, much more commonly, in my opinion. The latter are ideals and aspirations that will be matters of practice in actual life only for a minuscule proportion of any population in Theravāda civilization, quite irrelevant demographically but very important aspirationally. The stories about wisdom discussed here have, I submit, a wider audience even among the small educated elite within civilization than does "systematic thought." This is not because the stories are or appear to be simpler. On the contrary, they are often very much more complex and in need of sophisticatedly articulated interpretation than the simple four truths, five aggregates, and the rest. I am not saying that an educated elite are necessarily more sophisticated in terms of emotional intelligence than cereal-producing, uneducated peasants (I imagine the opposite might well be often true), just that appreciating the stories as written in the father tongue of Pali could only be the preserve of such an elite.

I am making a large claim: it is that narratives rather than texts of systematic thought ("doctrine") are the heart and humanity of the Pali tradition, and what is standardly presented nowadays as the "Theravāda." This is a modern word, and only applicable to part of the Pali textual tradition, albeit a large part quantitatively. *The Birth Stories* are indeed included in its canon, but in a collection, a "basket," called the *Khuddaka Nikāya*, which can mean either *The Group of Short (Texts)* or *The Short Group (of Texts)*. Neither of these names is accurate, since this group, or "basket" (piṭaka), is longer than all of the others. *The Birth Stories* alone are longer than any other "basket," with the possible exception of the *Saṃyutta Nikāya* (*The Group of Collected [Texts]*).

Pali systematic thought attempts to resolve value conflicts, by hierarchization and by the use of a very large number of interconnected lists. Narrative thought states them. In Charles Hallisey's words, stories are "discursive sites where Buddhists debated the scope and validity of the different ethical theories which they knew."[3] Human life, apart from systems of specialist askēsis, contains irresolvable value conflicts. *The Birth Stories* can be enjoyed and admired by everyone, for many different reasons, without being subjected to the classificatory categories of, for example, "the eightfold path," "conditioned co-origination," and still less—since in *The Birth Stories* it does not occur—nibbāna (nirvana). They express many of the aspirations of Theravāda civilization, and thence of its intellectual history.

1.2. WORDS FOR WISDOM AND EXCELLENCE IN WISDOM

There are, naturally, many words that could be translated as "wisdom" or "wise," English words that themselves have many meanings, like the Pali appropriate to different contexts. In Pali the most common and important are paññā and paṇḍita. It has recently been claimed that both of these words came from the same root, but this is not important to me. The root is √ jñā, basically meaning "to know." With the prefix pra (Pali pa-), in Sanskrit one gets prajñā, in Pali paññā. In Pali sometimes the j is dropped, so √ ñā, from which ñāṇa. The *Dictionary of Pali* gives for paññā "understanding, cleverness, discriminative knowledge, true, profound understanding," and for ñāṇa "knowledge, understanding." The words paññā and ñāṇa are as wholly unspecific and heterogeneous as of course are the words given in English dictionaries as synonyms or senses for them. The *OED* has for "wise": "having or exercising sound judgment or discernment; capable of judging truly concerning what is right or fitting, and disposed to act accordingly; having the ability to perceive and adopt the best means for accomplishing an end; characterized by good sense and prudence." All of these words, Pali and English, mean different things in different contexts. The English monk-translator Ñāṇamoli preferred "understanding" for paññā. The contemporary American monk-translator Thanissaro prefers, at least in the systematic texts he standardly translates, "discernment." This is accurate and useful in those contexts, but readers without Pali will not know that this is the same concept standardly translated "wisdom," for example in prajñā-pāramitā, translated as "the perfection of wisdom." Someone, no doubt in the nineteenth century, chose "wisdom," and because of lethargy in translation we are stuck with that as a general term.

The same thing can be illustrated by the translation of mettā, everywhere rendered "loving-kindness," although it is derived from mitta, "friend," and so "friendliness" is both obvious and correct. "Loving-kindness" in English derives from a sixteenth-century translation of the Hebrew word *chesed* in the Old Testament, used of God's love for Israel. What could be more inappropriate for Buddhism? One is between a rock and a hard place: a traditional, standard rendering might be vague or inappropriate to the text one is dealing with, even straightforwardly wrong, as with mettā; but making one's own choice risks being idiosyncratic, so that readers would have to take each translated text on its own, without being able to make connections with others using the standard rendering. Translation is both necessary and impossible.

Paṇḍita is often translated "wise," which is in many contexts acceptable, given the polysemy of the English word. It is used in *The Birth Stories* quite indiscriminately for all manner of knowledges and skills. It often appears in compounds, such as āmacca-paṇḍita (or paṇḍitāmacca), "wise minister"; kumāra-paṇḍita, "wise young man"; and in animal stories for wise dogs, parrots, and many other creatures. It also appears in proper names, such as Senakapaṇḍita, "Wise Senaka," whom we will meet below. In Sanskrit it later came to have the specific meaning of "learned," from which we get English "pundit," a word formerly used positively but now, in the age of spin doctors and television, often as pejorative.

It is not at all clear to me why the translation "perfect" for pāramī and pāramitā was originally chosen, nor why people have continued to use it. Nadia Comaneci scored what is always called a "perfect ten" in the 1976 Olympics. Others have scored that since, but Comaneci was the first and remains the most famous for it. The rules have changed, and it is now impossible. No one takes this to mean anything more than that the athletes who scored it were excellent gymnasts. Comaneci was for a time a uniquely excellent athlete in that sport. A score of 10 in all styles simply means that it is not possible to score any higher. Perhaps we might say that "this was the furthest one could go." Of course, it has nothing to do with such athletes as people. What can "perfect" or "perfection" mean, of people in toto, in modern English? Such a usage can have no sense. Why use them as translations in Buddhism?

Para and pāra both have the same range of meanings; "highest, supreme, further shore, the utmost reach or fullest extent." Pāramī and pāramitā are both nominal forms, called in Sanskrit vṛddhi (strengthened) derivatives from para or pāra, from the root √ pṛ, among whose meanings are "get over, overcome, bring to an end." Pāramī and pāramitā therefore mean, as in Monier-Williams's *Sanskrit Dictionary*, among other things "completeness, highest state." Edgerton's *Buddhist Hybrid Sanskrit Dictionary* gives "supremacy, mastery." Monier-Williams, following Sanskrit texts, takes -ita in pāramitā to be a past passive participle from √ i, to go, and thus translates pāramitā as "gone to the opposite shore," which is wrong. I prefer "excellence," but given the variety of meanings of "wisdom" in English, as also paññā in Pali, will ignore the polysemy of both "wisdom" and paññā and translate paññā-pāramī(itā) as "Excellence in Wisdom."

Why was "perfection" chosen in English? In a (so-called) religious sense it is borrowed, I think, from Christian theology, as so often where early Christian monks appear to have taken literally a sentence from the Latin version of Matthew's Gospel (5.48), where perfectus is the translation of Greek teleios, which means "to have attained one's telos"; telos means "aim, purpose." The English Standard Version has "You therefore must be perfect, as your heavenly Father is perfect." The Latin is "Estote ergo vos perfecti, sicut et Pater vester cælestis perfectus est." Accordingly, monks came to aim to be "perfect." In fact, the name of our Buddha Gotama, from birth, is Pali Siddhattha, Sanskrit Siddhārtha, which means literally "having attained his purpose, his aim." Strictly speaking this cannot be true, since he attained his aim only when he reached enlightenment. Later Buddhist intellectuals did, however, say that the lifetime of a buddha, during which there can be no other buddha, extends from his birth until the nirvana of his relics, in this latter case meaning, I suppose, just "disappearance." But this is never mentioned in discussions of the forms of excellence. I have no interest here (or anywhere) in exploring what "perfection" means in Christian theology. My interest is only that this seems to have been what lay behind the choice of "perfection of wisdom" for paññā-pāramī (itā) well as the other nine "perfections." In *The Birth Stories* the meanings of paññā are so many and various that we can only understand "excellence in wisdom" as meaning that the future

Buddha was aiming, gradually and certainly with hiccups, to go as far as one can go in every sphere he wanted to. The perfect all-rounder.

1.2.1. The Quotidian and the Supererogatory: Dhamma 1 and Dhamma 2

I will discuss Pali Buddhist wisdom in *The Birth Stories*, and tell many of them, with two distinctions in mind: explicitly between the quotidian and the supererogatory, dhamma 1 and dhamma 2, which I translate in both as "what is right"; and implicitly, for the most part, between forms of wisdom and wisdom seeking that are matters of practice or of textual trope. The latter are ideals and aspirations that will be matters of practice in actual life only for an infinitesimally small proportion of any population in Theravāda civilization, quite irrelevant demographically. But they are enjoyed and admired as themes in stories by everyone, as also is the idea, the imaginative possibility, that some people, somewhere, in the past or present, were or are actually doing such things, or aspiring to do so.

In *Nirvana and Other Buddhist Felicities*, in a chapter concerned with kingship and violence, I suggested that one make a distinction between these two modes or senses of dhamma: "dhamma 1 and 2."[4] I said there is an ethics of reciprocity in which the assessment of violence is context dependent and negotiable. Buddhist advice to kings in dhamma 1 tells them to not to pass judgment in haste or anger, but appropriately, such that the punishment fits the crime. To follow such advice is to be a "good king," to fulfill what the philosopher F. H. Bradley would have called the duties of the royal station.[5] This is what Peter Brown called nicely, in relation to the Roman Empire, "the gentle violence of a stable social order."[6] In a number of places in Pali an executioner's block, gaṇḍikā, is, astonishingly, prefixed with dhamma-, so that the compound is perhaps best translated here as "block of justice." I shall tell one of those stories below. Dhamma 2 is an ethic of absolute values, in which the assessment of violence is context independent and non-negotiable, and royal punishment, as a species of violence, is itself a crime, as in the *Temiya Jātaka*, also discussed below. The only advice possible for kings in dhamma 2 must be, as in that story, "Don't be one . . . renounce the world . . . leave everything to the law of karma!" Many birth stories recommend just this. Others, as a solution (of sorts) of the same problem, envisage the utopian absurdity of a nonviolent king.

Here I will use the categories dhamma 1 and 2 to correspond with what I will call the quotidian and the supererogatory. Paññā in quotidian dhamma 1 is skill is some particular domain. In *The Birth Stories* there is no Buddha, so naturally no dhamma 2 of the kind exemplified and promoted in the *Discourses* (*Suttas*) and *Monastic Rules* (*Vinaya*) texts, although the motif of renunciatory askēsis certainly is. Paṇḍita in dhamma 1 can be translated "wise," meaning skill in all manner of domains, as with "wise" and "wisdom" in English, certainly including knowledge, but also experience, prudence, shrewdness, being smart, and much else. I shall follow the convention of using "wisdom" and "wise" in all these contexts, precisely because of the useful vagueness, the polysemy, of the English words. I do not like the phrase "worldly wisdom," "the world" being a category of Christian theology that is not useful for sociological or narratological analysis.

The quotidian is a simple idea: matters of fact and aspiration (along with their opposites) that are part of everyday, ordinary, normal, usual life and thought. As I have said, paññā and paññavant, "wisdom" and "wise" in Pali, have various synonyms or words close in meaning—ñāṇa, medha, dhī, mati, viññu, and especially in *The Birth Stories*, paṇḍita, a "wise/smart/etc. person")—so for paññā and paṇḍita in many contexts there would be better translations of the Pali than "wisdom/wise": intelligence, sagacious, prudent, or others. The *OED* has for "wisdom": "[the] capacity of judging rightly in matters relating to life and conduct; soundness of judgment in the choice of means and ends, learning, erudition, etc." Wisdom in this context is often called "worldly" wisdom, but I do not find the idea of "the world" descriptively or (still less) analytically useful. "Quotidian" is more existentially accurate. "Supererogatory" is probably a word many readers will find unusual and initially difficult. It is actually also quite simple. The word has a genealogy in Catholic theology, but it was introduced into Anglophone philosophy in 1958 by J. O. Urmson, in a paper entitled "Saints and Heroes." The former is for me, as it was for Urmson, a term that can only be a metaphor in a Buddhist context, but the idea of "heroes," in the sense of "culture heroes," actual and/or textual, will be important in what follows. Urmson imagines the following situation. A squad of soldiers is practicing the throwing of live hand grenades; a grenade slips from the hand of one of them and rolls on the ground near the squad. One of them sacrifices his life by throwing himself on the grenade and so saving the lives of his comrades.[7] Now, doing such a thing cannot be regarded as a moral duty; no one would have blamed the soldier for not doing what he did. At the same time it is obviously an act that deserves moral praise. So an act of supererogation can be defined precisely: it is the doing of something that is morally praiseworthy, but the not doing of which is not blameworthy. The idea has, of course, had much discussion, though most of it concerns issues within philosophy (for example, whether and how Utilitarianism can accommodate the idea) that are not germane to my purposes here.

For me, in the first instance dhamma 2 is, analytically, simply the living of a celibate monastic life, itself supererogatory. Obviously not everyone should, or indeed could, live such a life. From the civilizational, macrosociological perspective attempted in the last chapter, the existence of a monastic order, especially a literarily and philosophically erudite and sophisticated one, was in premodernity a supererogatory luxury good, a form of conspicuous consumption on the part of the various elites who could be seen to be able to afford it, precisely because it went beyond the ordinary. In *The Birth Stories* discussed in this chapter, the supererogatory is exemplified by practitioners of askēsis, for whom a number of terms are used, to be discussed in 1.3.2 below.

What is quotidian Buddhist ethics? It is always said, in Buddhist texts as in secondary sources, that the basis of Buddhist ethics is what are normally called the "five precepts" (pañca sīla), which I would prefer to translate as the "five kinds of good moral character." They are to avoid (1) killing living beings, (2) stealing, (3) misbehaving sexually (for laypeople this means avoiding adultery), (4) lying, and (5) becoming intoxicated. But these are merely the most basic necessities of any successful human community. If everyone, or at least a majority, killed indiscriminately, stole as a way of life, were sexually promiscuous, told lies, and became drunk all the time, no community could survive, still less provide the peaceful continuity of a stable taxpaying (tribute-giving) peasantry supporting, as a way of life, kings and their administrations who themselves supported art, philosophy, institutionalized askēsis, and other sophisticated (and expensive) achievements. So what are the kinds of good moral character other than a basic civilizational necessity? As was argued in the last chapter, following K. R. Norman, when King Aśoka advocated dhamma, this was the "sort of dhamma [that] was moral and ethical, so that he could equally well have been a Jain layman."[8] There is nothing specifically "Buddhist" about the requirement and the process. One could say that this is "non-Buddhist" or "pre-Buddhist," though I do not mean by these words what previous scholars have taken in a chronological, positivist, and sociologically naïve manner. There is also much that is Buddhist about them, in the Theravāda case their entextualization and ritual enactment in Pali. If both Buddhists and Jains say that one should not go around killing people, then this, articulated in their own contexts—sermonized in relation to their own kinds of systematic thought, in their own buildings, temples, monasteries, and so on, with audiences composed of different sections of the elite and also, and gradually more and more as the centuries passed, any others (peasants) affiliated with them—then of course they are, separately and complementarily, both Buddhist and Jain.

Identity language doesn't have much use here. Everyone, elites, laypeople, and those practicing some form of askēsis, has to avoid murder (it is true, though, that some Hindu ascetics acted as soldiers, often mercenaries). The further type of askēsis, part of dhamma 2, consists in part in those practices undertaken by a very small number among the ideological elite, called by Hadot "spiritual exercises" and by Foucault "practices of self," which I shall explore in the next chapter. Ordinary kinds of good moral character, of which there are five or an expanded list of eight—vows for practicing which are taken by laypeople on ritual occasions and by the majority of modern "nuns"—and another of ten—undertaken by some "nuns" and all novices without specified end point—are called sikkhāpadas. Sikkhā (Sanskrit śikṣā) is from √ śikṣ, a desiderative of √ sak, to be able to, competent for; thus √ śikṣ is to want to be able, to attempt, to train. Pada is used in Sanskrit and Pali for many things, but here most simply a step or mark. These "steps in training" are not specialist askēsis but simply, as just said, the necessary competencies to be an acceptable and functioning member of ordinary society. There are, however, three further forms of training (the word -sikkhā is often appended to the compound words), which here do mean specialist askēsis.

These are usually given in the order adhi-sīla, adhi-citta, and adhi-paññā. The prefix adhi, like so many in Sanskrit and Pali, is used in many senses: here superior, higher, in addition. So these virtues and practices mean higher morality of the monastic kind, with more than two hundred rules to follow; higher (states of) mind, which is always explicated by texts and their commentaries as samādhi; "higher meditation" in all its forms; and "higher wisdom," which of course means the practices of getting rid of craving, attachment, and understanding Buddhist systematic thought in some profound way. This is "in addition" to the five or more precepts undertaken by laypeople, male novices, and contemporary "nuns." All of this is supposed to lead to the mysterious state of "salvation," nibbāna, nirvana. This word, nirvāṇa in Sanskrit, has become an English word, nirvana without diacritics, with a completely unspecific range of meanings.

1.3. INTRODUCTION TO *THE BIRTH STORIES* (*JĀTAKAS*)

What follows is a description of *The Birth Stories* in some of their varieties. As well as trying to appreciate the separate stories in themselves, I want to stress that they, like proverbs, fables, and other genres, what I will call in 1.4 "wisdom literature" as a cross-civilizational phenomenon, almost always were and are redacted in collections. This means that as well as their internal nature, which may and often does itself contain problematizations and conflicts of values, a collection as a whole clearly does this. Yes, perhaps individual stories, especially the long ones, were read or heard separately, but they would necessarily have been read or heard as coming from a collection, many or most of which the readership/audience would have been familiar with and remembered.

There are many different kinds and different collections of stories in Pali. I have chosen to discuss *The Birth Stories* (*Jātakas*), that is, *Past Lives of Our Buddha Siddhattha Gotama*. There have been and will be an infinite series of buddhas. This concentration on the *Jātaka* collection, despite the very bad translation in which most of it is available to English readers (1.3.9), is the largest single collected set of narratives one can use as an archive of Pali literature, and on many occasions of Pali elite Literature (the difference between "literature" and "Literature" with a capital *L* will be discussed below). There are many other texts that contain stories: in the canon many suttas; in the *Vinaya*; among those others translated into English are the commentary to the *Dhammapada*, the *Petavatthu* and *Vimānavatthu* and their commentaries, the *Udāna* and its commentary, and the commentary on the *Therīgāthā* (and into French the *Sīhalavatthu* and *Dasavatthu*). It would have been possible to use any or all of these texts, but I have concentrated on *The Birth Stories* because they are the longest and most varied collection, not dominated by other texts to which they are a commentary, for reasons set out below. They do indeed contain word commentaries on some of the verses, and it is often said the stories are a commentary on the last moralizing verse, as is the *Dhammapada Commentary*. This is largely untrue, apart from some very short stories (and even then). As I have said, they are usually said to be "popular," "folklore," "moral tales (especially for children)," and so on. They are none of these things. They are written in often complex and difficult Pali, as my students can attest. The prose sections often contain very long and linguistically sophisticated sentences, and the verses especially are often gnomic and especially hard to construe. The verses are often meant, in my view, deliberately to be playful and elite linguistic challenges. Here are two examples of the view I shall be rejecting. First, a piece of du haut en bas grotesquery, first published in 1880, alas by one of the greatest Pali scholars of the late nineteenth and early twentieth century and founder of the Pali Text Society, T. W. Rhys Davids. He says:

> In the Jātakas we have a nearly complete picture, and quite uncorrupted and unadulterated by European intercourse, of the social life and customs and popular beliefs of the common people of Aryan tribes closely related to ourselves, just as they were passing through the first stages of civilization. . . . We may still turn with appreciation to the ancient Book of the Buddhist Jātaka Tales as a priceless record of the childhood of our race.[9]

Commentary seems unnecessary or would be unkind to a great scholar. John Garrett Jones, in 1979 in one of the very few books devoted to *The Birth Stories* until Naomi Appleton's recent work, wrote:

> These are tales that can be passed on orally from parent to child, can be used in school for practice in reading, can be acted out in village festivals, can become subjects for murals and paintings, can live in a people's imagination. In the day-to-day life of the village, these stories are a constant reminder of the price to be paid for succumbing to greed or passion on the one hand and of the rewards attaching to the path of virtue on the other.[10]

Birth stories were and indeed are acted out in village festivals, usually different parts of them in different contexts. They are subjects for murals and paintings. And a few of them are morally simplistic, but most aren't. Proper understanding of the *Jātakas* as a species of adult literature produced by people just as intelligent and morally sophisticated as ourselves has scarcely begun. Alas, it needs translation and interpretation of these texts by scholars with competence in Pali equal or close to Rhys Davids's, a very rare achievement these days. I suspect Jones knew no, or at least very little Pali. Most of his examples are taken from the old and deficient translation discussed below. Who now, as an individual or group, would undertake a new translation of the whole collection? In the present circumstances and restrictions of university life it seems unlikely.

1.3.1. Pali Narrative Literature and Its Audience

Pali literature is usually understood as K. R. Norman says: "for the Indologist Pali literature means anything written in Pali irrespective of literary value in the accepted European sense of the word."[11] Literature with uppercase *L*[12] is indeed used for doctrinal, ideological, and historiographical texts; for liturgy, chants with what is called "magical efficacy" but better, "instrumental value," and other such things. The tradition of Pali texts also contains sophisticated conceptual analysis, interesting and useful apart from its "religious" value; many narratives, either independent or embedded in other kinds of text; both poetry and prose that can be ethically and aesthetically complex and also self-critical, and sometimes attains a level of sophistication that would deserve the Indian label of kāvya, complex and sophisticated Literature (Pali: kabba) often mislabeled "ornate"; comedy (sometimes of the slapstick kind: see *The Birth Story of the Turtle* in 1.3.5), and much else. Pali literature and Literature, precisely because of their being written and recited in a difficult prestige language, have necessarily been restricted to a very small and highly specialized audience. Most monks who are said to "know Pali" in fact usually know the small amount used in liturgy and chanting.

To repeat a phrase I have used elsewhere, the external, etic analyst should see Buddhists as human beings first and Buddhists second. That is, not everything they write and cherish is "religious." Pali Buddhist ideology is not something that encapsulates the world of those whom we (and they) might call "Buddhists," such that they can only look from inside it, but something within the world that they can accept, ignore, contest, or in other ways objectify.

Many years ago (starting in 1927), Maurice Winternitz wrote a *History of Indian Literature* in three volumes.[13] This is available on the Internet as .pdfs as well as in book form. Much, even most of this work is now outdated and not of much use. But his long section on the *Jātakas* is, in my view, still very useful indeed.[14] He does spend a lot of time discussing chronology, all of which in my view is pointless guesswork, and he does often address the question whether particular stories are "Buddhist" or not, which seems to me a waste of time. There are, as I shall exemplify below, and as Winternitz extensively exemplifies himself, comedy and tragedy both as episodes within the stories and indeed as whole stories, often problematizing, even satirizing Buddhist ideas or values. Why call this "non-Buddhist"? Can't monks and courtiers laugh and be moved like the rest of us? Don't Buddhists enjoy self-deprecating humor? Aren't the capacity to laugh at self-deprecating humor and to be moved by the artistry of tragedy themselves part of wisdom? I think so. As well as offering numerous summaries and sections of *Jātaka* stories (translated well), Winternitz offers a helpful, if on occasion old-fashioned list of many, indeed most of the kinds of story birth stories are. In his words, they are:

> 1. Fables, most of which, like Indian fables in general, aim at teaching Niti, i.e. worldly wisdom [an unfortunate phrase, in my view]. Only a few of them have the moral tendency as evinced in the ascetic poetry [that is, dhamma 2]. 2. Fairy tales, including many animal fairy tales, almost entirely in the style of the European popular fairy tales. 3. Short anecdotes, humorous tales and jokes. 4. Novels and even long romances, abounding in adventures, and sometimes with a greater or lesser number of [supplementary] narratives within the story. 5. Moral narratives. 6. Sayings. 7. Pious legends . . . many of them [belonging] to the common property of Indian ascetic poetry.[15]

There are also, as he exemplifies, sarcasm, parables, ballads in dialogue form or "in a mixture of conversational verses and narrative stanzas," with more or less direct analogies in, for example, the *Mahābhārata*, Aesop, and many other texts.[16] Winternitz's treatment is appreciative, even celebratory. And he gives useful summary versions of many stories. One of the very striking things about birth stories is how they (unlike the translations) avoid anachronism. They all take place, by definition, at a time when there is no Buddha, no founder of a sāsana. It is true that enlightenment is possible in birth stories, by those much understudied characters called pacceka buddhas (on whom see 1.4.3). In *The Birth Stories* pacceka buddhas do teach dhamma. However, this is dhamma 1, "what is right" in everyday human life. They know, in some unspecified way, but do not teach dhamma 2, which is the specialized Truth only available—in entextualized form—when there is, narratively, a buddha to teach it. Later texts are quite clear on this: "The Two Characteristics of Conditioned Things and Events," suffering and impermanence, are all too easy to understand, with or without the existence of a buddha to teach them.[17] A common birth story motif is of someone seeing examples of suffering or impermanence and then deciding to go to live in the Himalayas as a hermit. A common and to me rather nice motif is of someone seeing a yellow leaf falling to the ground and realizing that everything is impermanent, and then choosing the life of an ascetic as a response to the fact of death. But the third characteristic, true of both the conditioned and the unconditioned (nirvana), anattā, the absence of a self or anything permanent in human beings, can only be understood if there exists a buddha who can fathom its depths and reveal them to others by means of a historically institutionalized sāsana. It is very unfortunate that the standard English translation of *The Birth Stories*, done more than a century ago, is highly deficient, even offensive in some ways, as will be discussed in detail below, and highly misleading as to both the content and the style of the originals, simplifying, adding to, bowdlerizing, and in other ways not doing justice to the original Pali. Most or all of the audience of the birth stories, highly educated monks and literati at royal courts, would also have known Sanskrit, and both high and low registers of their respective vernaculars.

In Sanskrit such an audience is said to need to be śiṣṭa, "educated" or "qualified," precisely the opposite of what is so universally assumed. Michael Hahn, dealing with very sophisticated Sanskrit texts of riddles, the solving of Pali versions of which is a very frequent and important component of wisdom in birth stories, writes that such texts:

> give us a very good idea of what courses of study [were] at a Buddhist university in the first half of the eleventh century and the erudition and predilections of the professors there. Highly sophisticated works [such as riddles in poetically sophisticated verse] show that the professors of philosophy were by no means specialists in only one discipline of learning but regarded it worthwhile to spend some part of their knowledge and energy on such worldly topics like the intricacies of Sanskrit poetry.[18]

I think the idea of the "worldly" is not a useful category, and no doubt the kinds of "Buddhist university"—centers of advanced learning—in Theravāda civilization had some differences from those Hahn is referring to in India. I quote Hahn to suggest, as is surely obvious, that Buddhist learning does not consist solely in systematic thought, as so many introductory books now suggest, but also in narrative thought (far beyond that of the modern invention "The Life of the Buddha"), which itself also contains language of great sophistication, in riddles, proverbs, stories, etc. Even where there is no great linguistic complexity demanding extensive education, it is still a mistake to think birth stories are merely "popular." It is surely obvious—one only has to state the sentence to see the absurdity of what it says—that to think that if a story is, apparently, simple then the people reading it must be simple too. Personally, I like to read (and reread) *War and Peace*, *Anna Karenina*, *The Brothers Karamazov*, *Middlemarch*, *Madame Bovary*, *Mrs. Dalloway*, and all the other classics of Western Literature [*sic*, capital letter]. I also like to read philosophy. But I am also an avid consumer of detective novels, such as those by Elizabeth George and Anne Perry, and TV series such as *DCI Banks* and *The Fall*. Samuel Beckett, unlike myself one of the greatest literati of the twentieth century, who read novels, plays, and poetry in five or six European languages and wrote some of the most erudite and original novels and plays of the century, also loved to read thrillers and detective stories. Apparently among his favorites were Len Deighton and Conan Doyle. There is no reason to think that Buddhist literati were not the same: intellectuals can appreciate many literary genres, including (apparently) simple ones, which are often in fact not at all simple, without ceasing to be intellectuals.

It is unfortunate that we know next to nothing directly about the premodern court cultures in which Pali Buddhism flourished, and probably never will. Peter Skilling has written a very fine study of one such court culture, in Thailand (Siam) in the eighteenth century.[19] Grammarians were certainly, as their texts show, as experts in Sanskrit grammar, valued by courts also. Nor will we know much about the early centers of Pali education, save what we can glean from archeological remains. As ever, the evidence we do have comes from texts, and texts are unreliable witnesses, at least to event history. Texts, however, must have relied for their imaginative adventures at least in part on the world that they knew, on the contexts in which they were produced. Of course they could invent things: magical skills, flying through the air, enlightenment, and the like. But they had no genre analogous to modern science fiction. Although even in that genre there are limits to how distant from our own actual life such texts can go. What we can do in relation to *The Birth Stories* is to use them, one hopes judiciously, as evidence, borrow from what we know about court culture in South Asia more generally, more recent courts in Southeast Asia, and indeed elsewhere. We can try to move from what inside these texts seems repeatedly to be presupposed about court culture outside them.

We know that often kings held contests. Sometimes these contests were intricately philosophical, no doubt tedious after a while to both kings and courtiers. Maybe they appointed judges to listen on their behalf. *The Birth Stories* contain, I believe, only one debate on philosophical issues of any length (*The Mahābodhi Jātaka*), but numerous examples of debates on less technical matters, sometimes on the meaning of obscure, gnomic verses, and also often on the solving of riddles. They also had various other kinds of contests, such as those involving proverbs. One competitor would start with something like "a stitch in time saves nine"; the other would cap that with "more haste less speed"; then it was the turn of the first to try to cap that, and so on. The wisdom involved here is that which knows when and how a particular proverb relates to the context in which it is cited. We have collections of such proverbs, called in Pali and Sanskrit *nīti* texts, "good advice, "wise policy," or some such. In Sanskrit these were also called subhāṣita, "things well said." Thus, for example, there is in one Pali collection, after listing a number of qualities a good king should have, the toadying and bombastic "a bull among men endowed with the qualities just mentioned conquers the entire earth and (re-)distributes a pile of merit,"[20] which can be capped from another by the more challenging and realistic "a king and a wise man are never, ever, alike: a king is honored [only] in his own country, a wise man is honored everywhere."[21] Apart from the fact that one can almost always find one proverb to counter or cap another, it is important that, as I said in 1.2, like fables, birth stories, and the like, proverbs circulated in collections. The collections were usually organized into thematic chapters: the wise man, friendship, conversation, sons, servants, etc. The different chapters necessarily embody diversity: not a diversity that cannot, a priori, be arranged into some form of unified hierarchy of values, though it would be difficult to do so, given the range of topics addressed, but one that neither seeks nor is presented along with any such unification. I shall return to the issue of diversity and unity in the conclusion (1.4.1).

1.3.2. The Birth Stories: *Structure*

The *Jātakas*, usually translated, as I have, as *The Birth Stories*, is a large collection of over 500 tales. Modern texts often say the number should be 550 but is in fact 547. This is wrong: many of the shorter "tales" are simply extracts from longer ones, with their own title and sometimes a shortened "Story of the Present," but no text, so all we need to say is "over 500." They are allegedly about our Buddha, Siddhattha Gotama, in previous lives. He (it is always he) can be a human being, an animal, a god, sometimes Sakka, king of the gods, or, for example, a lower-level supernatural such as a tree spirit. Usually, though not always, he is the hero. Sometimes he is just an onlooker, taking little or no part in the story. Usually, though not always, he is a moral hero; sometimes he behaves badly.

The structure, very well known to students of Buddhism, never varies, although the lengths of the two parts do. First, there is the "Story of the Present," which is usually a short but occasionally a long episode about the present Buddha Gotama (sometimes with a narrative that is simply repeated in summary form in the "Story of the Past"). Typically monks are discussing some topic. The Buddha asks what they are talking about, they tell him, and then he tells them the "Story of the Past," which usually but by no means always closely resembles the events or at least the general tenor of the "Story of the Present." A common but unfortunate example is when a monk is hankering after his former wife and thinking of leaving the order to go back to her. The Buddha then tells a misogynistic story of how in a former birth the monk was mistreated by a woman, often with alarming violence. So now he should not leave the order. But misogyny is only present in a minority of the stories. A very short and perfunctory "conclusion" (literally "putting together," samodhāna) then identifies characters in the story with then present-day people, usually well-known monks, in this case the previously mistreated man with the present monk. The character standardly called within the "Story of the Past" the bodhisatta is, of course, by definition a former identity of Buddha Gotama. The fact that at the same time he is called by what he is in the story, an animal, a named or unnamed "wise man," or a named or unnamed ascetic, is one of the many ways (I shall return to this) actants within the narrative always have multiple identities, between which the narrative can move explicitly, or that are implicitly inherent in the story as it is told.[22]

As said above, *The Birth Stories*, like *Aesop's Fables*, have almost always been regarded, and dismissed, as folklore, or as children's literature, teaching allegedly uplifting morals but otherwise uninteresting. This is entirely wrong in both cases, both a priori and in relation to their content. In the first place, a priori one must remember that Pali is a learned language, as A. K. Ramanujan put it, a "father tongue" and not a "mother tongue," and therefore not comprehensible either by children or by those uneducated in Pali (that is, almost everyone), and used by no one, as Ramanujan puts it, in the kitchen. It is usually assumed, without any evidence whatsoever, that birth stories started out as folktales in low-register vernaculars that were then "translated" into high-register vernaculars or Pali. We have no evidence whatsoever as to whether this was true or not, and indeed it is obviously quite possible, perhaps usual, that the process was the reverse. As mentioned above, the prose parts of the stories are written in good, usually sophisticated and therefore, in a nonpejorative sense, difficult and enigmatic Pali. As so often in Buddhist Literature generally, where verses are inserted into prose, for whatever reason (and there are many) they are much more difficult than the prose, often using highly sophisticated poetic techniques such as (as mentioned already) the śleṣa, where a word or phrase is deliberately chosen because it can have two or more meanings. In a few texts these two meanings are one in Pali, one in Sanskrit. Learned indeed.

I have tried to show at length elsewhere in relation to the last and most well-known *Jātaka*, the story of Vessantara, and will also mention below that *Jātaka* stories can embody reflections on the contradictions and difficulties of even the most (allegedly) important of Buddhist values: they express rather than solve moral problems, in the case of the *Vessantara*, detachment and (excessive) generosity versus family love and prudence. Fortunately, Appleton and Shaw's recent translation has useful introductions to all the stories translated. Shaw's introduction to her translation of the *Vessantara* compares it insightfully to Shakespearean comedies and tragedies. Some *Jātakas* can be called short stories, some "epics."

> I would like to mention here a distinction taken from narrative theory never used, to my knowledge, in the interpretation of *The Birth Stories*, that is between constituent and supplementary events or episodes. To take, first, a simple and very familiar western example: Cinderella. There have been many versions of this tale through the centuries, and in them what are the constituent and supplementary events might well be, as in fact they always are, matters of interpretation and debate. But in the simplified modern version designed for children, the evil and oppressive Sisters, Cinderella as their victim, the Glass Slipper and the Prince are constitutive. Without any one of these any other version simply wouldn't be the same story. One can add as many supplementary events and episodes as one likes, but the four things just mentioned are fundamental to any telling of the story in its usual form. In the *Birth Stories*, when the relation between the Story of the Present and the Story of the Past is simple, which it is often not, the constituent events of the Story of the Past must, one would think, be those which correspond most accurately to those in the Story of the Present. But there are many cases where both Stories are long and complicated, and working out which people and events are constituent and which are supplementary are interesting matters of interpretation and debate.[23]

This is certainly the case with versions of the Vessantara story (in Sanskrit Viśvantara, often elsewhere Sudāna and translations of it). The Pali version is long and has many supplementary events. Ārya Śūra's Sanskrit version, written in very high kāvya style, is very much shorter, but it has the same constituent events as the Pali, although I would argue that the general tenor of it has more to do with politics and prudential government than with the melodramatic giving away of the children that is the heart of the Pali version. The constituent event in the "Story of the Present" in Pali and other vernacular versions that we might call the same, which occasions the "Story of the Past" in the *Vessantara*, is a "lotus-leaf shower," in which "those who wished to be made wet were made wet, while not even a drop fell on the body of anyone who did not wish to be made wet" (in Cone's translation). In the "Story of the Past" the event that corresponds to this at the end is a rain of jewels sent down by Sakka, the king of the gods. Vessantara gave some of this to "various families" and kept the rest for himself, with which he "established largesse." The similarity is rather tenuous. And of course one might well see the two dissimilar rain showers as purely formal and supplementary events, and others such as the character of the Brahmin Jūjaka and the highly melodramatic and central "giving away of the children" constituent. A Mongolian phrase puts it nicely: "If you want to cry, read the *Vessantara*; if you want to laugh read [some other story]."

Even more important than this is the question of how the *Vessantara* ends. In the Pali and most South and Southeast Asian versions, in both written texts and ritual performances, the prince returns to his natal city and becomes king. In some Nepali and Chinese tellings, however, he remains in the forest as a renouncer (even in some versions giving away his eyes, as does King Sibi [Śivi] in another famous story), while his son Jāli returns to become king. In my view, Vessantara's return home to be king is a constituent event: he ends up combining in one person the contradictory values of good kingship (involving, eventually, violence through justified punishment) and nonviolent renunciation. So his remaining in the forest makes that version a different, though of course closely related, story. Others may disagree. But such disagreement is in the nature of Literature: How can one put an end to interpretations of Hamlet? Which events in that text are constituent and which supplementary?

1.3.3. Apparently Simple Stories: A Familiar One from Aesop, and a Buddhist One

An allegedly "didactic" tale from the European collection known as *Aesop's Fables*, "The Fox and the Crow," is very widely known. There are countless versions available, again in prose, verse, cartoons, and on the internet. Here is a version, taken deliberately from a book called *Aesop Without Morals*:

> A crow who has stolen some meat perches in a tree. A fox catches sight of him and, wishing to get the meat, stands there and begins to praise him for his size and beauty, telling him that of all the birds he might appropriately be king and that he certainly would be if he had any kind of [good] voice. The crow wants to show the fox that he does have such a voice and so drops the meat and produces a great [ugly] croaking noise. The fox runs up, seizes the meat and says, "Friend Crow, if you had any kind of sense, you would be completely equipped to be king of all."[24]

At the outset of this version we are told, as does not happen in the majority of tellings, that the crow stole the meat (usually it is cheese): already moral complexity is introduced. In another version a farmer puts some poisoned meat in a field to kill rats. The crow steals it, and when the apparently clever fox eats it he dies an agonizing death. Pride comes before a fall, perhaps. Aesop's stories circulated with many different morals, set at either the beginning or the end. The book I have just quoted from gives a moral for each story in an appendix. For this one it is "this fable is appropriate for a senseless person." Others are "beware of flatterers," "this is a story for fools," and the like. In yet other versions, particularly Christian ones, the cheating fox is obviously guilty of wrongdoing and so is the villain of the piece. The moral is then "virtue is forgotten in the pursuit of ambition." In yet others, the fox dies before the crow, who is delighted and cries, "God, you have avenged me!"

In the seventeenth century Jean La Fontaine wrote a book of fables adapted from Aesop in sophisticated French verse, intended it seems for young ladies of the court who otherwise could only read the Bible and what he saw as rather dull religious tracts. The ending of his version of the crow and the fox is "Le Renard s'en saisit, et dit: 'Mon bon Monsieur / apprenez que tout flatteur vit aux dépens de celui qui l'écoute.'" "The fox seizes it [the cheese] and says, 'My dear Sir, learn that every flatterer lives in dependence on the person who listens to him.'" Quite normal, it may seem at first sight. But one can interpret La Fontaine's verse more carefully, as meaning that a flatterer can only exist if there are people not immune to flattery, that is, the latter are necessary parts of the relation. One suggestion is that he was offering a joking critique of royal theater, mocking the stereotypical characters of the courtesan, who flatters those in power to get what she wants, and those in high positions of power who foolishly give it to them. Another interpretation (my own) suggests that a flatterer depends for his very existence on the existence of fools whom he can persuade: to be a flatterer is to be caught, imprisoned in a necessary duality of which he is but one pole.

But whatever the moral, whatever the interpretation, my point is that the stories circulated not because of their usually bland and simple moral. Do we really need an animal fable to teach us that we should be careful of flattery, or try not to be fools? The story circulated because it is a good story, not because of anything it supposedly teaches us.

Here is an analogous Pali tale (II 158ff, #208), entitled *Suṃsumāra Jātaka* (*The Birth Story About the Crocodile*), which I will give in summary (as in the cases of all birth stories discussed hereafter.) The future Buddha is a big monkey who lives on one bank of the Ganges. In the river lives a crocodile. His wife is first described as his bhariyā, the normal word for a human wife, thus "Mrs. Crocodile," a humanized form who speaks. Elsewhere she is suṃsumārī, the ordinary word for a female crocodile. She becomes pregnant and longs to eat the big monkey's heart. In a humanized identity with a voice she is cruel and disgraceful; as a crocodile she is just being carnivorous, as all crocodiles are. Mr. Crocodile thinks of a means (an upāya) to get it and goes off to try to do so (hen-pecked, uxorious, devoted?). He reaches the monkey and asks why he is living in such a crowded and dreary place. On the other side of the river, he says, deceiving the monkey as to his real intentions, there are trees with excellent fruits, sweet to eat. He offers to carry the monkey on his back across the river to eat them. The monkey, stupidly and perhaps greedily, agrees. Once in the river the crocodile starts to sink into the water. The monkey, finally showing some intelligence, asks the crocodile what is happening, and he tells him the truth. The monkey says, "Sir, we monkeys don't keep our hearts in our chests, for if we did, then jumping around at the tops of trees as we do, our hearts would be crushed to powder." Instead, he says, they hang them from fig trees: he points out to the crocodile a tree on the bank he previously lived on (figs do vaguely resemble hearts, I suppose). "Take me there and I will give you my heart." The (Mr.) Crocodile does so, and when they arrive the monkey jumps off the crocodile's back and exclaims joyfully, "I have cheated you (the verb is √ vañc, always used for wrongdoing in Pali), foolish crocodile, keep however many fruits (hearts) you want. Your body is big but your wisdom (paññā: intelligence) is small!"

What is this story about? What, if anything, is its moral? The "Story of the Present" says that it is about the evil monk Devadatta's attempts to kill the Buddha. He is always the villain in Pali stories, cited in the "Story of the Present" and/or the conclusion as the present-day equivalent of miscreants of all sorts in the past. The crocodile (Devadatta) first deceives the monkey (the future Buddha) in not telling him his real intention but giving him a false invitation.

The monkey foolishly climbs on the crocodile's back. When the crocodile does tell the truth, it is unwisely, because of the dénouement of the story. The monkey then deceives him by speaking of the heart-shaped fruits. Thus both the crocodile and the monkey show foolishness; both also tell lies. This is a unique birth story: it is the only one in which the future Buddha tells a lie. Is the story telling us to avoid stupidity? Is it that we should save our skins even by lying? Or is it just, again, a good story about the coexistence and alternation between trust and deceit, truth telling and lying, foolishness and ingenuity? If you want a simple moral, your guess is as good as mine. I think the resistance to one-sided interpretation is the point. This and so many other examples of "didactic literature" are, in fact, vignettes of multiperspectivalism, nuggets of inscrutability.

1.3.4. Some Quotidian/Dhamma 1 Stories: Friendship, and for Parents, Justified Violence

Having a good friend is a monastic virtue, although here it is a vertical connection resembling that of patron and client, which is so often what "friendship" means cross-culturally, as in the Roman amicitia. One's good friend (kalyāṇamitta) is one's advisor monk (ovādaka-bhikkhu), a senior monk who chooses one's meditation subject according to one's temperament and in general gives good advice, which no doubt it would be unwise not to follow. Friendship, in both the vertical sense—patronage—and the horizontal—friendship between equals—is an extremely common motif throughout proverbial (*Nīti*) texts, with such verses often repeated in *The Birth Stories*, regularly by the future Buddha as an ascetic. Sometimes the uttering of such verses is a constituent event; more often they are given as supplementary homilies offered usually by the hero of the story. Friend stories are very often between animals, either of the same species or across species, including those otherwise considered permanent enemies, such as a lion and a jackal or a snake and a mongoose. There are also stories about friendship between a human and an animal. The kinds of virtue shown by such a friend are on the one hand kindness, helping his human friend out in distress, discerning who are friends or enemies; on the other hand, especially, gratitude. Here is one about friendship between humans, starting from a childhood horizontal relation and moving to an adult vertical one. The main story is given in the "Story of the Present," as quite often, with the "Story of the Past" simply saying that in the past everything happened just as in the present. The story concerns Anāthapiṇḍika, a very well-known rich supporter of the Buddha, who is an actant in many stories.

The story, the text says, is about a friend of Anāthapiṇḍika's, with whom as a child and pupil of the same teacher he played with mud pies. His friend is called Kālakaṇṇī, "Black Ears," an unfortunately inauspicious name. When they are grown up Kālakaṇṇī falls on hard times and is not able to make a living. He goes to Anāthapiṇḍika, now a rich banker, who employs him as business manager. Some other employees in the house, however, treat him badly, telling him when to stand up, sit down, and eat. One day some of Anāthapiṇḍika's friends and colleagues come to him and tell him not to allow this sort of thing to go on in his house: "He is not your equal, he is ill fated, unfortunate: why do you have anything to do with him?" Anāthapiṇḍika replies, "A name is just a matter of convention. The wise do not make a name the measure (of someone). It is not right to behave (in a certain way just) because one has heard something auspicious. I will not get rid of a friend with whom I played with mud pies just because of (his) name." One day he goes to a village that pays him taxes and leaves the manager to protect his house. Some burglars come, thinking the house empty, but Kālakannī knows they are there and starts such a noise that they discard their weapons and run away. The next day people come, see the weapons, and praise Kālakannī excitedly: "Today, if there had not been such an intelligent guardian of the house, burglars would have got in as they wished and the whole house would have been ruined. The banker is fortunate to (be able to) rely on such a firm friend." Anāthapiṇḍika comes back and they tell him what happened. He replies, "A name is not the measure; a friendly attitude is the measure," and gives him even higher wages. He goes to the Buddha and tells him what happened, and the Buddha tells a "Story of the Past." In it the overall narrative voice says simply that the same thing happened as in the "Story of the Present."[25]

Respect for parents is expressed and celebrated in many stories. *The Birth Story About Sāma* (#54, *Sāma Jātaka*—Sāma is a proper name) is very well known.[26] It is gentle, then violent, but overall compassionate. It is long and has two constituent magical events: Sāma's birth and his revival from apparent death. It is a campū (melodramatic, tragic, and romantic tale). In the "Story of the Present" a monk is in the habit of giving what he receives in alms, food, and clothing to his mother and father. Some other monks reprimand him and in displeasure tell the Buddha about it. The Buddha summons the monk and congratulates him, saying that he too in the past supported his parents. In the "Story of the Past" two beings in a Brahma world, which is genderless and sexless, are reborn as the son and daughter of two families of hunters. Their names are Dukūlaka and Pārikā. Their parents arrange a marriage between them, but they do not want to have sex and refuse to act as hunters. They then renounce and go to live in the Himalayas. Sakka, king of the gods, sends his handyman Vissakamma to build for each of them a leaf hut and arrange the necessities for an ascetic life. They dress as ascetics, and by the power of their friendliness all creatures around them feel the same thing and do not kill one another. Sakka comes down and looks after them. But one day, realizing that they will go blind, he tells them they should have a son to look after them, and thereby "follow the way of the world (loka dhamma)." Dukūlaka firmly refuses, and Sakka tells him to touch Pārikā's navel with his hand (this itself a slight breach of the usual norms of an ascetic life). He does so at the time of her period, and the future Buddha comes down from a heavenly world and enters her womb. When he is born he is called Suvaṇṇasāma, "he who has the same color as gold." When he reaches the age of sixteen, on one occasion his parents leave him in the leaf hut and go out to look for food. They are bitten by a snake and go blind. Sāma then looks after them for some time. One day the king of Benares goes into the forest to hunt, and after some short episodes shoots Sāma with a poisoned arrow. This is, apparently, a fatal wound; Sāma vomits blood, but he still has some time to live. The text seems deliberately ambiguous about whether in fact later he dies or not. Often language is used that normally means death, and on one occasion his mother is even made to use technical systematic language that certainly does describe the process of death. But it also says things like "he lost consciousness," which may not mean that he actually dies. This may be conceptually confusing, but it is clearly narratively useful. He exchanges a long series of verses with the king, during and at the end of which he repeatedly laments his parents. The king, listening to his laments and realizing that he himself might go to hell for his misdeeds, decides to stay and help look after Sāma's parents. He goes to the hermitage and tells them what has happened. They want to see Sāma, and the king leads them to him. They both, along with a goddess who was Sāma's mother seven lifetimes before this one, make an act of truth.[27] After the mother's and father's acts of truth Sāma turns from one side to another. Sāma's mother, the goddess's, act of truth is followed by Sāma's "recovery" (nirogatā—an unusual word meaning literally "lack of illness") and his parents regaining their sight. The king, who has by this time had a change of heart, Sāma, and his parents go back to the hermitage, where Sāma instructs the king on the ten dhammas of a king (a very common motif throughout *The Birth Stories*). The king goes back to Benares, performs acts of merit, and at death goes to heaven. Sāma and his parents live a life of supernatural practices and at death go to the Brahma world. In Buddhism one can't say "and so they lived happily ever after," since there is no "ever after" in a world always and everywhere characterized by impermanence.

But it is a fairy story that expresses and celebrates an important virtue of dhamma 1, caring for parents.

Justified violence is, of course, explicit in all the stories where a king hands out justice. The ethical and narrative principle of reciprocity, central to dhamma 1, requires it, since crime is inevitable in the quotidian world. But it is present also in stories where people or animals kill for revenge. In what seems always to be called *The Birth Story of the Cat* (#128, *Bilāra Jātaka*), although the villain in the Pali version is a jackal (sigāla), the "Story of the Present" is about a fraudulent monk.[28] In the "Story of the Past," the future Buddha is a mouse with an entourage of many hundreds of other mice. A jackal wonders how to deceive them and eat them. The future Buddha mistakes him for a moral character and asks his name; it is, the jackal says, Dhammika, perhaps "the Righteous," or more ponderously "He who does what is right." He comes up with a plan to eat the last in a row of mice as they walk along. He catches the mouse at the rear, chews and swallows it, and washes his mouth (presumably to deceive the bodhisatta about what he is doing). Through this the entourage of mice gradually becomes attenuated. The future Buddha sees that something is wrong and decides to test the jackal by himself taking up the rear. The jackal tries to capture him, but the future Buddha-mouse criticizes him, saying that his righteousness is not real, just a disguise. He then jumps at the jackal and bites his throat, killing him. The other mice come back and eat the jackal, making a sound I suppose we might translate "munch munch," or "crunch crunch" (murumurā). Then the text adds a short supplementary event, which shows that the story has been to some extent deliberately witty: when the mice eat the jackal, it is only those who come first who eat it, not those who come later, the obvious point being that there is no meat left for them. Get in first! Likewise, in *The Birth Story About the Crane* (#38,

Baka Jātaka), a crane deceives some fish and eats them, and the story ends with a crab avenging them by biting the heron's throat.[29] The future Buddha, reborn as a tree spirit who sees the whole thing, congratulates the crab and speaks an ironic verse: "The person skilled in deceit (nikati-paññо) does not find happiness completely. Just like the heron skilled in deceit [only] found success from the crow!"[30]

1.3.5. Comedy

So there are stories that offer examples of quotidian wisdom, some of which confound and challenge the reader/audience by offering perhaps irresolvable ethical and value dilemmas. There are also stories that seem quite obviously intended to be, or at least to contain, comedy, intended to entertain rather than sermonize. Here are two, the first an outright slapstick comedy about a monkey and his penis, *The Birth Story About a Turtle* (#258, *Kacchapa Jātaka*), and the second, *The Birth Story About Temiya* (#538, *Temiya Jātaka*), a more subtle problematization by means of farce of a popular theme elsewhere in the stories, kingship and renunciation.[31] In the case of the first story the earliest (upper-class) translator found it so scurrilous that he translated it into Latin: we can't have the unruly and passionate lower classes inflamed by such a tale, can we? It has recently been translated into English, twice. God help civilization.

In *The Birth Story About a Turtle*, the future Buddha is an ascetic in the Himalayas who lives in a leaf hut. During the day he standardly sits at the door of his hut in meditation, sitting still. A bold and dissolute monkey is in the habit of putting his penis in the ascetic's ear and ejaculating, to which the ascetic remains impervious. One day a turtle emerges from the Ganges and because of the heat falls asleep with his mouth open. Seeing another opportunity, the monkey ejaculates into his mouth. The turtle wakes up, closes his mouth, and so bites on the monkey's penis. In great pain the monkey runs to the ascetic, holding the turtle in his hands. The ascetic "makes a joke" (davaṃ karoti) by comparing him to a Brahmin with a bowl full of food in his hands. The monkey admits his stupidity and asks the ascetic to release him. The ascetic, chatting with the tortoise, makes another joke, that tortoises and monkeys are from different families (in India, different castes) and so shouldn't have sex with each other. The turtle, pleased with the joke, opens his mouth to laugh and so lets go of the monkey's penis. The monkey runs away, vowing never to come back.

Isn't this entirely a joke? What moral can we draw? Don't put your penis in the wrong place? Don't disrespect ascetics and turtles? Don't, simplistically, be foolish? Unusually, the impersonal and omniscient narrative voice interrupts the "Story of the Past"—whose narrative voice is, formally speaking, that of the Buddha—by remarking that in this story "it seems [*sic*: kira] that the future Buddha was practicing excellence in patience (forbearance, endurance, khanti, Sanskrit kṣānti)." This, like so many of the morals added to Aesop's fables over the centuries, is obviously a later addition, appropriate for only a small part of the story. Was it just pious (and pompous) monks bowdlerizing a funny story? Is the mention of excellence in patience itself an ironic joke? This is quite possible, it seems to me. Monks surely like to laugh too, sometimes in a self-deprecating manner: is this not itself an element of wisdom? (Many old and young monks whom I have had the good fortune to meet laugh a lot.) And audiences in courts were certainly used to bawdy humor and its use in mockery. In any case, for a modern interpreter to follow the first of these alternatives, that the story is "about" excellence in patience, is likewise bowdlerizing the story, on the grounds that "religions" must be serious and tell stories in order to sell something.

The second story is less obviously comic on the surface level, but it is full of implicit farcical comedy, in my reading, which underlies the narrative throughout. It is also a melodrama. It is the first of the last ten *Jātakas*, the *Mahānipāta* (*The Great Section*), which is very frequently, at least in modern times, painted on temple walls. It is sometimes also called the *Mūgapakkha Jātaka* (*The Birth Story of the Dumb Cripple*).[32] The "Story of the Present" says that it is about "The Great Renunciation" (that is, the Buddha's) and in the schema of the ten forms of excellence this is number 3, excellence in renunciation. It is, as I have said, a subtle and clever farce, though this genre category should not be taken in the pejorative sense in which the word is often used nowadays. Thus for the latter, the *OED* has not only "Something as ridiculous as a theatrical farce; a proceeding that is ludicrously futile or insincere; a hollow pretense, a mockery," but also, more simply and generously, "A dramatic work (usually short) which has for its sole object to excite laughter." The story's humor is restrained and understated. Another definition of farce I found in an online dictionary is also appropriate: "a light, humorous play in which the plot depends on a skillfully exploited situation rather than on the development of character." The future Buddha indeed remains the same throughout the two main situations of the story (his being tested and tempted in the royal court, and then living in the forest), from the moment of his birth until the end. This is not a bildungsroman.

Here is a summary of the story, giving for the most part the constituent events but not the supplementary ones, albeit that I will make the argument that one scene that might seem at first reading to be a supplementary event is in fact a constituent one.

When the future Buddha, Prince Temiya, is just a month old, he sits on his father's lap while he judges criminals. The future Buddha sees that his father orders that one of them receive a thousand lashes with spiked whips, one be sent to prison in chains, one be struck on the body a thousand times with swords, and the last be impaled on a stake. The Great Being becomes terrified and fearful: "Alas, because he is a king my father is doing terrible things, which will take him to hell."[33] Remembering his own past lives, he reflects, "I was king (here) for twenty years, and (as a result) cooked for eighty thousand years in hell. Now I have been reborn again in this criminal house. If I become king I will again endure great suffering in hell." Then the deity who lives in the umbrella comforts him, saying, "Dear Temiya, don't be afraid. If you want to escape from here, act as if you can't walk properly, even though you can; act as if you are deaf and dumb, even thought you're not. Take on these three characteristics so as not to show your wisdom (paṇḍitabhāva)."[34] Over the next sixteen years, as he grows up, the king, his wives, and courtiers try various means to make him show that he is not really handicapped. They leave him thirsty and hungry, but he does not cry for milk or food; they offer him playthings, but he is not interested. They try to frighten him by putting him in a house and setting fire to it, by getting an elephant to pretend to attack him, and by letting snakes loose near him that have had their teeth removed and mouths tied up, but in no case does he move. They have dances performed in front of him and the other children, but though the others laugh and enjoy themselves, he says and does nothing, reflecting that there will be no laughing and being happy for him in hell. They have someone pretend to attack him with a sword, to no avail. They have conch shells blown suddenly and loudly near him from behind hiding places, but he does not react; likewise, they try drums and suddenly lighting lamps in the dark; they smear molasses all over him and let flies bite him; they leave him unwashed for a year; they heat water under his bed; all to no avail. When he is sixteen, thinking that at this age everyone feels sexual desire arise, they have him bathed and ornamented like a god and bring beautiful women to dance lasciviously and sing for him. But he restrains his breathing so that his body becomes rigid, like a Buddha image. The women are afraid to touch him, thinking him a nonhuman spirit.

Finally the king consults soothsaying Brahmins, who advise that he should be taken to the charnel ground and killed. At this his mother weeps, saying, "Dear young Temiya, because of you I have not slept for sixteen years, my eyes are shriveled up from weeping, (I feel) as if my heart were breaking with grief. I know that you are not crippled, deaf, and dumb: do not make me (live) without a lord."[35] But he ignores her and so is taken away from the city to a part of the forest made to look like a charnel ground by the gods. Then the future Buddha, wondering if the chariot driver will be able to overpower him physically, takes hold of the chariot and lifts it up as if it were a toy (this is the scene standardly represented in modern temples). He starts to live as an ascetic, and his father comes to visit him, accompanied by his army and the entire population. The future Buddha preaches a sermon to them, at the end of which everyone takes to ascetic life in the forest. A neighboring king, hearing that the king of Benares and his people have renounced, enters the city to seize the kingship of Benares. He sees that all the houses and stores have been left open and that the palace is empty, with seven kinds of costly jewels abandoned there.

Next, in a telling detail I regard as constituent of the story as a farce and not as a supplementary one in a tale of renunciation, the king, thinking that there must be something dangerous about all this abandoned wealth, sends for some drunks who have remained in the city and asks them which gate the king went out through. They tell him, and he goes to the forest also, where he and his entourage also renounce. Yet another king does the same, so "three kingdoms were cast aside."[36] Elephants and horses revert to living wild in the forest, war chariots disintegrate, coins from the (royal) treasuries are scattered about the hermitage like sand. Everyone becomes destined, at the end of their life, to be reborn in the Brahma worlds. Even the animals, the elephants and horses, their minds calmed and inspired by the company of the group of sages (isi-gaṇa), are reborn in heaven.

There are many ways, it seems to me, this is obviously farcical. How, to ask but one realist question, could one forest have enough space, roots, and fruits for the people of three kingdoms? Where did they urinate and defecate? The motif of animals giving up their normal natures and becoming calm is a familiar textual utopian fantasy. The detail about the drunks left in the city is only an apparently supplementary event: I take it to have been deliberately inserted there as a constituent event by the redactors of the story, introducing a moment of realism to help create the impression of farce. Some people were, like the overwhelming majority of its readers/listeners, immune to the charms of forest renunciation, preferring alcohol (though probably not too much of it, like the drunks in the story).

The long sequence of attempts to make the future Buddha as a child either reveal his true humanity through suffering or fear or be charmed out of it, which takes up a third of the text, is by turns amusing, absurd, frightful, and entirely fantastic: a child behaving that way?! Parents would have allowed themselves a wry smile at this.

1.3.6. Talking-Animal Stories: Why Do People Tell Them?

Telling animal stories, so very common in *The Birth Stories*, is such a familiar practice worldwide, known from childhood on, that it might seem odd to ask why we tell them. But I will now ask the question explicitly and give some preliminary answers, though I am sure there is a great deal more to say. Much of what I will say here, though not all, has been said before.

First, of course, it is just because they are entertaining: a good example where the pleasure of the text is the confrontation with the unfamiliar. How striking and fearful to have Little Red Riding Hood with the Big Bad Wolf disguised as her grandmother! There are a very large number of versions of this story, dating back to peasants in tenth-century France. How much unusual fun there is in Goldilocks and the Three Bears! But one can essay more than this.

There is an inherent irony in such stories, where the animals obviously represent in some way (in fact, in various ways) forms of humanity. We can be shown to be, sometimes by turns, foolish, wise (or apparently so), thoughtful, impetuous, greedy, cruel, and so many other things, either by exaggeration or by the sheer fact of our being, whether explicitly said or just by implication, worse than, the same as, or better than the animals in the stories. Narratively there is an inherent and endlessly fascinating oscillation between two identities, necessarily two actants in the same animal/human character: merely animals but, because they speak, human. Forgive me what is called in the book I got it from a "schoolboy joke." A horse and a cow are energetically debating some question, without resolution. A dog who has been lying nearby gets up and tells them the answer. The horse turns to the cow and says, "Amazing! A talking dog!" Even in this perhaps silly example, there is a discernible and to some extent subtle changing of frames: the first in which we accept the fact of animals speaking in a story as normal and unobjectionable, the second in which we are brought to the realization of the frame in which such an absurd story is set. By this means we therefore objectify immediately, and come to interpret the narrative first in one frame and then in another. Such is true, surely, of the monkey and the crocodile (and his wife) in the story just told. A female animal or Mrs. Crocodile? Both.

The identities of the animals are often stereotypes: in India lions, kings of animals, are noble and brave, but also on occasion arrogant, proud, and foolish. Cats, foxes, and jackals are cunning (the last also greedy), snakes dangerous and duplicitous, owls (unlike their Western counterparts, who are often wise) ugly and ferocious, and so on. There are also natural enmities between species, perhaps the most renowned being between mongooses and snakes. But they can also act or speak out of character. In this they may be said to resemble the medieval commedia dell'arte, where stock characters, often denoted by standardized masks or costumes, or even placards with moral terms written on them, moved through standard stories—usually comedies but sometimes also tragedies and mixed forms—played by actors who offered improvised speeches or dialogues as commentary on local politics, bawdy or irreverent humor, and other things, but often also remarks that were not what was expected from the stock character. Some American readers may not understand this; British readers will: such stories, stock characters, remarks about contemporary politics and the like, all happen in Christmas pantomimes.

In this, of course, speaking animals, commedia dell'arte, and pantomime characters represent what all of us are: at one and the same time predictable characters but also capable of acting or speaking out of character. If we had no predictable character but acted and spoke always as multiple, changing characters, we would suffer from multiple personality disorder, or worse, schizophrenia. If our characters were completely unchanging, we would be tedious to the point of inhumanity.Here is a story where an animal acts in character—that is, in a character ascribed to it. In the "Story of the Present" there is a well at a place called Isipatana (which often figures in Buddhist stories). The future Buddha is an ascetic living there with a group of others. A jackal is in the habit of defecating and urinating in the well and then leaving. The Buddha chases it away and tells the "Story of the Past." In this same well, he says, presupposing the text of the "Story of the Present," a jackal is in the habit of fouling the well. Some of the ascetics catch the jackal and take him to the future Buddha, who exchanges verses with him. The future Buddha says:

> Some old ascetics in the forest worked hard to make this well. Why, good sir, do you defecate on it? The jackal replies: This is the proper nature (dhamma) of jackals; we defecate where we have drunk. This has been the proper nature of my ancestors. You should not complain! The future Buddha replies: Of those whose proper nature is this, what can be their improper nature be [i.e., when they do wrong]? Let me not see your proper or improper nature anywhere! And then the future Buddha sent him away.[37]

There are many stories where one or more animals act in unexpected ways, different from their normal natures as we know them in other stories. A short and pleasant little whimsy is the story of an elephant and a dog, in *The Story About Repetition* (*Abhiṇha Jātaka* #27).[38] A dog is in the habit of going to a royal elephant's stall to eat the food that drops to him from the elephant's mouth. He becomes friends with the elephant and will not eat without him. The two became inseparable; they play by having the dog take hold of the elephant's trunk and swing back and forth. One day a villager buys the dog and takes him away. The elephant refuses to eat, drink, or bathe. The king dispatches his minister (the future Buddha, called paṇḍita) to find out why. He discovers that the elephant is grieving because of the absence of his friend. He tells this to the king, who recovers the dog. The dog runs to the elephant, who takes him with his trunk, puts him on his head, and weeps. Then he lets the dog down and has him eat first. The king exclaims of the future Buddha, "He (even) knows the hearts of animals!"

One of the most popular animal stories is *The Hare in the Moon*.[39] Four animals, a hare, a monkey, a jackal, and an otter, live in close proximity. They are called both "friends" and "wise" (paṇḍita). The hare regularly gives sermons to the other three. On the day preceding an uposatha day—a day on which one observes abstinence, gives gifts, and so on—the hare urges his friends to practice the observances, in particular giving to beggars. The otter goes off and finds some fish that a fisherman has buried in the ground. The otter digs them up, holds them up, and shouts, "Does anyone own these?" Not getting an answer, he takes them home. Is this theft? The jackal goes and finds, in an absent field watcher's hut, a spit for cooking meat, a lizard, and a pot of milk curds. He also asks if they have an owner, and getting no answer, takes them home. Theft again? The monkey goes into a wood and finds some mangoes (not, this time, belonging to anyone else). The hare reflects that he has nothing to give: human beggars won't eat grass, which, as an animal, the hare lives on. So he forms the intention to offer his own body as meat. As is usual in such cases of high or extreme virtue, the seat on which sits Sakka, the king of the gods, grows hot. He looks down, sees what has happened, and comes down to earth. He asks the first three animals for alms, and they give him some of the food they acquired, properly or not. But when he comes to the hare, who has nothing, the hare announces his intention to roast his own flesh as his gift. Sakka creates a fire and the hare jumps into it. But due to Sakka's power, the fire feels to the hare ice cold, and of course does not roast him. He asks what is happening; Sakka reveals himself and says he came just to test the hare's virtue (character, or morality, sīla). Then he squeezes a mountain, takes its juice (a nice touch), and draws with it a picture of the hare on the moon, so that his good qualities will be known for the rest of the eon. Like so many others, a just-so story.

1.3.7. Just-So Stories

The idea of just-so stories is taken, of course, from Rudyard Kipling's collection of whimsical tales that explain, in a humorous manner, how certain things came about: "How the camel got his hump," "How the rhinoceros got his skin," "How the leopard got his spots," and so on. Here is one from the *Jātaka* collection, *The Birth Story of the Pot* (*Kumbha Jātaka*, #512, V 11–20), an odd title, as many of them are. In the "Story of the Present" there are five hundred women friends of Visākhā, who is always a firm supporter of the Buddha and here behaves, as usual, fittingly. The other women get drunk and behave insultingly before the Buddha, dancing, singing, making improper gestures with their hands and feet, and generally making an unseemly commotion. He sobers them up with a display of magic; Visākhā asks him how drinking alcohol started, and he tells the "Story of the Past." It begins in a forest with a man called Sura.[40]

There is a tree that branches into three parts, at the base of which is a hole "as big as a wine jar." Rainwater collects in it, and myrobalan fruit and rice get into it. The sun's heat ferments the liquid and it turns red. Birds come to drink from the hole in the hot season, get drunk, and fall down. They sleep for a while and then fly off singing. Similar things happen to dogs, monkeys, and other animals. Sura sees what happens, drinks himself, and is taken with a desire to eat meat. He roasts some birds that have fallen down drunk by the tree and spends a couple of days "dancing with one hand and eating meat with the other." Then he goes to an ascetic called Varuṇa, who lives in the forest, to drink and eat meat with him. That is how the words surā and vāruṇī, both terms for kinds of alcohol, arose, from the names Sura and Varuṇa. The two men take some of the alcohol to a nearby town, where they sell it to the king. This lasts him a couple of days, and he asks for more. The two men fetch more from the forest, but then take note of the ingredients and start brewing it in the city. The townsmen get drunk, and it is "as if the town were empty." The two men then ply their trade in the cities of Banaras and Sāketa, with the same results. Then they come to Sāvatthi and tell the king that they need the ingredients and five hundred jars to brew alcohol. To guard the jars, they tie a cat to each one. As it is brewing some alcohol overflows the jars, and the cats drink it, become drunk, and fall asleep. Mice come and bite off their ears, noses, teeth, and tails. The king thinks the two men must have made poison and has them beheaded. But then the cats wake up, move around, and play. The king realizes it is not poison and prepares to drink it himself. At this point Sakka, the king of the gods, thinking that if the king starts to drink "all India will be destroyed," comes to earth disguised as a Brahmin with a jar of alcohol in his hand. But instead of selling it to the king, he gives voice to a long series of verses expounding the evils of alcohol. The king, persuaded, has the jars broken, lives a life observing the kinds of good moral character and giving gifts, and becomes bound for heaven. But the story ends on a wry note: "But in India drinking alcohol became widespread."

The story, like Kipling's, is full of verbal and other witticisms, absurdities such as animals getting drunk (are human drunks not equally absurd?), and a final reflection that undercuts the whole just-so trajectory. Is this a happy ending? I imagine some of the less well-behaved monks, and certainly courtiers, would have been amused, the latter perhaps raising their glasses to the storyteller.

1.3.8. Karma and Rebirth: Explanation or Forms of Identity (Actant)?

It is often said that *The Birth Stories* are told to exemplify the law of karma: good is recompensed by good and bad by bad. One major influence on this way of thinking was Max Weber, who studied karma from the point of view of the problem of theodicy. Like so much else in Weber's lexicon, this had its home in Christian theology: How can one reconcile the existence of an omnipotent and benevolent God with the real existence of evil? Weber broadened this to ask: how can belief systems in general explain the existence of evil and suffering? He concluded that karma was "the most complete formal solution of the problem of theodicy," "the most consistent theodicy ever produced by history."[41] It is not, because it does not resolve the problem of the ultimate origin of evil and suffering: karma has no beginning.

In the Christian case, the problem of theodicy is precisely where real evil and suffering originate: from an omnipotent and benevolent God? How so? In *The Birth Stories*, the very structure, connecting the "Story of the Present" with the "Story of the Past" and then connecting them with an entirely perfunctory conclusion, may be said to presuppose karma, particularly when—as by no means happens always—the "Story of the Past" is a direct analogy to the "Story of the Present." It is very often said in modern secondary sources that the birth stories illustrate the idea of karma. They usually do not: that is, apart from the perfunctory and quite formalistic putting together at the end, there is only rarely a direct statement that event A in the "Story of the Present" is connected to and "explained" karmically by event B in a past life. There are transitions from one life to another, sometimes preserving the same gender and the same species, but more often just a bland "and so he/she went to heaven," or "to the Brahma worlds." Such connections, however, are rarely long-term and serial. Just one story to another and no more.

In understanding how the discourse of karma works in the actual life of Buddhists, one should follow Charles Keyes and distinguish between efficient and ultimate explanations. Efficient explanations are those that might actually achieve something in the world: fertility, cure of disease, passing exams, whatever. They have, as he says, both "explanatory and prescriptive aspects." Just as with modern medicine, one might have no idea what the explanation is. Who, apart from medical specialists, knows exactly what viruses, cancer, schizophrenia, and so much else are, or how they are caused? Often specialists don't know either: they just know how to treat them, using science, more efficiently than with any other knowledge system. Many people wish also to have recourse to fantasy, in case rational science fails to achieve a cure of physical or mental illness: witness the frequency of supernaturalist icons in hospital rooms.

What is the ultimate explanation in case efficient practices fail? Pessimists—or as I would say, realists—may simply conclude that there is no such explanation. Many people in the West will turn to ideas such as "God's will" or "fate." People called Hindus and Buddhists may likewise turn in the first instance to one or other of the panoply of efficient explanations and practices: witchcraft, possession, disturbance of bodily "humors," the ill favor of some local, small-scale deity, and so much else of the same genre. But if these efficient solutions fail, some people may simply shrug their shoulders and say, "It's his or her karma," in the same way as people refer to "God's will" or "fate" as a means of not simply accepting the situation as having no explanation at all. Common to all these ultimate explanations or reactive phrases is the idea that there is a rationally and morally ordered universe, even if one has no idea how it works and it has not offered the desired outcome in any particular situation. Likewise, in the Buddhist case, people hope that, say, spirit mediums are able to exorcise the sick. If they can't, people will turn to the inexplicable and incomprehensible karma when all else fails.

Intellectuals in the tradition, primarily in texts, will try to comprehend it, as in the twenty-four kinds of conditioning relation elaborated in the Abhidhamma text the *Paṭṭhāna*. Even these intellectual-textual constructions can be used in instrumentalist ways, as when the twenty-four kinds of conditioning relation and other Abhidhamma texts are recited at funerals. These intellectual-textual constructions are not held to be wholly explanatory: only a buddha, and no ordinary person, knows, it is so often said, how karma actually works.

But my interest here is not in these anthropological issues, important though they are, but in the textualist uses of the idea. It is a way of construing identities, their establishment, imagined connections, and disconnections, which together produce stories, comprehensible only to what has traditionally been called the "omniscient narrator" and his audience. Omniscience, in a quite different sense, is also said to be to the aspiration of a future Buddha as an actant within the stories. In many modern novels, of course, the narrative voice itself is to be construed as having a particular, sometimes deceptive character, itself also therefore an actant within the narrative. But in traditional premodern narratives such as the birth stories, the overall narrative voice is omniscient. In narrating the text, this omniscient narrator is behind everything, even the "Story of the Past," which is, within the story, narrated by the voice of the present Buddha Gotama, a fact almost always forgotten as soon as the story starts to be told. Of course this narrative voice of the Buddha refers to "the future Buddha" in the third person in every story.

We all have multiple identities, as child, parent, student, teacher, engineer, accountant, politician, person at home, person in public, and so on, all of which can be connected or disconnected as identities of the same "person," whatever that means. If we suffer from multiple personality disorder as a pathology, we may end up confined to a mental hospital. But most of us live happily with different identities in different contexts. In the birth stories there are many multiple identities. Overall, of course, there is the double identity of the present Buddha in the "Story of the Present" and conclusion, and the future Buddha as an actant, usually the hero, of the "Story of the Past," often denoted straightforwardly within the story by the word bodhisatta or Mahāsatta, "Great Being." This is the case even when, for example, he is an actant such as an animal or tree spirit. In such stories, as I have said, there is always the perhaps only implicit double identity of the animal or spirit as an animal or spirit, in the case of animals with the characteristics of that (often constructed and conventionalized) species, and that of human beings seen as likewise foolish, clever, brave, wise, etc. Karma and rebirth are narrative ways of connecting identities one to another, superimposing one on another. This is triply or fourfold the case with the Buddha: himself as an allegedly historical actant in the "Story of the Present," and always at least twofold in the "Story of the Past": the future Buddha and the person he is in that life. When he is a talking animal there is always a corresponding human identity presupposed, and so the identity is, implicitly if not explicitly, fourfold.

So the stories do not so much illustrate the ideas of karma and rebirth as use them as narrative devices. Once again, for the external analyst karma and rebirth do not exist. One has to find other, external ways of understanding them.

1.3.9. Caveat Lector: Currently Available Translations of the Jātakas

I must, I fear, in this section make some very negative remarks, already mentioned in passing, on the frankly appalling translations of the birth stories that nonspecialists in Pali (that is, almost everyone) have had to read for more than a century now. I have mentioned the prejudice that these stories were simple didactic literature, aimed very often indeed at children. An Oxbridge translation team, under the general editorship of E. B. Cowell, produced at the turn of the twentieth century a translation of the entire collection, in six volumes, which reflects this assumption.[42] The translations generally get the events of the stories correct, or close to it.

How could they not? But there is a complete chaos of multiple, very often inaccurate or inappropriate translations of the same words, and single English translations of different Pali words. The translations are often quite unsuitable to the psychological and sociological complexities of the texts and to the situations contained in them. The very careful avoidance of anachronism is ignored, or not noticed: thus dhamma becomes often "the Doctrine," which in *The Birth Stories* it is certainly not. How could it be, when there is no Buddha to have discovered it? Other English versions of the stories, widely available in book or pamphlet form, in cartoons and on the internet, have merely copied, as far as I can see, usually with even more simplification, this old and bad translation. Worst of all is the condescending assumption that because these are children's stories the complex, sophisticated, and often beautiful verses can be translated into English rhyming verse, which produces offensive doggerel. Words are added or ignored at will if they do not fit the desired English rhyme. Here is one example, in itself perhaps innocuous in terms of the accuracy of the general rendering in its narrative context but completely misleading as to the tone. A verse, which occurs in a number of places and in a number of different contexts in the collection, is in Pali quite simple: "āsiṃ seth'eva puriso na nibbindeyya paṇḍito / passāmi vo 'haṃ attānaṃ yathā icchiṃ tathā āhu." At Ja VI 43 Appleton renders this, correctly, if not entirely literally (what is a literal translation?): "You should take heart. A wise person should not give up. I see how I myself got what I wanted [i.e., in this story]."[43] In his translation of the story, which has this verse at Ja VI 43, Rouse refers his readers to his own translation of IV 269, which is: "Hope on, O man, if thou be wise, nor let thy courage tire Myself I see, who now have won the goal of my desire."[44] In his translation of the Pali at I 267, Lord [*sic*] Chalmers offers an even more absurd and mistaken rendering, which like Rouse's adds words to get the desired rhyme: "Toil on, my brother; still in hope stand fast, / Nor let thy courage flag and tire. Myself I see, who, all my woes o'erpast / Am master of my heart's desire."[45]

Adding English words or ignoring Pali ones happens in the translations of almost all verses throughout the six volumes. Perhaps, charitably, we might say that an English reader in the twenty-first century can try to make allowances for the prose style and inconsistencies, as well as the doggerel verses, albeit that in many places he or she will simply not be able to understand what is being said. Uncharitably, one might say that this is exactly what members of the late-Victorian upper class would produce as a rendering of Oriental moral fables, which were to them obviously simplistic and childlike. Why did the committee do all that work?

Here is a more serious example, of prose, where the English translation has misled an influential scholar in quite typical ways. It occurs in the *Vessantara Jātaka*. In the preface to the second edition of Cone's translation, Gombrich states that the *Jātaka* "had been translated into English only once before, by W. D. H. Rouse in 1907. That version we found neither attractive nor accurate. We were unable to profit from it in preparing our own."[46] At Ja VI 546 in a passage, quite astonishing, like very many other *Jātakas* as a whole for the intensity and oscillation of the emotions expressed and incited, Vessantara speaks to his son as he is about to give him away. Immediately before, in the very next sentence, the text says that Vessantara puts a ransom price on his children "like someone valuing oxen." The Pali of the sentence preceding this is: "tāta jāli kiṃ tvaṃ mama dānavittabhāvaṃ na jānāsi ajjhāsayaṃ me tāta matthakaṃ pāpehi." Cone renders this: "Dear Jāli, do you not know that giving brings me gladness? Help me to realise my aspiration."[47] Rouse's version is: "My son Jāli, don't you know that I have gladly given you away? So do that my desire may attain fulfilment."[48] Spiro, writing anthropologically of Burma with a—to me useless and offensive—psychoanalytic interpretation of Buddhist monasticism as narcissism, italicizes the words "my desire" to contrast

Vessantara's love for his son with his "desire" for omniscience, understood in a psychoanalytic manner.[49] The word ajjhāsaya, "aspiration," is in fact very rarely, if ever, translatable as "desire," in the English sense(s) of that word. The word vitta, which Cone translates "gladness," can have a variety of meanings, some of them quite different from each other, and more than one of them may be in play here.

There may be several kinds of what Indian literary theory calls "suggestion" (dhvani) and "double/multiple meanings" (śleṣa). A sympathetic reading would attempt to tease these out, albeit perhaps in the form of a footnote, though this is often undesirable in translations. The word matthaka at its simplest means a human head, but also the top or summit of a mountain. So Cone's rendering "fulfilment" is not a literal translation (what could be?), though it is good, and semantically accurate in a general sense. As an interpretation I have suggested elsewhere that the sense of "mountain" may have the dhvani that a buddha's omniscience is for Vessantara the man a far off and lofty one, as indeed it is, since he doesn't attain it until two lives later as Siddhattha Gotama. Perhaps, as I put it, Vessantara is trying to persuade himself as much as the children. The next few scenes, indeed the story as a whole, show at length that the identity of the man (actant) Vessantara is in painful conflict with that of the bodhisatta Vessantara.

So, caveat lector, let the reader beware. Those old translations, of the complete collection though they are, are very misleading, to say the least. Over the years one or two better translations of individual *Jātakas* have appeared in journals. Margaret Cone's accurate and elegant translation of the *Vessantara* appeared in 1977, reprinted in 2010. In 2006 Sarah Shaw's excellent selection of twenty-six of them appeared in the Penguin Classic *The Jātakas*.[50] Very welcome is Naomi Appleton and Sarah Shaw's

(2015) two-volume translation of the ten last and longest stories, *The Ten Great Birth Stories of the Buddha: The Mahānipāta of the Jātakatthavaṇṇanā*.[51] These new translations, along with their sometimes quite extensive introductions, are now by far the best point of entry into the birth stories. Some scholars have published books on particular subjects that contain useful summaries of the stories, though not extensive translations of them.

1.4. ON "WISDOM LITERATURE" AS A CROSS-CIVILIZATIONAL CATEGORY

It is unfortunate that the category "wisdom literature" has come to have the very specific sense of a few books of the Old Testament, along, sometimes, with some contemporaneous literature from areas of ancient Mesopotamia. It would be better, in my view, to use the phrase to refer to a whole range of literature, worldwide, that offers advice, moral and otherwise; examples to follow or not follow; stories to reflect on and ponder over, sometimes simply to enjoy. The phrase "didactic literature" is sometimes used in this context, but this seems to me problematic. On the one hand, if a story does nothing else but offer some bland, simple, familiar, and so quite likely boring moral, can it be "literature" in the appreciative sense? On the other, perhaps all literature is didactic, in the sense that it always offers moral issues to reflect on, examples to ponder, or, as one says in the contemporary USA, a number of "take-home points" to think about. But it would surely be philistine at the least to say, for example, that *Anna Karenina* or *Madame Bovary* is "about" the dangers of adultery.

One needs to have some restrictions, although there will always be marginal cases. I am thinking, to use firstly Western categories, of such texts, usually short but also long, as are called proverbs, apothegms (maxims or gnōmai), fables (notably, of course, the many versions of those ascribed to Aesop), exempla (as used, for example, in medieval sermons), the largely medieval category of "mirrors for princes" (principum specula, Fûrstenspieg el) offering them advice, just as "wise ministers" (paṇḍitāmaccas) so frequently advise kings on attha, "good (wise) policy," and dhamma, "(doing) what is right," in *The Birth Stories*. Sanskrit works such as the *Pañcatantra*, which are in fact collections or series of discrete fables, are set in frame stories where they are alleged to be advice given to young princes. Some such research has been done, into stories that clearly diffused from India: the collections *Pañcatantra as Kalilah and Dimnah*; *The Story of the Buddha as Balaam and Josaphat*; individual stories such as *The Brahmin and the Mongoose.*[52] But we need more.[53]

Narratives occur in almost all kinds of Buddhist text: in the collection of *Suttas* (*Discourses*); in the *Vinaya* monastic rules, where each rule is introduced by a story giving the occasion on which the Buddha (allegedly) promulgated it; and also in other parts of these texts. The only genre in which stories—indeed, even grammatically complete sentences—do not occur is the *Abhidhamma* (*Further Doctrine*), for reasons I will explore in the next chapter. Commentaries to *Abhidhamma* texts do have many stories.

It is important that such kinds of text, proverbs, fables, birth stories, circulated in collections. There are proverbs, fables, etc., that exemplify or offer for reflection many different "morals" or perspectives. Wisdom then consists in knowing which proverb, which fable, applies to which situation. The kind of comparative project I am envisaging would compare and contrast the kinds of collection and context in which such wisdom literature circulated—both literary form and narrative content.

1.4.1. Wisdom in Systematic Thought

This section can be brief, since wisdom in this sense is so often presented in widely available introductory and other books, and online, as "Buddhist doctrine" or "Buddhist thought." The idea of "wisdom" is, naturally, that textual world where something called "enlightenment," which does not exist in the historical world, is used as a category applied to either aspirants to nirvana or those who have attained it. Wisdom is here said to mean various things, all of them "spiritual." What is meant here is, for the external analyst, the gradual and then complete introjection of Buddhist ideology. Wisdom here is "seeing things as they really are": that every conditioned existent is unsatisfactory and impermanent; that every existent, conditioned or unconditioned (that is, nirvana), is without self; or the doctrine (and general idea) of dependent origination; or the understanding as well as the practice of bhāvanā, askēsis, and the like. The enlightened person is "wise," a "sage." It is not at all clear to me why the word "wisdom" is used here in so many modern translations. But in the fantasy world of "spiritual" achievement it is, like enlightenment itself, an empty category, a prize, as it were, which to the external analyst means nothing. Just a word. The word, of course, turns up in many lists, the standard for which the typical textual form is that of the list (without finite verbs: see 2.3.2); very common, for example, is the threefold analysis of bhāvanā (askēsis) as sīla (morality), samādhi (concentration), and paññā (wisdom). Less often there is a threefold analysis of paññā itself, as cinta-maya, arrived at through reflection; sutta-maya, arrived at through listening (to texts); and bhāvanā-maya, arrived at through askēsis.[54]

There are others. Here again, why "wisdom"? I don't know. The commentary to the canonical text *Cariyā-piṭaka* (*Basket of*

Conduct), which gives short versions in verse of seven of the ten forms of excellence, describes them at length in abstract terms. Here are a few small extracts from it (in Bhikkhu Bodhi's translation).

> How many are there? In brief, there are ten. These have come down in the texts in their specific character. As it is said: "How many qualities are there, Lord, issuing in Buddhahood?" "There are, Sāriputta, ten qualities issuing in Buddhahood. What are the ten? Giving, Sāriputta, is a quality issuing in Buddhahood: generosity, virtue, renunciation, wisdom, energy, patience, truthfulness, determination, lovingkindness, and equanimity are qualities issuing in Buddhahood." . . . "What is their sequence?" (4) Wisdom is mentioned immediately after renunciation: (a) because renunciation is perfected and purified by wisdom; (b) to show that there is no wisdom in the absence of meditation (jhāna), since concentration is the proximate cause of wisdom and wisdom the manifestation of concentration; (c) in order to list the causal basis for equanimity immediately after the causal basis for serenity; and (d) to show that skillful means in working for the welfare of others springs from meditation directed to their welfare. (5) Energy is stated immediately after wisdom: (a) because the function of wisdom is perfected by the arousing of energy; (b) to show the miraculous work the bodhisattva undertakes for the welfare of beings after he has reached reflective acquiescence in their emptiness; (c) to state the causal basis for exertion right after the basis for equanimity; and (d) to state the arousing of energy right after the activity of careful consideration, according to the statement: "The activity of those who have carefully considered brings excellent results." . . . (4) Wisdom has the characteristic of penetrating the real specific nature (of phenomena), or the characteristic of sure penetration, like the penetration of an arrow shot by a

> skillful archer; its function is to illuminate the objective field, like a lamp; its manifestation is non-confusion, like a guide in a forest; concentration, or the Four (Noble) Truths, is its proximate cause.[55]

This, as is no doubt all too obvious, has its own kind of complexity (and difficulty), but it is not that of narrative.

1.4.2. Wisdom in Narrative Thought: Excellence in Wisdom and Wise Person (Paṇḍita) Stories

The ten forms of excellence are obviously a later and rather clumsy imposition on the stories. Some texts, including the biographical introduction to the final birth story collection, do mention various birth stories as exemplifying the ten forms of excellence, but these exemplifications are often opaque, and the stories referred to only rarely say—or in some cases do not say at all—that they are "about" (ārabbha) the excellence attributed to them. The last ten birth stories are allegedly about the ten forms of excellence, but the attributions vary, and both the Vidhurapaṇḍita (note the name) and the Mahosadha birth stories are said to be about excellence in wisdom. The words paññā and paṇḍita occur, naturally, a great many times in the over five hundred birth stories, all of which would be impossible to cover here. As a principle of limitation I will discuss briefly some of the stories that are directly said to be "about excellence in wisdom" (paññā pāramiṃ ārabbha), and then a very few of the dozens of stories that are about or refer to someone (men, women, gods, animals) who is called "wise" (paṇḍita). The words are often used in striking and unexpected ways. I will mostly leave paññā and paṇḍita untranslated, or use the stereotypical "wisdom" and "wise."

The Birth Story of the Tiṇḍuka Tree (#177, *Tiṇḍuka Jātaka*): In the "Story of the Present" monks are discussing the Buddha's excellence in wisdom.[56] The Buddha, in the usual narrative form, says that it is not only now that he has paññā, and tells the "Story of the Past." The future Buddha is the leader of eighty thousand monkeys. Near their dwelling place is a village where grows a tiṇḍuka tree, sometimes inhabited, sometimes not. When it is uninhabited the monkeys come and eat the tiṇḍuka's sweet fruits. But at one time when there were many people there, with a fence around the village and a gate, the monkeys could no longer take the fruit. One night, when the villagers are asleep, against their leader's advice the monkeys creep up to the tree in the middle watch of the night and begin eating the fruit. A villager who got up because of his bodily needs gives the alarm and the people, armed with bows, other weapons, and stones, surround the tree, intending to kill the monkeys at dawn. But the future Buddha comforts them (literally "made them breathe easily)," saying that they will find something to divert the villagers. They are rescued by his nephew, Senaka, who sets fire to the village, distracting the attention of the people, thus allowing the monkeys to escape. They do so, bringing a fruit for Senaka. Here, it would seem, the (unnamed) future Buddha's paññā consists in his capacity to comfort his monkeys. The story's hero, the one who saves the day, is his nephew Senaka.

The Birth Story of the Full River (#214, *Puṇṇanadī Jātaka*): The future Buddha is a king's chief priest, who advises the king on wise policy and what is right.[57] At one time the king listens to the words of paribhedakas (loosely "malevolent ministers," but on the word see below), so he becomes angry with his chief priest and banishes him. But later, remembering the chief priest's good qualities, he sends him a letter containing some verses and some crow's flesh tied up in a white cloth. Three of the verses—the first starts with the words "a full river," thus the story's name—are riddles. Both the verses and the crow's flesh are a kind of test-riddle such that if the chief priest is paṇḍita he will understand them. The story does not say explicitly what the answers to the riddles are, but the commentary explains that the answer to each one is "a crow." A full river, for example, is often called kākapeyya, "drinkable by crows," i.e., when they can stand on the riverbank and drink. The chief priest, obviously solving the riddles mentally and knowing that the flesh is a crow's, concludes (in verse) that he must be once again in the king's favor, since if the king has crows he must also have other, more beautiful birds, such as swans, curlews, and peacocks, and then he goes home.

In itself the story is, as so often, concerned with solving riddles as wisdom. It has, I think, at least one further but entirely implicit level of meaning, one that would be accessible only to a sophisticated and knowledgeable audience who knew Pali, and which solves the enigma, or the riddle, of what the story is really about, other than the rather bland story of the king's riddles (none of which, remember, is solved in the text itself), the crow's meat, and the return of the exiled future Buddha. The word kāka means in the first instance a crow, as an onomatopoeia because of the ugly sound that bird makes. But then, according to Monier-Williams, it means, as applied to a person, "(metaphorically as an expression of contempt); an impudent or insolent fellow." *Critical Pali Dictionary* has "greedy, impudent, short-sighted." The word paribhedaka is from √ paribhid, which means literally "break up," and thence paribhedaka is (*Pali English Dictionary*) "a disturber of the peace." The word is often used in *The Birth Stories* and in commentaries to them, as here, to refer to malevolent ministers who break up the peace of a well-functioning kingship by reviling the future Buddha, normally the king's chief priest or minister, and so causing dissent. Here, the verbal riddles whose answer is "crow" and the crow's flesh, once understood, signify that there are malevolent ministers at court. The future Buddha's verse suggesting—but not saying explicitly—that he has solved the riddle and deciphered the king's meaning means that he knows that there are more beautiful birds at court (that is, benevolent ministers) and he can return safely. So the story itself is a kind of riddle to be deciphered by the audience: its form reflects its content. Not a children's story.

The Birth Story About a Barley-Meal Bag (#402, *Sattubhasta Jātaka*): The "Story of the Present" merely mentions excellence in wisdom and refers to itself as being in the *Mahā-ummagga* (*Mahosadha*) *Jātaka* (dealt with below).[58] There monks praise the Buddha in a series of epithets found often, as having "great wisdom, wide-ranging wisdom, joking wisdom, quick[-witted] wisdom, sharp wisdom, crushing contrary views." Before telling the "Story of the Past," the Buddha remarks, as often, "now I have paññā, but in the past when my knowledge (ñāṇa) was not ripe [or: not cooked] I was wise to the extent that I was practicing for the sake of knowing Enlightenment."[59] In the "Story of the Past" the future Buddha becomes minister-advisor to a king. When he speaks, "it was as if the time of a Buddha had arisen throughout the kingdom . . . and he spoke with the elegance of a Buddha."[60] Then the real story starts. A young Brahmin wife with an old husband is dissatisfied sexually and takes a lover. She sends her old husband to get money enough to hire a maid, giving him a leather bag with barley meal, some made into cakes and some not. He gets the money, then turns back. At a place where there is pleasant (presumably clear) water, he eats some barley, then without tying up the bag goes to get some water. While he is gone a black snake gets into the bag and eats some barley. The Brahmin comes back, ties up the bag, and goes off.

A tree spirit sees him and says: "Brahmin, if you stay on the road you yourself will die. If you go home today your wife will die," and disappears. The Brahmin, not being able to see the spirit, "terrified with fear of death," goes to Benares. People tell him that wise Senaka (Senakapaṇḍita) is about to teach dhamma (i.e., dhamma 1) with the elegance of a buddha and with a sweet voice. He does so, sees the Brahmin sorrowing, and asks him why he is upset. The Brahmin tells him what the spirit said. Wise Senaka reflects on the different kinds of death and as he does so realizes that there must be a snake in the Brahmin's bag. He knows precisely by his knowledge of skill-in-means (upāyakosallanāṇen'eva) and "as if seeing with a divine eye" what has happened and what the spirit's words mean: if the Brahmin stays on the road and opens the bag again to eat and puts his hand in it, the snake will bite him fatally; if he goes home, his wife will do the same thing.

Cross-examining the Brahmin about what happened, he tells him to undo the bag and hit it with a stick. The Brahmin does so; the snake comes out and is caught by a snake charmer, who sets it free in the forest. The Brahmin speaks some verse in praise of Senaka and says that it was a good thing for Senaka to have found him and to see that he possessed "good wisdom" (sādhupaññaṃ). He then offers Senaka money, which he refuses. Senaka has the Brahmin's bag filled with a thousand pieces of money and tells him to go home. When he cross-examines him again, about the reason for his journey, the Brahmin tells him. Senaka devises a strategy by which the Brahmin can go home, keep his money, and get rid of his wife's lover, which is successful.

In what does Senaka's wisdom consist? He does not know by supernatural means, since the text clearly says he worked out what had happened as if (viya) by a divine eye. One could use that overworked and entirely vague word "intuition," which doesn't explain anything. I think the text is like a detective story. The future Buddha works out from the initially obscure and, to the rest of us, indecipherable evidence, in a Sherlock Holmesian or Philip Marlowe-like manner, what the tree spirit's enigmatic words mean: inordinately skillful but an empirical deduction. In later giving the Brahmin advice and practical assistance on how to punish the wife and get rid of the lover, is he wise, savvy, smart? All of these things.

The Birth Story About a Needle (#387, *Sūci Jātaka*): As in *The Birth Story About a Barley-Meal Bag*, the "Story of the Present" here merely mentions excellence in wisdom and also skill in means, and refers to the "Story of the Present" in the *Mahā-ummagga* (*Mahosadha*) *Jātaka*.[61] The future Buddha is born into a poor family of metalworkers. Not far from his village is another one of metalworkers. The principal smith there has a daughter who is very beautiful, like a heavenly nymph. The future Buddha wants her as a wife, so he makes an extraordinary needle that can pierce the blade of an axe but also float on water. He then makes seven sheaths capable of the same things. The text comments, "how he made it cannot be described, as the acts of future buddhas succeed through the greatness of their knowledge." He goes to the nearby village and at first calls out that he has a needle to sell. Eventually he comes to the house of the principal smith, who tests the needle with the blade of an axe and water six times. Each time, what his onlookers think was the needle is in fact a sheath over it. When they finally get to the needle, it passes the same tests as the sheaths. The principal smith gives the future Buddha his daughter in marriage. After they have lived there for some time, the principal smith dies and the future Buddha succeeds him as principal smith. A love story with the hero passing a series of tests to win his girl.

The Birth Story About Suppāraka (#463, *Suppāraka Jātaka*): The "Story of the Present" has monks again praising the Buddha's wisdom, giving a series of epithets similar to that in *The Birth Story About a Barley-Meal Bag*.[62] In the "Story of the Past" the Buddha is born as the eldest son of a ship's captain. By the age of sixteen he has attained mastery in seamanship, and when his father dies he succeeds him as the ship's senior captain. He has paññā and is endowed with knowledge. When he is on board, no ship comes to any harm. But because his eyes are struck by salt water so often he goes blind. He goes to work for the king as assessor, assessing the value of elephants, horses, and other valuables by passing his hand over them. On a series of days he assesses the value of various animals and jewels, and each time the king gives him only eight pieces of money (kahāpaṇas). He thinks, *The king sees such wonders and he gives me only eight pieces of money. These are the wages of a barber! He must have been born to a barber. What's the point of such service to a king?* and goes home. Then some merchants need a captain for their ship. Knowing that Suppāraka is both paṇḍita and "skilled in means" (upāya-kusalo), they ask him. After initial reluctance he accepts. The ship passes through six seas, in each of which lie gold, silver, and jewels. On each occasion the future Buddha gets hold of the valuables but keeps them from the other sailors. The sixth and last sea is too dangerous to sail on, so he makes an act of truth, to the effect that since he reached the age of maturity (viññutā, literally "intelligence," even "wisdom") he has not killed a single living being. The ship escapes, and though the journey has up to now taken four months, it returns home in one day, as though it possessed magic power. The ship drives up overland until it reaches Suppāraka's door. There he distributes the gold, silver, and jewels to the sailors and tells them not to sail again. Suppāraka's wisdom, or perhaps simply skill, is threefold: as previous knowledge of seamanship at the beginning of the story, as blind assessor of valuables, and again as seamanship at the end, along with astuteness in regard to the valuables.

The Birth Story About Great Enlightenment (#528, *Māhabodhi Jātaka*): The Māhabodhi (the future Buddha's name) is the only story that contains moments of explicit and sustained conceptual argumentation, odd and inadequate though they are. The future Buddha is an ascetic who lives in a royal park for twelve years. The king has five advisors, who each hold a different philosophical and ethical doctrine. As judges they all accept bribes. The future Buddha takes over as judge and makes judgments according to what is right. The previous advisors persuade the king that he is their enemy, plotting to kill him, and one day the king agrees. A dog, thinking in language, stands at the door as the future Buddha is about to enter the palace and barks. The future Buddha, "by his knowledge of the meaning of all sounds," returns first to the park and then to the Himalayas and then to a forest in a frontier village. The advisors kill the queen and say that Mahābodhi has done it. Knowing what is going on, Mahābodhi eats the flesh of a monkey, dries its skin, and wears it as clothing. He returns to the royal park and sits on a stone slab. The king arrives and the future Buddha tells him what he has done with the monkey skin, and how it has been of great service to him. The five advisors accuse him of murder. The future Buddha asks them how he is guilty according to their doctrines, which are explained briefly, and he refutes them all. The king ties the advisors up with dog leashes, sprinkles cow dung over them, and exiles them. The future Buddha stays on for a few days, advising the king to be diligent, and returns to the Himalayas.

The five doctrines are analogous to, but not the same as, a much-discussed sutta, the *Sāmaññaphala* (*The Fruits of Asceticism*)—the passage has analogies elsewhere. That text has at the beginning a series of six positions, to which the Buddha opposes a long and elegant account of the Buddhist Path.[63] But be that as it may, the story of Mahābodhi as a whole is also decidedly odd. Can wisdom kill a monkey and use its skin as trickery to (seem to) refute opponents? Make of the story what you will. It is, apparently, "about excellence in wisdom!"

The final two birth stories said to be about excellence in wisdom that I will deal with are *The Birth Story About Wise Vidhura* (#545, *Vidhura-paṇḍita Jātaka*) and *The Birth Story Sbout Mahosadha* (Mahosadha is the future Buddha's name).[64] The latter story (#546) is sometimes, in Sri Lanka and in Rouse's translation, called *Mahā-ummaga Jātaka*, *The Birth Story About the Great Tunnel*, because of the episode at the end about building a tunnel to gain victory in war. They are both very long, and it will be impossible to recount them fully here.

The Birth Story About Wise Vidhura has many affinities with the Sanskrit Mahābhārata: people, their names, places, situations. The narrative, though containing many episodes, is continuous in both prose and verse. The verses also contain throughout a great deal of nīti-style dhamma 1 advice. The following is a very brief summary. Vidhurapaṇḍita is the minister of King Dhanañjaya, who rules in the city Indapatta in the kingdom of Kuru. Vidhurapaṇḍita advises him on good policy and what is right, and teaches people dhamma with the elegance of a buddha. He is often compared to a buddha in the text. Four kings, who were friends in a former life, come to the royal garden and "practice asceticism" together. They are: the son of Dhanañjaya Koravya (himself also called Dhanañjaya), who is addicted to gambling but nonetheless rules his kingdom according to what is right; Sakka, king of the gods; Varuṇa, king of the nāgas; and the king of the supaṇṇas (mythical birds, usually natural enemies of nāgas). Sakka asks who has the most virtue (good character, sīla). They each speak a small section of prose and a verse. They ask Vidhurapaṇḍita to judge; he says they all have equal virtue. When Varuṇa arrives back in the nāga realm he tells his wife, Vimalā, about Vidhurapaṇḍita, and she wants to hear a dhamma talk from him. In order to do so she pretends to have a desire to eat Vidhurapaṇḍita's heart and asks Varuṇa to get it. He tells their daughter Irandatī to find a husband who can do it. A yakkha (a class of spirits), a slave called Puṇṇaka, falls in love with her. After an exchange of verses with the king and queen of the nāgas, he goes to his uncle, King Vessavanna, who gives him permission to leave. Puṇṇaka flies off on his horse through the air to the Kuru capital. He plays dice with the king and wins many things, including Vidhurapaṇḍita.

After a very long series of verses in which Vidhurapaṇḍita explains good conduct, what is right, and so on, which also have significant narrative content, Vidhurapaṇḍita prepares to leave. As he is putting on his outer cloak, the narrative voice says, to the contrary of what is said in the "Story of the Present," that he is "making excellence in resolve his ideal." Puṇṇaka flies away with Vidhurapaṇḍita and places him on the summit of a mountain. He tries various magical means to kill him, to no avail. Then they have a conversation, in which Puṇṇaka explains the situation. Vidhurapaṇḍita gives him a persuasive dhamma talk and asks to be taken to the nāga realm. There he gives the king another dhamma talk and dissuades him from trying to get his heart. Then he gives the nāga king and Vimalā yet another dhamma talk. King Varuṇa gives Irandatī to Puṇṇaka. King Dhanañjaya has a dream that portends Vidhurapaṇḍita's return. Puṇṇaka takes Vidhurapaṇḍita back to the city and Irandatī to his own city. Vidhurapaṇḍita recaps his adventures, at great length. Dhanañjaya tells the residents of the city of his dream. Many different classes of people honor Vidhurapaṇḍita with food and drink. He teaches them dhamma, and everyone goes to heaven after death.

This is an adventure story and a romance. One might call it a picaresque novel—as the *OED* says, this is "a genre of narrative fiction which deals episodically with the adventures of an individual"—though without the negative or mischievous qualities the hero usually has in Western examples. Some of the characters, though not many, do have negative qualities, notably Vimalā and Irandhatī. The thread that holds the story together is the combination of the hero Vidhurapaṇḍita and the nāga Puṇṇaka. Talks on dhamma (obviously dhamma 1) are frequent, mostly in verse, and though within the text given to characters are also clearly meant for its audience or readership. A variety of different species are involved, especially humans and nāgas. It is so long, like *The Birth Story About Mahosadha*, that unless it was given in a marathon all-night session it must have been given in episodes.

The Birth Story About Mahosadha (#546, *Mahosadha Jātaka*) is, as I have said, so called because Mahosadha is the name of the hero.[65] It is alternatively called *The Birth Story About the Great Tunnel* (*Mahā-ummagga Jātaka*) in some recensions, because the building and use of a city, a smaller secret tunnel, and a great tunnel is one of the most important constituent events. This section is, in fact, only 40 pages out of 149, and itself contains supplementary events, such as verses irrelevant to the constituent events of the story. Unlike the previous story, the *Mahosadha* is truly episodic, consisting mainly, along with the relatively short episode of the city and tunnels, in questions and riddles, with only the wisdom of the hero Mahosadha as the tenuous thread that holds them all together.

Twelve episodes of the birth story occur elsewhere in the collection as complete *Jātakas*. I will first give a summary version of the story, with summary versions of some passages, omitting many I see as supplementary events (others might disagree: there are a great number) and giving many constituent events in summary form. I also make some commentarial remarks of my own, enclosed in square brackets. After that I will cite some remarks from Shaw's introduction to her translation, as I think they make some very thought-provoking comparative suggestions for ways of reading and interpreting the story. So, first the story.

In the "Story of the Present" monks are praising the Buddha's wisdom, using the list of epithets given above in the "Story of the Present" of *The Birth Story About a Barley-Meal Bag* (#402, *Sattubhasta Jātaka*). In the "Story of the Past" here the king of Videha has four paṇḍitas, Senaka, Pukkusa, Kāvinda and Devinda, who advise him on what is right. On the day of the future Buddha's birth the king has a dream that frightens him. Senaka tells him, "Don't be frightened by this, Great King; it is an auspicious dream, and there will be prosperity." He explains, "Great king, a fifth paṇḍita will arise (who will surpass everyone)." However, during the story the four advisors become adversaries of the future Buddha, who constantly outclasses them in wisdom. As he is being born, the king of the gods, Sakka, places a healing herb, osadhī, in his hand (thus his name). His mother the queen takes the herb to a merchant who has had a headache for seven years, and it cures him. When Mahosadha is seven years old he is as beautiful as a golden statue, once again reminding the readers/audience of his identity as the Buddha in the future. At that time Senaka belittles an achievement of the future Buddha to the king, who sends him to Mahosadha with instructions to test the young paṇḍita. What follows is a very long section, or rather a series of questions and episodes, showing the boy's paññā, or his status as paṇḍita. Their titles are the piece of meat, the oxen, the threaded necklace, the (cotton) thread, the child, the (dark) lump, the carriage, the stick, the skull, the snake, the cock, the jewel, the calving, the rice, the sand, the pool, the garden, the ass, the jewel, the chameleon, the goat, and the rich and the poor. It is worth giving the story of the child in full, since it is such a remarkable analogy to the judgment of Solomon, which has become paradigmatic in Western histories of wisdom.

A certain woman takes her baby and goes to the Mahosadha's pool to wash her face. She bathes her child and sits him down on her clothes while she goes to wash her face and bathe. At that moment, a certain yakkhinī (a female spirit) sees the child and wishes to eat him. She takes him and says to his mother, "This is a lovely child, is he yours?" The mother says, "Yes, lady." "May I give him something to drink?" the yakkhinī asks. The mother replies, "Yes, do feed him." So the yakkhinī takes him and plays with him for a little while, and then starts to run away with him. When his mother sees this, she rushes after her and grabs her, saying, "Where are you taking my baby?" The yakkhinī says, "Where did you get this baby? It's mine!" As they are having this argument they pass by the wise man, who hears the commotion. He calls the women and asks them, "What is it?" When he hears the case, although he sees at once that one is a yakkhinī, by her having red eyes that do not blink, he says, "Will you abide by my judgment?" "Yes, we will," they both agree. So he draws a line and places the baby in the middle of it. He tells the yakkhinī to take the child by the hands and the mother to take him by the feet.

Then he says, "Now, pull the child: the one who can pull it to her keeps him." So they both pull. The child, pulled in both directions, cries out in great pain. The mother lets go of the child as if her heart were being broken, and stands there in tears. The wise man asks the assembly, "Is it the heart of the mother that is tender toward the child, or she who is not the mother?" "It is the heart of the mother, wise man," they reply. Mahosadha asks, "Is the one who held on to the child the mother, or the one who released him?" "The one who released him," they reply. "Do you know who it is who took the child?" "We do not know," they reply. "She is a yakkhinī who took the child to eat him." "How do you know that, wise man?" "Because her eyes are red and do not blink, and she leaves no shadow, and she has neither fear nor compassion." Then he asks, "Are you or are you not a yakkhinī?" "I am." "And why did you take the child?" "To eat him, sir." Mahosadha admonishes her: "You are a blind fool. Because you did wrong in an earlier life, you were born a yakkhinī. Now you are also doing wrong, and are a blind fool." He establishes her in the five precepts and sends her on her way. The child's mother says, "May you live for a long time, wise man!" She sings his praises, and goes away with her child.

In each of the questions the future Buddha shows himself to be paṇḍita, possessing paññā. When he reaches sixteen, Queen Udumbarā thinks, *He is now a grownup; his reputation is great: it is time to find a wife for him.* She and the king arrange a marriage. Mahosadha, however, thinks, *I will not be happy with a wife I have not chosen; I'll find one for myself.* He goes and finds a girl called Amaradevī. He finds out by an exchange of hand gestures that she is not married, and their courtship consists largely of exchanges of riddles and tests, some of those given by the future Buddha quite cruel. But finally they marry and the future Buddha lives with her in happy accord, and gives instruction to the king about wise policy and what is right.

After further sections with riddles and contests, the future Buddha starts to fortify the city, including building a new city and two tunnels, a smaller and a greater. I will not attempt to summarize the complicated war between King Videha of

Mithilā, whose advisor is the future Buddha, and King Cūḷani Brahmadatta of Uttarapañcāla, whose advisor is the Brahmin Kevaṭṭa. There is a long series of episodes, involving parrot spies, human spies, violence and the threat of it; a siege of Mithilā frustrated by the cleverness of the future Buddha; the use of the tunnels, which are lighted and decorated; a moment of technology where there are eighty major doors and sixty-four minor doors, all of which have contraptions such as a catch, which when pressed makes all the doors close; a dhamma fight (dhamma yuddha) between the future Buddha and Kevaṭṭa, which the future Buddha wins through a clever stratagem; a secret meeting; the fraudulent offer of Cūḷani Brahmadatta's beautiful daughter to Videha; and, at the end, a female ascetic. The future Buddha, and others, are called paṇḍitā and said to possess paññā.

Such a summary cannot do justice to the length and complexity of the tale, which is not easy to follow. In conclusion to my discussion of it, I can do no better than to quote some sections from Shaw's introduction to her translation, which give a number of useful comparisons to Western genres:

> Through riddles, questions, answers to apparently insoluble problems, advice to kings, intelligence gathering, planning and forethought, the Bodhisatta brings his great wisdom, or perhaps more accurately in the situations described, his extraordinary ingenuity, to sort out the immense difficulties, challenges, and dangers that face him and other characters. . . . Words associate with wisdom—bhūri or paṇḍito—are explicitly mentioned throughout, both applied to the Bodhisatta, and, challengingly, to other characters, some good and some bad, in a way which forces us to confront what is meant by this essential, but difficult, perfection. . . . It is very long, and in modern terms something we would class a great and absorbing read, with all the skilfully suggested elements

> of suspense, danger, and uncertainty we associate now with literary genres including folk, popular, court, and now globally marketed bestseller novels designed to grip, entertain, and mystify. It even includes a "hightech" element in the various contraptions that guard the city from attack and which allow the tunnel to be lit throughout. So there are plentiful tropes and storylines that fit well, for instance, the often strictly conventionalised demand of nineteenth- and twentieth-century Anglophone genre novels, including detective "whodunits," mysteries, spy-thrillers and sensation fiction of various kinds. . . . From a theatrical point of view, its appeal also has many affinities with other global dramas, including elements of the highly complicated intrigue and misunderstanding that animate the energetic and fast-moving machinations of Jacobean melodrama, the farce, and Sanskrit drama. It even, in some of its paradoxical components, echoes the tragic drama of ancient Greece. It has, in the grandeur of its hero and some female characters, an occasional sense of the heroic that aligns it with Homeric and Greek epic. . . . It deploys elements we can recognise from Romantic ballads, mediaeval riddles and ancient cultures from the east and west, and folkloric puzzles and rhymes, common to many cultures. . . . Rhys Davids . . . tracing related elements in the mediaeval and ancient cultures of Asian and European nations, estimated that Mahosadha contains about a hundred and fifty varied stories.[66]

I have given this long citation not to impose Western categories on the *Jātakas* in an Orientalist manner, as some politically correct readers might charge, but to try to demonstrate, by juxtaposing the stories with various different kinds of Western literature and theater, as some of my discussions of other birth stories have done already, what it means to read them or at least many or most of them, especially the longer ones, as adult literature. The *Mahosadha* is an excellent example of what I called earlier wisdom literature as a worldwide category. The fact that it has, as Shaw claims, bad characters said to be endowed with wisdom shows that we need to think about what it means that some of the stories challenge the most revered of Buddhist values, just as does the great *Vessantara*, which has even greater in-your-faceness, if I may put it that way, with no convincing solution, or indeed no solution at all, to its central moral dilemma.

By now it is probably quite clear that in a very large number of birth stories good people and animals, and sometimes bad ones, are called paṇḍita. In many cases it does not seem that "wise" is the best translation: some other word, "skillful," "prudent," "knowledgeable," or whatever, seems better in English. There are numerous stories where the category is unexceptionable and straightforward, and the characters so described, male and female, are simply in some way admirable. The word often appears in compounds, such as paṇḍita-purisa (wise man); āmacca-paṇḍita or paṇḍitāmacca (wise minister of a king), who advises him on (wise) policy (which can concern military strategy) and what is right; kumāra-paṇḍita (wise young man); and in animal stories where wise dogs, parrots, and many others offer advice to others, often their followers. It also appears in proper names, such as Senakapaṇḍita, "wise Senaka," whom we have met. Sometimes who the word actually applies to is unspecific, as in "wise men say (paṇḍita vadanti or something similar)." The now entirely commonplace maxim "fools rush in where angels fear to tread," first written by Alexander Pope in 1711, was modified in a song about falling in love by Elvis Presley in 1961: "wise men say, only fools rush in . . ." Scarcely specific conceptually.

If paṇḍita can be, like "wise" in English, used for qualities or skills that are not intrinsically good, as in the *OED*'s "having the ability to perceive and adopt the best means for accomplishing an end," then it would seem that wisdom in this sense is a form of skill, not necessarily a moral quality. The birth story where this is most strikingly the case is *The Birth Story About Sulasā* (#419, *Sulasā Jātaka*; Sulasā is the heroine's name). The main story is told in the "Story of the Present." A female servant of Anāthapiṇḍika goes to a park wearing an expensive ornament. A thief, intending to kill her and take it, plies her with fish, meat, and alcohol.

He takes her from the garden to somewhere more private. She realizes his intention and asks him to get her some water from a well. As he is leaning over the well, she pushes him into it, but thinking that this will not be enough to kill him drops a large brick on his head. She tells the story to Anāthapiṇḍika's wife, who tells it to Anāthapiṇḍika, who tells it to the Buddha. The Buddha says, "Now is not the first time that this slave girl has been endowed with wisdom (paññā: shrewdness?) occurring (in a way) appropriate to a situation . . . in the past also she killed him."[67] In the "Story of the Past" Sulasā is a prostitute in a brothel of five hundred women. In the town there is a thief who terrorizes the townspeople. They catch him and are taking him to the place of execution when Sulasā, standing at a window, sees him and falls in love with him. She thinks that if she could free him she could give up her bad life and live with him, and frees him by sending a thousand pieces of money to the chief constable. But after three or four months of marriage he decides he can no longer live there and plans to kill her and take all her very expensive jewelry. He tries to trick her by saying that he owes lot of money to a tree spirit and they should go repay him. When the two of them get to the tree spirit, he tells her the truth: he wants to kill her and steal the jewelry. She, conceiving a plan to kill him rather than be killed, pretends to walk around him in reverence but pushes him in the back over a steep cliff. He is crushed to pieces and dies. The spirit who lives on the mountaintop (the future Buddha) speaks verses that begin with: "It is not only a man who can be paṇḍita; a woman is paṇḍitā if she is attentive in all circumstances. It is not only a man who can be paṇḍita; a woman is paṇḍitā if she can quickly discern what is useful."[68] I cite this story not because a woman is said to be paṇḍitā, which is said quite often elsewhere despite the ubiquitous misogyny in the stories, but because here being paṇḍita consists in committing murder when necessary—"worldly wisdom" indeed.

1.4.3. Words for "Renunciant" and "Renunciation"

All of the people described in the previous section are called paṇḍita or said to possess paññā. In *The Birth Stories* they are often renunciants. The most common word for "renunciant" is isi (Sanskrit ṛṣi—pronounced rishi, a word of uncertain derivation), usually rendered in modern translations and secondary sources as "sage" (with the *s* often uppercase), or "seer." This choice seems to have been taken from the ancient Sanskrit use of ṛṣi as the name for the ancient sages or seers who, at the beginning of time, heard the Vedas and began their oral transmission. It may also be influenced by the standard English translation of the Greek seven sages or the seven wise men of the seventh to sixth century BCE, a title given to philosophers, statesmen, and lawgivers who were renowned in the following centuries for their wisdom. As a translation of isi I prefer the rather unspecific and bland "ascetic," one who takes what the stories call isi-pabbajjā (renunciation as an ascetic), that is, one who lives a special kind of life of celibate askēsis. The compound isi-pabbajjā is used, obviously, to differentiate this kind of pabbajjā from that of a novice Buddhist monk or nun (which must precede upasampadā, ordination as a bhikkhu or bhikkhunī), in reference to which the word is used as a technical term. *The Birth Stories*, as I have said, are remarkably almost wholly devoid of any form of anachronism. Stereotypically "renunciation as an ascetic" involves someone, usually but not always a male, and very often a king, leaving a city or a village to live a celibate life in a forest, in the Himalayas, either alone or in a group. The word pabbajjā is from Sanskrit √ pra-vraj, "leave, go out." This is not a formal ritual but simply means either leaving places of normal human habitation or living as a celibate ascetic in a town, often in a king's garden in or near the palace, where such ascetics sometimes, like ministers elsewhere, advise the king on good policy and what is right. Those who do leave normal human habitation (it is always wrong to say that they "leave society") have to go to human habitations for loṇa and ambila (salt and citrus fruit), both necessities of good health.

As a literary trope, becoming an ascetic often opens stories, starting the narrative on its way, or ends stories, providing closure. Thus, a typical (stereotypical) example is the *Mudulakkhaṇa Jātaka* (#66, *Characterized by Being Weak Jātaka*).[69] In the past, when Brahmadatta is king of Benares, the future Buddha appears in the Kāsi kingdom in a rich family. When he attains the age of reason he learns all kinds of knowledge thoroughly, but abandoning objects of lust takes isi-pabbajjā, and, making preparations (for meditation) by means of the kasiṇas (see chapter 2.4.8), attains magic knowledge and other achievements, and lives in the Himalayas passing his time in the pleasures of meditation. One day for the sake of salt and citrus fruit he comes to Benares. There, in another standard topos of South Asian narratives, he falls in love with the queen and loses his ascetic powers, but at the end of the story he regains them, and sitting in the air teaches dhamma to the king. He flies to the Himalayas and no longer comes to the "paths of humans." As he develops the four ways of living like a Brahma, his meditation is uninterrupted, and after death he goes to the Brahma world.

There is a special subset of such ascetics, called pacceka buddhas. The etymology of this word is difficult to determine, but it was rendered in Sanskrit as pratyekabuddha. Pratyeka means single, and so pacceka buddhas have been understood in secondary sources as "solitary buddhas" who live alone and do not teach, but this, at least in *The Birth Stories*, is wrong. These stories, as I have said, assiduously avoid anachronism, in that they all take place, by definition, at a time when there is no Buddha, no founder of a sāsana, that is to say no tradition characterized by continuity simultaneously of both institutions and ideas. But attaining enlightenment and being thus freed from rebirth is possible in birth stories, by pacceka buddhas. The crucial feature defining a pacceka buddha, as was said above, is that although he can attain nirvana (though this word is never used in "Stories of the Past"), he does not found a sāsana. In the birth stories pacceka buddhas often live in groups, and they do teach dhamma. But this is dhamma 1, "what is right" in the everyday world of human life. They do not teach dhamma 2, which is the specialized truth only available—in texts—when there is a buddha to teach it. Many texts are quite clear on this: the two characteristics of suffering (unsatisfactoriness) and impermanence are all too easy to understand, with or without the existence of a buddha to teach them. A common story motif is of someone seeing examples of suffering and then deciding to go to live in the Himalayas as a hermit. A nice motif, again common, is of someone seeing a yellow leaf falling to the ground and realizing that everything is impermanent, and likewise choosing the life of an ascetic. But the teaching of anattā, the absence of a self or anything permanent in human beings, can only be known and understood if there exists a buddha who can fathom its depths and reveal them to others by means of a historically institutionalized sāsana. And this is what pacceka buddhas do not do. All of these figures may or may not practice tapas, austerity, of one sort or another, and so can be called tāpasa, "renunciants" in this sense.

1.4.4. Diversity and Unity

It seems to me true, indeed no more than common sense, to say that we live (experience) diversity; we (may) think (construct) unity. One does not have to think unity: one can leave the diversity of everyday life in place. More than once Max Weber quoted James Mill's remark that "if one proceeds from pure experience, one arrives at polytheism."[70] Weber used Mill's remark metaphorically: "polytheism" for him referred not to supernaturalist ideas and practices but to the many "value spheres in the world [that] stand in irreconcilable conflict with each other." He opposed any attempt on the part of intellectuals to impose a unifying ideology on it. And diversity is what *The Birth Stories* (and proverbs) express. As a collection they give voice to, and indeed I would go so far as to say they celebrate, the diversity and complexity of everyday life and its values. Buddhists are human beings first, Buddhists second. Buddhist systematic thought, by contrast, attempts a unifying ordering of the universe, in explanatory and descriptive schemata of unlimited applicability, such as the fundamental explanatory language of karma; the subsumption of all ills in the category of dukkha, suffering or unsatisfactoriness; the insistence on impermanence and death; and above all the central conceptual category of saṃkhata, conditioned things/events, along with its negation or contradictory category—the asaṃkhata, unconditioned, i.e., nirvana—as a necessary corollary, which together represent and account for everything that exists.

It is a simplified version of Buddhist systematic thought constantly presented in secondary sources and introductory textbooks as "early Buddhism." But in my view this is, as Samuel Beckett so finely put it, to get things arsy-versy. As the earliest art-historical evidence shows, it was Buddhist narratives that preceded intellectual rationalizations. Only by the middle of the first century CE had the committee called Buddhaghosa unified the universe in the terms just mentioned and produced a fantasy in which the Great Man had produced unified systematic thought from out of his "enlightened wisdom" immediately, without difficulty, as a rationally ordered whole, like Athena, goddess of wisdom, directly from the head of Zeus.

Let me repeat: I am not saying that systematic thought was the preserve of intellectuals while narrative thought was "popular." I am saying that even among that very small part, speaking demographically, of any Theravāda civilization that knew enough Pali to read or listen to texts in that father tongue, stories were central to their experience, precisely because they represented that experience as it was, and is, in value terms, as Weber put it, polytheistic. Stories such as the *Jātakas* were on occasion moral fables; they were just as often entertaining and very often thought-provoking reflections on life, its complexities and conflicts.

1.5. CONCLUSION

Reading Pali stories not as "religious" literature offering for sale some moral or "spiritual" tidbit but as elite Literature that entertains (seriously or lightly) its readers or listeners—who are, for the Pali versions, as I have insisted, an educated monastic or court audience—allows us to escape religious studies' all-too-common equation of civilizations with what it sees as "systems of religious belief," and also the sociological naiveté that sees such systems as permeating the whole of a civilization. Even so distinguished a materialist historian as Fernand Braudel of the Annales School makes what I view as these mistakes, by taking "ideas" (by which he means, unintentionally, ideological-elite ideas) as foundational: he introduces *A History of Civilizations* to its high school readership by describing civilizations as geographical areas, societies, economies, and "ways of thought." In relation to the last, he says that:

> in every period, a certain view of the world, a collective mentality, dominates the whole mass of society. . . . These basic values, these psychological structures, are assuredly the features that civilizations can least immediately communicate one to another. They are what isolate them and differentiate them most sharply. . . . Here religion is the strongest feature of civilizations, at the heart of both their present and their past. . . . The ceaseless constraints imposed by geography, by social hierarchy, by collective psychology and by economic need . . . These realities are what we now call "structures." . . . These are the "foundations," the underlying structures of civilizations: religious beliefs, for instance, or a timeless peasantry, or attitudes to death, work, pleasure and family life.[71]

This may be true of the systematic thought of different traditions. It is not so true of narrative thought. Some stories did travel, not unchanged of course, from India across the Islamic world and into Europe. To appreciate, for example, the crow and the fox, the monkey and the crocodile, and the turtle, monkey, and ascetic, for instance, "being Buddhist" has no relevance.

Buddhists are people first (who can enjoy stories from anywhere), "Buddhists" second. If narratives are, as I assert, the heart and humanity of the Pali tradition, then they are not, as Braudel says, "what isolate [civilizations] and differentiate them most sharply." I am not arguing for a narrative version of perennial philosophy: everybody is the same underneath. I am arguing for a literary analysis of what are called religious texts, and the possibility of understanding them, at least in part, by comparisons with texts that are read in the West as literature, with all the respect and acknowledgment of the unending possibility for interpretation that Western literature has. I made a no doubt inadequate attempt to do this in relation to the *Vessantara Jātaka* twenty years ago, in chapter 7 of *Nirvana and Other Buddhist Felicities*. In this book I have compared *The Story of Wise Senaka*, very briefly, to a detective story: "the future Buddha works out from the initially obscure and, to the rest of us, indecipherable evidence, in a Sherlock Holmesian or Philip Marlowe-like manner," the meaning of the tree spirit's words. The much older quote from Winternitz given in 1.3.1 lists a number of genre terms that might be applied to *The Birth Stories*, giving some but not extensive comparisons to justify the use of them. Recently Sarah Shaw has, promisingly, compared the Vessantara story to *The Merchant of Venice*, and to what she refers to as "Shakespearean dramas, mediaeval Western mystery plays, and ancient Greek tragedies and comedies."[72] This, I think, is the direction the study of Pali Literature ought to go.

Part Two

PRACTICES OF SELF

2.1. MY INTENTIONS IN WRITING THIS CHAPTER; HADOT AND FOUCAULT ON THE DESIRABILITY OF COMPARISON

This second section[1] derives from two intentions of mine. First, as I have said repeatedly, the actual percentage of relevantly educated people who read or listened to Pali texts in Pali, of both narrative and systematic kinds, must have been in any premodern Theravāda civilization demographically infinitesimally small. The percentage of people who not only read about, as did monks and some educated laity in court cultures, but also actually engaged in practices of self assiduously and as a full-time lifestyle must been even smaller, confined to the monastic order, celibates in homosocial institutions. But as I have also said, the number of people in the contemporary anglophone world who not only read, say, the works of David Hume or James Joyce but also actively try to understand them intellectually and historically is likewise a tiny percentage. But in the intellectual historiography of the "West" these two authors are indispensable. I have insisted that the diversity expressed in Pali narrative thought (stories) is more central to the tradition than the unity envisioned by systematic thought, especially as simplified in modern textbooks and introductions. Nevertheless, writing in the academic tradition of intellectual history, as I take myself now to be doing, it is impossible to ignore Buddhist ideas and the practices of self that were prescribed by them or juxtaposed to them. Nineteenth-century scholars, as well as many now, have not only thought and think that their expertise in the language(s) necessary—difficult as this is to attain, requiring many years of study—gives them, as it obviously does, authority in linguistic matters, but also have thought that that kind of expertise made and makes it possible for them to write about philosophy, sociology (of both the macro- and micro- kinds), historiography of more than the positivist-empirical kind, and other things with some comparable kind of intellectual authority. Sometimes their attempts to do so seem, to me anyway, of spectacular naïveté.

In this book I claim no such authority, although I have tried over the years to familiarize myself to some extent with those disciplines, and I have tried in this book to enter into those fields of study in an exploratory way. It is for readers to decide whether what has resulted has any persuasiveness or interest. So, to repeat, demographically tiny but civilizationally of great importance, practices of self and the texts in which they are described and prescribed remain of signal importance to the intellectual history of the Pali tradition. In writing about them in this section, I found the conceptual intricacy of sections 2.3 through 2.3.2 in itself fascinating and rewarding to reflect on. Readers who do not share this view may pass directly to 2.3.3, where the point of it all is summarized. In 2.4 and thereafter, I hope that my exploration of practices of self will be more interesting, or at least more true to the tradition, than the simplified version of Buddhist "meditation" usually now presented, where the two forms, samatha/samādhi, calming/concentration, and vipassanā (insight) are seen as the only possibilities, complementary or opposed to each other as one or another author may think.

The second reason for writing this chapter, indeed for writing the entire book, is to provide some comparative material to the work of Pierre Hadot on—to use the standard slogans—"spiritual exercises" and "philosophy as a way of life," and to that of Michel Foucault on "practices/technologies of self" and "subjectivity and truth."[2] As I shall demonstrate in a moment, this is not an idiosyncratic quirk of my own, but something they both wanted and looked for. One of the problems with their wonderfully inspiring work is their lack of attention to the social and institutional context of the ideas they were writing about. In the Theravāda case, on a micro level, which I have not at all attempted, this would look at, among other things, the institutions of the monastic order, what I have called celibate homosocial institutions, from social, economic, geographical, architectural, and other perspectives, as well as at the variety of kinds and sizes of them. In the ancient Greek case it seems, according to Philip Mitsis, that there were scarcely any institutions in the physical sense.[3] When we speak of "Stoicism" or "Epicureanism," he says, we are speaking in the same intellectual way we speak of Wittgensteinianism or the tradition of Ayn Rand. Hadot makes some occasional and vague references to institutions of education. I have attempted, perhaps rashly, to provide a much larger context—the civilizational—in which to set Pali narrative and systematic texts produced by an educated monastic elite and intended for others of that kind, as well as for well-educated people in royal courts (of which, admittedly, I have provided no serious empirical study).

Hadot, along with others such as Martha Nussbaum, have insisted that philosophy in the ancient world was a therapeutic way of life, a set of spiritual exercises in which the goal was not merely the acquisition of knowledge about the world but the transformation of the knowing subject.[4] There are very many obvious parallels with Buddhism, as others have pointed out. The Buddha as healer cures the disease of suffering by the therapy, inter alia, of detachment. One should remember here that the word *spirituel* in French does not mean quite the same thing as the English word "spiritual." The word for "mind," for example, is *esprit*, and so in some contexts at least one might translate *exercises spirituels* as "mental exercises." Hadot's work is entirely confined to the Hellenistic and early Roman Imperial epochs, but he did, in his later work, suggest the need for comparative studies:

> Despite my hesitations about the use of comparative studies in philosophy, I wanted to end this chapter by emphasizing the extent to which the description, inspired by Buddhism, that Michel Hulin [a contemporary French philosopher] has given of the existential roots of the mystical experience, seemed to me close to the characteristics of the ideal of the Ancient Sage, so striking did the resemblances between the two spiritual searches appear to me to be. . . . I think, indeed, that these [Hellenistic and early Roman Imperial] models correspond to permanent, fundamental attitudes which all human beings find necessary when they set about searching for wisdom. . . . I was for a long time hostile to comparative philosophy because I thought it could give rise to confusions and arbitrary parallels. Now, however, as I read the works of my colleagues [here he cites some contemporary French philosophers] it seems to me that there really are thought-provoking analogies between the philosophical attitudes of antiquity and those of the Orient. . . . Perhaps we should say that the choices of life we have described—those of Socrates, Pyrrho,

> Epicurus, the Stoics, the Cynics and the Skeptics—correspond to constant, universal models which are found in forms specific to every civilization, throughout the various cultural zones of humanity. This is why I mentioned earlier a Buddhist text, as well as some considerations by Michel Hulin, who was inspired by Buddhism: because I thought they could give us a better understanding of the Greek sage.[5]

Foucault, in a lecture originally given in English at the University of Vermont in 1982, says first that he agrees with Habermas that there are in all societies the three techniques of production, signification, and domination, and he adds:

> But . . . I have come gradually to realize that there is in all societies, I think, in all societies whatever they are, another type of technique: techniques which permit individuals to effect, by themselves, a certain number of operations on their own bodies, on their own souls, on their own thoughts, on their own conduct, and this as a way to transform themselves, to modify themselves, and to attain a certain state of perfection, of happiness, of purity, of supernatural power, and so on. Let's call this kind of techniques a "technique" or "technology of self."[6]

In a remarkable interview in Japan in 1978 with a Japanese specialist in French theater and literature, published as "The Theatre of Philosophy" ("La scène de la philosophie"), he suggested a comparative project:

> In the history which I am trying to make of techniques of power in the West, techniques which concern bodies, individuals, conduct, the souls of individuals, I have been led to accord

> a very important place to Christian disciplines, to Christianity as formative of Western individuality and subjectivity, and, to tell the truth, I would very much like to be able to compare these Christian techniques to Buddhist or Far Eastern spiritual techniques; to compare techniques which up to a certain point are close to one another; after all, Western monasticism and Christian monasticism were influenced by, copied from Buddhist monasticism, but with a completely different effect, since the principles of Buddhist spirituality must tend towards a disindividualization, to a desubjectification, to pushing individuality truly to its limits or beyond its limits, with the aim of an emancipation from the subject. My project would be first to get to know a little about that, and to see how, through apparently very similar techniques of asceticism, of meditation, through this overall resemblance one arrives at entirely different results.[7]

Foucault's phrase "Buddhist or Far Eastern spiritual techniques" is now, in the circumstances of a globalized world and increased knowledge of it, rather quaint, and either annoying or charming depending on one's level of charity. Perhaps he used it because the interview took place in Japan. I find the remarks about "a disindividualization, to a desubjectification . . . pushing individuality truly to its limits or beyond its limits, with the aim of an emancipation from the subject" a little vague, or at least difficult to interpret as they are. I will attempt to offer here, as I and many others have done elsewhere, something a little more precise in 2.3 and 2.4.13 below.

I hope that these citations from Hadot's and Foucault's work will attest that the comparative project I am here aiming at, however inadequate it may be, is something of which they would have approved.

2.2. AN ISSUE OF TRANSLATION: "THE SELF"?

I want to interject in this section and the next some remarks about translation. I do not want to insist that my own choice of translation is necessarily correct and always to be used, but I do want to raise some issues that may not be familiar to those who do not read Foucault in French. Translations standardly refer to "the self," with the definite article "the." In ordinary English, one never uses such a phrase—"I hurt the self on the knee." It is only used in philosophical or other complex discourses. In fact Foucault overwhelmingly uses not *du soi*, which contains the definite article and would be translated as "of the self," but "*de soi*," which does not contain the definite article and which I have translated here as "of self." This is, I admit, equally distant from ordinary usage. Sometimes the French can be translated better by a quite different phrase in English: thus volume 3 of his *History of Sexuality* in French, "Le souci de soi," is always translated and referred to as "The Care of the Self," as if it were "Le souci du soi," but "Le souci de soi" would be much better simply as "Caring for Oneself."[8] This reflexive use of the word "self" does not imply any metaphysical or otherwise transempirical concept. It is no more metaphysical than "I hurt myself on the knee" or "I'll do it myself." This distinction between ordinary language and metaphysical versions of "self" is vital, I think, to any comparative endeavor in this domain, and certainly with Buddhism, which teaches, as is well known, that there is ultimately no such thing as a permanent unchangeable self beyond experience, where everything is changing, including oneself.

Pali texts, like those in any other language, contain necessarily and ubiquitously reflexive uses of the word "self," and any stories would be impossible without persons, characters—what I have called, following narrative theorists, narrative actants. The Buddhist distinction between ordinary language uses of words like "self" and "person" and the specialist idea of the nonexistence of such things is standardly referred to in secondary sources as the distinction between conventional and ultimate truth. I discuss this in 2.3.1 and 2.3.2, where I will offer a detailed linguistic and conceptual analysis of the distinction and what I think are more accurate translations. Without such a distinction in interpretation, Pali literature as a whole would be entirely incoherent. Theravāda systematic "ultimate truth" could not possibly be a civilizational phenomenon, just the preserve of a few very odd people who could not speak a language comprehensible to anyone else, as Pali texts themselves clearly recognize. In fact, they could not speak a language at all, just recite lists of lexical items to one another. Theravāda civilization is not based on a lesser truth, but on a truth (just as true, in its own way, as is "ultimate truth") that is, as I shall translate it—consensual.

2.2.1. Caveat Lector Again: Some Misleading but Symptomatic Mistranslations

It is very unfortunate that the available translations of Hadot and Foucault, though generally admirable and correct, are also unreliable in a number of places, sometimes important ones. Here are two examples where the translation gives the opposite of the original. They are both examples of what are called "false friends": words in French and English that look the same but in fact have different meanings.

The first is from Hadot. In the first quotation from his work in the previous section I gave one sentence as "it seems to me . . .

that there really are thought-provoking analogies between the philosophical attitudes of antiquity and those of the Orient." The original French, on page 419 of *Qu'est—ce que la philosophie antique?*, is "il me semble . . . qu'i l y a réellement des troublants analogies entre les attitudes philosophiques de l'Antiquité et de l'Orient." The English translation, on page 278 of *What Is Ancient Philosophy?*, gives "it seems to me that there are really troubling analogies between the philosophical attitudes of antiquity and those of the Orient."[9] The relevant words are *troublants*/troubling. The English "troubling" means "worrying, causing distress or anxiety," which is precisely the opposite of what Hadot means. In French *troublant* can mean this, but it can also mean (altering the *OED* grammatically) "agitating and destroying (quiet, peace, rest); breaking up the quiet, tranquility, or rest of a person, stirring (one) up." Also given in dictionaries are "disturbing," "causing a change of mood or attitude" in the sense of shaking one out of a previous sense of settledness and ease. Thus there is in French the pleasant "une femme troublante," "a woman who shakes one up," that is, an attractive one. Hadot means, of course, that the analogies he has discovered between the philosophical attitudes of antiquity and those of "the Orient" have shaken him out of a previous sense of settled security with the uniqueness of "the philosophical attitudes of antiquity." I have chosen to use the word "thought-provoking" as a translation because this, I think, gives the sense of the word as Hadot uses it. He does not mean "worrying, causing distress or anxiety."

In a short piece on academic work, *Dits et écrits*, Foucault writes, beautifully, that it is "ce qui est susceptible d'introduire une différence significative dans le champ du savoir, au prix d'une certain peine pour l'auteur et le lecteur, at avec l'eventuelle récompense d'une certain plaisir, c'est à dire d'un accès à une autre figure de la vérité."[10] The English translation *Ethics, Subjectivity and Truth*, trying to give, I suppose, a literal and therefore, apparently, accurate translation has: "That which is susceptible of introducing a significant difference in the field of knowledge, at the cost of a certain difficulty for the author and the reader, with, however, the eventual recompense of a certain pleasure, that is to say of access to another figure of truth."[11] There are three main problems here, though quite a few of the words could be better translated. The first two problems are perhaps minor: *peine* is stronger than "difficulty": it means "penalty, punishment, pain, suffering." The author and reader have to pay the price for their work; they must suffer in doing it. "Figure of truth" is, to me, entirely unclear in English. French *figure* (which can mean simply "face"), as well as English "figure," mean primarily (*OED*) "shape, appearance." That is, figure means here "shape, appearance, form." The work of author and reader might result in truth appearing differently to them than it did before their work. But the third is the worst. French *eventuel* and English "eventual" are seriously false friends: the French means only "possible" where the English means (*OED*) "that will arise or take place," "ultimately resulting." What Foucault means is that the suffering of author and reader might result in truth appearing in another way, not that it will be the (inevitable) result of the difficulty they (temporarily) experience. Foucault's French is much stronger: their suffering will not necessarily have the "eventual recompense" of a new appearance of truth: it might result in nothing.

So, as in 1.3.9, caveat lector, let the reader beware. It is very unfortunately the case that, as I am attempting in this book, to offer material from Theravāda Buddhism to compare with Hadot and Foucault requires a detailed knowledge of both Pali and French. I say this not to show off, but as I hope to have demonstrated and will show further in this chapter, it just is the case, empirically provable, that working from existing English translations puts one at a significant distance from the texts, which can, on occasion, make detailed study of them into looking through a glass, very darkly.

The next three sections, 2.3., 2.3.1, and 2.3.2, may be hard going for readers who are not familiar with either philosophical or grammatical analysis. For them I suggest moving on directly to 2.3.3, where I attempt to summarize what has been going on in the previous three sections.

2.3. NO SELF, BUT MANY WORDS FOR PERSONS

It is well known, and treated in many books easily available to readers of this one, that the most basic and important idea of Buddhist systematic thought is the denial that there is any permanent, continuing self behind experience, and across the series of lives in saṃsāra: the doctrine of anattā, non-self. What people are is a collection of five constituents (khandhas), literally "heaps" but often translated "aggregates." I suppose this is because each khandha is a heap composed of many impermanent, indeed momentary events aggregated into categories. The word attan (its stem form, not one used in discourse), however, is used in many ways, most obviously as a reflexive pronoun for all genders and numbers: in the masculine singular ahaṃ attānaṃ vinemi, I train myself, in the feminine singular sā attānaṃ vineti, she trains herself, in the masculine plural te attānaṃ vinenti, they train themselves. It can also be used in an oblique case as an adverb: sā attānaṃ attanā vinet, she trains herself by herself, that is, (as is always necessarily the case, in the end) alone, without the help of anyone else. The word also appears often at the end of compounds, bhāvitattā, someone (male or female) who has trained him- or herself. So far, so obvious. But at the same time there are many terms by which persons and other such beings are referred to, in Pali texts and by any sane person, such as, for example, its entire narrative literature. These are words such as "person" (puggala), "man" (purisa), "woman" (itthī), "god" (deva or devatā), and other supernatural beings (of many kinds), nāgas (magical snakes), individuals of any species, people with proper names, and so on. There is the interesting term attabhāva, literally "the state of being a self" (better, "a subject" or "a subjectivity"), which can simply refer to the physical body, or to the individual of each lifetime. The former is rather like the English phrase "the murder weapon was found on the person of the accused." Rebirth is explained as follows. During a lifetime, what one calls "myself" or "the person I am" is in fact a collection of aggregates, each of them a category of impersonal events. Consciousness is just a series of changing events, as Pali texts like to say, just like milk turning to curds and whey. In this series consciousness happens to be connected, temporarily, to instances of the other four aggregates, notably the body. At death this connection is broken, and the series of events of consciousness becomes connected to another body, in a moment called that of "re-linking" (paṭisandhi). And then a new attabhāva, a new person, a new state of subjectivity, starts, until it too arrives at death, and so on (and on). The self-reflective nature of consciousness, a subject to which of course Buddhist philosophers devoted a great deal of attention, can be most briefly explained by the short sentence in English: consciousness reflects itself, not a self.

Is this a chaos of self-contradictory nonsense, the existence of persons and other individual beings irresolvably conflicting with the denial of self? No, of course it isn't. The Pali imaginaire is not the rambling of a schizophrenic. The main way

Buddhism has explained this apparent textual-linguistic aporia is by distinguishing between two kinds of truth, "consensual truth" and (what I call, for the sake of brevity) "ultimately referential truth." These have in the past been conventionally and imprecisely called "conventional" and "ultimate truth." In the former, persons can be referred to. In the latter, only dhammas, "existents," in the sense of "states" or "qualities," can be referred to. Crucially, they cannot, unlike the referents of words in consensual truth, be subdivided into component parts. The number of them varies: one calculation has eighty-two, classified under four general headings: one unconditioned dhamma; nibbāna (nirvana); consciousness (mind, citta), which has one member, and associated mentality (cetasika), which has fifty-two members; and physical phenomena (rūpa), which has twenty-eight. Throughout Sanskrit Buddhist philosophy, it was a matter of dispute whether the word *dharma* in this particular sense referred either to classes of dharma, types, or to individual, subliminal events within those classes, tokens. This is a difficult issue not addressed by Pali scholastic sources. For reasons I will go into in section 2.3.2, ultimate truth can only consist in lists of nouns or adjectives, without verbs: that is, "ultimately referential truth" is not expressible in a language.

2.3.1. Consensual Truth and Ultimately Referential Truth: A Linguistic Analysis

What has traditionally been translated as "conventional truth" is Pali sammuti-sacca. Sacca (Sanskrit satya) means "truth." It can also mean "reality," which has caused a certain amount of interpretive anxiety. The word sammuti was Sanskritized as samvṛti and taken by other Buddhists working in Sanskrit and

Tibetan to be from the root √ vṛ, to cover, with the prefix sam: thus it was taken to mean something like "the truth covering (the way things really are)," or some such. Much creative thought was engendered by means of this mistake; but mistake it is. In fact the word is from the root √ man, to think, with the prefix sam. Prefixes often add no meaning in Sanskrit or Pali, but here sam adds the meanings "together" or "along with." Mati is a verbal noun from √ man, "thought" or "thinking," (just as there is gati from √ gam), changed to muti by a phonological process called the labialization of vowels.[12] Thus sammuti-sacca or sammati-sacca mean, put loosely, "that which is true when we/people are thinking together, along with each other." It refers to what people agree on in normal circumstances, what there is a consensus about, what we agree that words refer to. It is important that ultimately referential truth can only be verified by individual experience, not by any collective process. Sammuti-sacca, that which is verified by collective agreement, truth by/of consensus, is in the terms of Sanskrit grammar, which have become English words, in the *OED*, a tatpuruṣa. I prefer the looser "consensual truth" (which is a karmadhāraya—on these grammatical terms see the next section), which sounds to me better in English. It is the truth of the world that we, as persons, live in together, talk to each other about, etc. "Ultimately referential truth," is, I fear, rather more complex. I will present the explanation in numbered sections.

1. The fundamental conceptual point is that consensual terms such as "person," "man," woman," etc. can be broken down into their constituent parts, as they are, for example, in "mindfulness of the body," to be described later. Ultimate "states" or "qualities" (dhammas) cannot be thus broken down, or as one

says nowadays, deconstructed. To go on now I will have to turn to the linguistic analysis of these compounds. Note, however, that the main analytical terms have now become English words, which can be found in the *Oxford English Dictionary*: tatpuruṣa, karmadhāraya, and bahuvrīhi.

2. Sammuti-sacca is grammatically a tatpuruṣa (= "his man," "the man of him," i.e., the king) called a "dependent determinative," where in the case system of Sanskrit and Pali the first member of the compound would be in a different case than the second if the words were separate. English examples are side door (= a door at the side, where "side" refers to the place where the door is), fact finding (= finding facts, where "facts" is the object of the verb "find"). Thus sammuti-sacca is truth of (because of, by means of, etc.) consensus. My translation "consensual truth" is thus technically inaccurate, since "consensual" is an adjective. In Sanskrit and Pali a compound where the first member is an adjective describing the second, and where the two words would be in the same case if separated, is called a karmadhāraya, a descriptive determinative, like "blackbird" or "greenfinch" in English.

3. This is not so with paramattha-sacca. At the first level of analysis it can indeed **be translated** like sammuti sacca, that is to say if one takes the compound as consisting of only two members it is a tatpuruṣa, "the truth of (what is) paramattha." But what does paramattha mean? This too is made up of two members, parama and attha. And now things get more intricate.

4. Parama means "ultimate," "highest," etc. At the first level of analysis, if one takes it to have only two members, it is a karmadhāraya; thus parama-attha can be "ultimate (highest, etc.) attha." But what does attha mean here? It can mean "aim" or "goal," and so paramattha used as a karmadhāraya, "highest

goal," is a synonym of nibbāna (nirvana). But to explain how paramattha-sacca is complementary to sammuti-sacca requires a philosophical analysis as well as a linguistic one.

5. The word attha (Sanskrit artha) has very many meanings, among which are "aim, goal, intention." Dictionaries standardly also give "sense, meaning," but this is philosophically incomplete. It can also mean "that which is referred to." The first step in attaining precision here requires going back to one of the most famous papers of the twentieth century (and still nowadays: it was in fact written in 1892), Gottlob Frege's "On Sense (Sinn) and Reference" (Bedeutung, sometimes translated as "Denotation").[13] This, of course, has given rise to an enormous philosophical literature, but the basic idea is simple. Frege's most popular example was this: the two phrases "morning star" and "evening star" have different senses, since "morning" and "evening" are not the same. But they both refer to (denote) the planet Venus; that is, they both have the same referent.

6. The second step in attaining precision here is to go back once again to an analysis of compounds in Sanskrit and Pali language. The word attha (and Sanskrit artha), "aim," "goal" in philosophical contexts, is best taken, in my view, as reference rather than sense. Parama-attha here is what is called a bahuvrīhi. This term means in the first instance "much rice" (i.e., it is a descriptive determinative), but it is used to denote a class of compounds that are adjectives, so it means here "much riced," that is, "rich." Such compounds can be understood by taking their two members, A-B (however internally complex each might be), usually "of whom the B is A." Bahuvrīhi means a person "of whom the rice is much (a lot), i.e., rich." There are many examples in English: "free-range eggs" ("of whom the range is free"); "seaside fun fair" ("a fun fair of which the front is at the seaside"), etc. Thus paramattha means "of which the reference is ultimate."

7. All, or almost all words in both kinds of truth succeed in referring (unlike, to use a classic example from Western philosophy, "the golden mountain," or in Pali the postulates of non-Buddhist philosophy such as the "atoms" of the Vaiśeṣika), to the nature and person(s) of the Sāṃkhya, which do not exist in either form of truth and so cannot be referred to. A classic Sanskrit example is "a barren woman's son." "Person," "man," "woman," "Christopher," etc. succeed in referring to what the speaker intends to talk about. But their reference is not ultimate, because the words exist in consensual truth and their referents can be deconstructed into their constituent parts. Words in ultimately referential truth refer to dhammas, a very difficult use of the word that I follow Rupert Gethin in translating "states" or "qualities," both physical and mental, of experience, which cannot be so deconstructed. The example given in a text I shall discuss momentarily is "eye contact" (cakkhu-samphassa). Both "eye" and "contact" (i.e., contact between the eye and its object) are ultimate and cannot be deconstructed. Therefore, on the linguistic level I would translate paramattha-sacca precisely as "the truth (of states/qualities) whose referent is ultimate." This would be clumsy in English, so I would interpret, rather than translate, the compound as "ultimately referential truth."[14]

8. It is vitally important to bear in mind that consensual truth and ultimately referential truth are both truths, and both of them are parts of the Buddha's teaching. Some verses found in many texts make this quite clear:

> The Buddha, best of speakers, spoke two truths: the consensual and the ultimately referential. There is no third. Words [used by] agreement [constitute] truth because of the consensus of people (loka-sammuti-kāraṇā); words whose referent is ultimate [constitute] truth because of the existence of qualities. Therefore no

falsehood is produced when the Teacher, lord of the world, skilled in commerce, employs the consensus.[15]

The word "commerce" is vohāra, which can, like its Sanskrit counterpart vyavahāra, refer also to both mercantile and legal exchanges. It is very commonly found in contexts such as these. There is a sense of "commerce" in English that captures the sense nicely, although it has become obsolete: the *OED* has "intercourse in the affairs of life; dealings . . . interchange (esp. of letters, ideas, etc.), communication." "Of good commerce" is "agreeable (etc.) in intercourse," "pleasant to meet." *Webster's* has as its first sense "social intercourse, dealings between individuals or groups in society." Note also that the verse explicitly denies that commerce, consensual truth, is falsehood: it is one kind of truth.

9. The passage cited above continues by giving eight reasons "The Blessed One teaches in terms of persons." They include the reflection: "if it is said 'the aggregates, elements, and sense-bases feel shame or fear of doing wrong,' ordinary people do not understand and are confused, or [even] become antagonistic. But if it is said that a woman, man, etc., feels shame or fears doing wrong, [they do not]." The same thing is said of seven other things, including feeling friendliness (mettāyanti–mettā as a noun will be discussed in 2.4.6 as a practice of self), and sentences such as "The aggregates accept a gift." To say instead "a person accepts as a gift" is "what people want (to hear)." Naturally, the Buddha uses ordinary language "without being attached to it." The same three verses are given elsewhere,[16] except that at the end the last half-line is vohāro ariyovaso, which means "this commerce is [also] noble." "Noble" here is a technical term; referring to people it can have some other senses, but here it is the more general "follower of the Buddha." It means, in modern categories, "to be counted as 'Buddhist.'"

10. Another text makes the same point, albeit in a more conceptually intricate way. This is the opening of the commentary on the Abhidhamma anomaly "concepts of persons," a passage that uses the verb √ vid. Linguists are divided as to whether this is one root that developed two meanings or two roots, "to find" and "to know." It is most usually used in contexts such as these in the passive, "is found," Pali vijjati, Sanskrit vidyate. Much discussion has been engendered throughout Indian philosophy because the word can mean "is found/known" epistemologically and/or ontologically. That is, it can mean "is known" or "exists." I think, for reasons that will become clear, that in the passage I am about to discuss it must be taken epistemologically, that is, "is known," "is found (in a certain discourse, in a kind of truth)." The passage discusses various kinds of concepts, of which the two relevant here are the concept "of what is found and the concept of what is not found" ([a]vijjamāna-paññatti): a concept of what is found is the designation of a good or bad quality that exists, is real, is found by means of what is truly, ultimately referential.[17] Correspondingly, a concept of what is not found (i.e., in that first form of truth) is "the designation of things like woman, man, and the like, which are established merely by the way people speak" (loka-nirutti). There is also a concept of something that does not exist, is not an object in any way whatsoever, such as a fifth truth or the atoms, nature, person, and the like of (non-Buddhist) thinkers. This (kind of) concept "is not in the scope of the teaching." A fifth truth is nonexistent because there can only be four. "Atoms," etc., are theoretical postulates of Hindu intellectual traditions. They cannot be referred to successfully.

11. It is because of the addition of this second kind of "concept of what is not found" that I think one must take (a)vijjamāna, in the cases of both ultimately referential and consensual truth here,

as "(not) found" epistemologically, in any kind of discourse. The referents of consensual truth such as "woman," "man," etc. are not found in ultimately referential truth, but they do indeed exist within that form of human life and discourse which establishes consensual truth, which is both "noble" and "within the sphere of the teaching."

2.3.2. Grammatical Roots, Conjugation, and the Implied Subject: Why Ultimately Referential Truth Cannot Be a Language

Ancient Indian grammarians, lost in the mists of time, with quite extraordinary acumen discovered under ordinary language a set of grammatical roots: that is, linguistic items that could not appear as such in any spoken or written sentence, but which, with the appropriate transformational rules (here one recalls Chomskyan linguistics), could generate ordinary language. Any sentence in Sanskrit or Pali must have a verb and a subject.[18] Using a Pali example with a Sanskrit root, for reasons I will not go into here: one starts from a root, say √ kṛ, "to make" or "to do." To construct an indicative sentence one moves first to a strengthened present stem kar; next one adds a connecting vowel o. Thus one has, as a present stem and not yet a word, "karo." One completes the process by adding a conjugational ending (called a vibhakti in Sanskrit, vibhatti in Pali), mi, si, ti, (I, you, he/she/it), etc. Thus karoti, he/she/it, "makes" or "does." This verb is a complete sentence because such conjugational endings as mi, si, ti, according to the grammarians, contain in themselves a reference to an implicit agent, Sanskrit kartṛ, Pali kattā. There may be explicit subjects, and words in other cases, such as kumbhakāro kumbhaṃ karoti, "a potter makes a pot," but such other words are not necessary additions to a verb to make a complete sentence.

Now, to put together these grammatical rules and categories with Buddhist ontology. First, Buddhist grammarians agree with their Sanskrit counterparts that conjugated verbs always have an agent, a kartṛ or kattā, as the subject, referred to explicitly or implicitly. But Buddhist systematic thought insists, as has been explained in 2.3, that there exists no such thing as an agent, in the sense of a continuing phenomenon as the subject of action. This means that the agent necessarily implicit in any conjugated verb, to which such endings as mi, si, and ti refer, can only be found, referred to, in consensual truth. Ultimately referential truth therefore must consist only in separate linguistic items, not sentences with conjugated verbs. It cannot be discursive in any normal sense. It can only be lists of nouns and adjectives. Lists are extremely common throughout Buddhist and Brahmanical texts, both systematic and narrative. This is highly important: ultimately referential truth cannot be a language. So the interpretive analysis found in some contemporary secondary sources, that in principle (whatever that means), consensual truth could be "reduced to" ultimately referential truth, is quite wrong. It is in fact an egregious imposition of Western categories on Buddhist thought, here the idea that consensual truth could be reduced to ultimately referential truth, in the same sense that in reductive materialism consciousness events could be, in principle, reduced to brain states (itself quite wrong, in my opinion, but that is another matter).

Accounts of practices of self are in sentences, so there is an agent. Although what is being analyzed, recollected, concentrated on, etc. may well be one of the lists of items permissible in ultimately referential truth, the analyzer, reflector, concentrator is him- or herself, an agent in the realm of consensual truth. But not absolutely always. In a short but remarkable passage of the *Path of Purification*, Buddhaghosa sternly admonishes his audience:

> There is no elimination of View for someone who thinks "I see with Insight, Insight is mine." Mental Formations see Mental Formations with Insight, think, determine, comprehend, define [them]. [Likewise] There is no elimination of pride for someone who thinks "I see excellently with Insight, I see pleasantly with Insight." Mental Formations see Mental Formations with Insight . . . There is no mastering of attachment by [thinking] "I am able to see with Insight." Mental Formations see Mental Formations with Insight. . . . [19]

Even here, however, grammar and its need for an agent arise implicitly in the present participle gaṇhato, from √ gṛh, basically "to take" but by extension (as in English) "think": "for someone who thinks." The Latin poet Horace put it well: "naturam expelles furca, tamen usque recurret" ("You may drive nature out with a pitchfork, but she will constantly hurry back").[20]

2.3.3. What Has All This Been About?

The previous sections tried to explain in some detail what "consensual" and "ultimately referential truth" are, and what the words mean. The most important point for understanding Buddhist practices of self is simply this: ultimately referential truth cannot contain conjugated verbs, of whatever kind. Writers of introductory textbooks have to describe the "Three Baskets of the Canon" and are often at a loss to know what the Abhidhamma actually is, so use vague phrases such as "which discusses psychological and philosophical subjects." In fact most books of that basket, leaving aside the anomalous[21] *Kathāvatthu* (*Points of Debate*) but not the *Puggalapaññatti* (*Concepts of Persons*), are more like dictionaries or encyclopedias, which consist overwhelmingly (one cannot say always, but at least almost always) of lists of nouns and adjectives. Strikingly, the only significant exceptions to this are passages that describe what we would call "meditative" practices of self, where the practitioner is described, or his or her actions are prescribed, using ordinary verbs. So if one is looking for Buddhist practices of self, one cannot find them solely or even mainly in ultimately referential truth. Consensual truth is inescapable. To be sure, these dictionary lists can be important, as in insight (vipassanā) practices, especially since the Burmese teacher Mahasi Sayadaw introduced, in the mid-twentieth century, the practice of labeling: that is, using nouns or adjectives mostly from ultimately referential truth to give names to passing mental and physical states. But in premodern and still ubiquitously in modern practices, there is a pluralism of truth.

2.4. BUDDHIST SPIRITUAL EXERCISES, PRACTICES OF SELF

As has often been pointed out, there is no common word in either Pali or Sanskrit that translates the English word "meditation." Bhāvanā means "development" and is used for the whole ensemble of things one might include under the heading "practices of self." Bhāvanā is an overall process, not a specific activity. Samādhi is a word with many, often quite different meanings throughout Buddhist and Hindu vocabularies. In Pali it is usually used in the present context for practices of concentration, which is a good enough translation.[22] Specific words often taken in modern times, particularly by modernist Buddhists, to be coextensive with "meditation" are in fact particular activities within bhāvanā: the two most common are sati (mindfulness) and vipassanā (insight). There is a verb, √ jhā/jhāyati, for which the *Dictionary of Pali* gives "meditates, contemplates, thinks upon, broods over, is thoughtful or meditative." There is a very rare action noun, jhāyana, which could be translated "(the act of) meditating," but it is so rare as to be irrelevant here. The Sanskrit counterpart verb is √ dhyai/dhyāyati, for which among other more familiar senses Monier-Williams gives, pleasantly enough, "think of, imagine, contemplate,. . . to brood mischief against, to let the head hang down (said of an animal)." From √ dhyai in Sanskrit comes dhyāna, in Pali jhāna, from √ jhā, which is not used for the act of meditating in general but only for a particular level or kind of achievement in it, sometimes called "meditation level" but better as "kind of absorption."[23] "Level" is in a preliminary way useful here, not only because the kinds of achievement are arranged in a hierarchy but also because they are correlated cosmologically with various Buddhist heavens, which are imagined to be literally one on top of the other. In what follows I shall try to find English words that more precisely describe the activities grouped under bhāvanā.

In the sections that follow I will be depending, for convenience, almost entirely on Buddhaghosa's *Path of Purification*, since it is so easily available, though I will not be following its ordering of issues and practices, nor in most cases its vocabulary. I use this text both because its treatment provides a number of contextualizing discussions and many anecdotes, which I find useful and interesting, but also, more important, because my interest is external and analytic, and I will be using existential, ideology-free vocabulary into which the categories of the Path of Purification are quite readily translatable. Certainly, because the practices are so bound up with and expressed in words from the Buddhist ideological lexicon, this will not always be possible. Buddhaghosa claims that his entire work is a commentary on a single verse from the canon: "a wise man, making his foundation morality, and developing mind and wisdom, [that] resolute and adept monk will disentangle this tangle."[24] The word for "tangle" is jaṭa, interpreted as craving, which is like a thicket of bamboos. It may also connote, remind people of, the tangled hair of many non-Buddhist ascetics. The words "mind" and "wisdom" are interpreted as, among other things, concentration and insight.

It is important to say, and to emphasize, that alongside or within his exposition of and prescriptions for development (bhāvanā) Buddhaghosa constantly illustrates what he says with stories and anecdotes, which serve both to elucidate and to lighten up the otherwise austere prose and verse of his text. Much as I would love to recount some of them, for reasons of space I must leave them out. Ñāṇamoli's translation is available on the web, so the reader of this book who cares to can read any number of examples.

2.4.1. Chanting, Paying Respects, and Devotional Ritual

The title here is taken from a chapter in Sarah Shaw's *Introduction to Buddhist Meditation*. As she explains, these are not merely propaedeutic to "meditation" proper but are, or at least can be, forms of it.[25] There are chants done by monastics alone as part of monastic ritual, by monastics and laity together, and by monastics for laity. Perhaps the form of chanting most familiar to laity is that done by monastics at funerals, which can sometimes be affairs of great elegance (and cost). The chants done at funerals are lists taken from the Abhidhamma, appropriately enough, as the dissolution of consensual truth into ultimately referential truth resonates with the dissolution of the dead person's body into its constituent parts.

Here is, if I may, a small anecdote from my own experience. At Wat Suthat, a large and very well-known monastery in Bangkok, every evening at 6:00 there is a session of Pali chanting, which lasts about an hour. If you want to get a place in the main hall, you have to get there early, as by 6:00 it is full to overflowing. Others have to sit outside on metal or wooden seats. The chanting is led by a single monk at the front using a microphone, facing away from the lay audience and toward the Buddha image.[26] In a way he and everyone present are chanting to the image. There are chanting books (Thai: nang seu mon piti) one can read from, but it is remarkable how many of the regulars know so many chants by heart, even though they probably understand little or nothing of what they mean, apart from the simple opening ones such as buddhaṃ saraṇaṃ gacchāmi ("I go to the Buddha for refuge"). No doubt many go there after work, aiming for such things as health, success in education or business, and the like. Pali is the language of power and truth, and so, it is hoped, chanting in it will be efficacious in achieving such goals. This is often dismissed as "popular Buddhism," which I think is wholly a mistake, but that is not my subject here. My point is quite different: the chanting is done very fast, with no breaks between sentences. This means that everyone, the leading monk included, has to stop every now and then to take a breath. Then, in order to rejoin the chant properly, one has to start again at exactly the right place, on exactly the right syllable. This takes, as I know to my cost, a considerable effort of concentration. Although chanting is not categorized by Buddhist texts as falling into one of the overt categories of bhāvanā and is not one of what Buddhaghosa calls, in the usual translation, the forty "meditation subjects" (kammaṭṭhāna), it is certainly, when done well, a kind of concentrative self-development.

Likewise, there is paying respects to monastics, especially senior ones, and to Buddha images, a topic badly in need of more ethnographic and textual study, as well as genealogical study of the English word so often used in such contexts, "worship." So-called devotional ritual involves learning to know what to do and how to do it, and to pay attention when one is doing so. These things can be done more or less successfully, more or less elegantly. It is a shame that Buddhist studies and religious studies have not given more attention to elegance as a virtue and an aspiration. I don't mean show-off big shots, just ordinary Buddhists going about their business with care. Like any and every form of performance art, chanting, paying respects, and devotional ritual require training, askēsis, and concentration, whether the devotion and respect are given by monastics or laity. They are certainly spiritual exercises and practices of self in Hadot and Foucault's senses: in each and every repetition, done with concentration, they change the knowing subject, which is more important than changing what is known, which stays the same. Buddha images and the forms of paying respect to them remain the same. In Foucault's words, "spirituality" is distinguished from "philosophy" in the following ways:

> We could call "spirituality" the pursuit, practice and experience through which the subject carries out the necessary transformations on himself in order to have access to the truth. We will call this "spirituality" the set of these pursuits, practices, and experiences, which may be purifications, ascetic exercises, renunciations, conversions of looking, modifications of existence, etcetera, which

> are not for knowledge but for the subject, for the subject's very being, the price to be paid for access to the truth.[27]

To be sure, the "truth" of which Foucault speaks here, as also Buddhist ultimately referential truth ("seeing things as they really are," yathābhūta-dassana), are—allegedly—"higher," "more sophisticated," and so on, than these apparently simple acts of Buddhist piety. But everyone, even that tiny minority of virtuosos who go on to seek enlightening truth, has to start somewhere, and that somewhere is here. It is a shame that the word "piety" has come in the modern world to be double-edged, with always the possible connotation of fraud, self-righteousness, and bombast that Jane Austen and George Eliot were so good at skewering. Perhaps "training in reverence" would be better for this askēsis.[28]

2.4.2. Bodily Deportment and Social Location: The "First Sermon"

In the previous section I was dealing with attitudes and practices of both laity and monastics, as I shall again in some later sections. Here I will be discussing issues that apply only to monastics. The *Path of Purification* is addressed only to monks, but at the time of its writing there existed women who were recognized as properly ordained, so we can take its prescriptions and ideals to apply to nuns also. But the text says "monks," so I shall follow that here. Modern ethnographic evidence shows that many of the same requirements and expectations apply to women who practice Buddhist askēsis also, often more exactingly.

I will start with dress. In a general sense, any kind of shared dress is a uniform: contemporary fashion is just a series of uniforms, worn temporarily until something new comes along (better said, is offered for sale in the sad and often ugly civilizational process of modern consumerism). It is striking that across the world ascetics and their supporters pay a great deal of attention to details of dress, which we can rightly call uniforms, and to public perception of them. Even the fearsome naked nāgas of India, who often in the past acted as soldiers, even mercenaries, pay great attention to their appearance: their naked bodies are smeared with ash, preferably from cremation grounds; their hair is carefully braided into dreadlocks. They are not clean. They are instantly recognizable, aside from their nakedness (some do wear a small jockstrap). Even the more extreme practices of some of them, such as holding one arm in the air until it atrophies or tightening a hand into a fist in such a way that the fingernails of one hand grow though the palm, produce a kind of appearance meant, among other things, to make such ascetics into celebrities to be gazed on by their supporters (and others). Nakedness, ashes, and distortions of the body are their uniform.

Most other kinds of ascetic uniform, again across the world, are meant to project an image of care, tidiness, and cleanliness, as indicators of matching inner states. Here are two descriptions of the comportment of a good Buddhist monk. The first is from the *Visuddhimagga*, in Ñāṇamoli's translation:

> [A monk] is respectful, deferential, possessed of conscience and shame, [he] wears his inner robe properly, wears his upper robe properly, his manner inspires confidence whether in moving forwards or backwards, looking ahead or aside, bending or stretching; his eyes are downcast, he has (good) deportment, he guards the doors of his sense faculties, knows the right measure in eating, is devoted to wakefulness, possesses mindfulness and full awareness, wants little, is contented, is strenuous, is a careful

> observer of good behavior, and treats the teachers with great respect. This is called (proper) conduct . . . having entered a house, having gone into a street, he goes with downcast eyes, seeing the length of a plough yoke, restrained, not looking at an elephant, not looking at a horse, a carriage, a pedestrian, a woman, a man, not looking up, not looking down, not staring this way and that.[29]

The second is from Michael Carrithers's anthropological study *Forest Monks of Sri Lanka: An Historiographical and Anthropological Study*. He says:

> This image of the graceful, restrained monk is ancient and powerful in Sinhalese Buddhist society. According to Buddhaghosa's Introduction to his commentary on the Vinaya [the monastic rules], the Indian Emperor Aśoka was first attracted to Buddhism by the sight of such a monk walking past the palace. Today, Buddhist laymen have a clear image of this style of deportment: on more than one occasion laymen imitated it for me. It is characterized by, in Ray Birdwhistell's terminology, small range—movements tend to be restricted rather than broad; and low intensity—they are slow rather than abrupt. Perhaps our nearest equivalent is the deportment of a well-brought up lady: the voice is gentle, the knees kept together, the arms held close to the body. [Perhaps one should add now, an old-fashioned upper-class lady.][30]

Birdwhistell and the discipline he founded, kinesics, seem to have largely been forgotten now, which is unfortunate.[31] One simple way to describe what he was doing (though this is a term he did not like) is "making a survey and analysis of body language."

In many, perhaps all Buddhist practices of self, in which external behavior and internal phenomenology are thoroughly intermingled, it is hardly original to suggest that we are confronted with a form of social theater, in which the presence of an audience, even if it is an imagined one, is not only desirable but necessary, as a constitutive part of theater. A dress rehearsal is not the same as a theatrical performance with an audience. I don't know (indeed, I can't imagine) what goes on, or is supposed to go on, in the mind of a good actor or actress when they are concentrating intensely on a part they are playing or rehearsing, but in the Buddhist case the monk's inner experience is supposed to mirror, or rather be part of the performance: he is acting out his inner state, showing what is inside to those who are outside. He not only "wears his inner robe properly, wears his upper robe properly," and so on, but "he guards the doors of his sense faculties . . . is devoted to wakefulness, possesses mindfulness and full awareness."[32]

At this point I will insert what might seem to be a digression—although I hope it will not be taken as such—owed for the most part to Oliver Freiberger, about what is called in Buddhism "the Middle Way."[33] It is worth going into some detail here, in my opinion, both to set right what is an extraordinary mistake made in so many secondary sources and to exemplify again the ideal monk's carefully positioned social performance. The text is construed by tradition to be the Buddha's First Sermon. The most well known and most often cited version of this text is in part grammatically incoherent, which suggests a process of editing, or rather mis-editing. It is not a newspaper account of what the Buddha actually said first, but what, somewhat mangled now grammatically, some writers wanted him to be thought of as saying first. One so often reads that the Middle Way is between the life of a householder, given over to sense pleasures, and that of extreme self-mortificatory asceticism. According to legend, Siddhattha Gotama experienced both of these, the first as a prince in his palaces and the second for six years after his leaving home to be an ascetic, before he accepted a bowl of milk rice from the woman Sujātā and sat under the Bodhi tree to attain enlightenment. But here is a striking example of the truth hidden in plain sight. In fact, what the text says is unambiguously: "dve . . . antā pabbajitenā na sevitabbā" ("there are two ends [extremes] that are not to be followed by one who is a renouncer").[34] That is to say, the Middle Way here has nothing to do with householders: it is about the right way to practice renunciatory askēsis. The second extreme is easy to translate and understand: "there is devotion to self-mortification, which is painful, ignoble, and useless." It is the first extreme, no doubt, that has caused the misunderstanding. It is not, indeed, at first sight semantically easy to construe: "yo cāyaṃ kāmesu kāma-sukhallikānuyogo hīno gammo pothujjaniko anariyo anatthasaṃ hito." (Literally, if a little woodenly, "there is devotion to the pleasure arising from desire in relation to the objects of desire, which is inferior, connected with villages, lived individually, ignoble, and useless"; or "the pleasure that arises from desiring desirable things. That is, not as part of an organized community, a saṅgha").

I. B. Horner, in a striking piece of English upper-class superciliousness, to whose translation so many nonspecialists are condemned, has: "that which is, among sense-pleasures, addiction to attractive sense-pleasures, low, of the villager, of the average man, unariyan, not connected with the goal." She adds a number of footnotes, for example, on gammo, which she translates "of the villager" (which means she assumes, despite the text, that this is a layperson). Another debatable term, whose explanation is gāma-vāsinaṃ santako ("belonging to village dwellers"), meaning, I think, more "common" than "pagan." "Boorish" would be better. Santako ("the property of") is satirical: these renouncers haven't renounced, they are owned by the villagers they depend on so closely for a living. Then, for pothujjaniko, in her version "of the average man," she comments, "ordinary, of the many-folk, the 'blind' and fools." Three things: first, the word kāma is one of those that in Sanskrit and Pali can mean both a subjective emotion and an external state or thing. Bhaya, for instance, means both "fear" and "danger." Thus in "kāmesu kāma-sukhallikānuyogo," the first kāma refers to objects of desire (what the commentary here, making a standard distinction, says is vatthu kāma, "desirable things"); the second, within the compound, means subjective desire for such things (what the commentary refers to as kilesa-kāma, "desire connected with mental defilements"). This says nothing about what "desire" or "desirable" means, but it certainly does not mean sexual desire or its objects. We are talking about renouncers, remember. Second, the word gamma (from gāma, Sanskrit grāmya, from grāma) means "to do with village(s)." As Freiberger suggests persuasively, given that this is something specifically not to be followed by renouncers, it must refer to some kind of asceticism that the Buddha is saying should be avoided. Most likely this is a familiar South Asian stereotype: scruffy layabouts who live close to villages for the sake of an easy life and a free lunch, doing nothing apart from perhaps performing the occasional ritual for villagers (and, in many modern cases in India, smoking a very great deal of marijuana). Ordinary people are frightened of them (usually because of their actual or possible magic powers) or disrespectful, or both. In any case, these ascetics do not follow the kind of restrained and supervised practices of self the Buddha wishes to recommend. Third, the word pothujjana (from puthu -jjana, Sanskrit pṛthak-jana) means "separate." Puthu/pṛthak taken adverbially means "separately, individually, singly." I have taken it as meaning living separately from a saṅgha, a specific community, and thus not subject to any discipline.

Gary Tubb has recently shown that in Sanskrit epics pṛthakjana means "excluded from (some specific) group."[35] This could mean what I have just said, living separately from a saṅgha, or it could also be being used in a technical sense, where puthujjana refers specifically to someone not included in the group of those who have attained one of the four stages to enlightenment, and who thus are in this sense the group of "noble ones." So anariyo (ignoble) would have this technical sense here also.

The point of all this discussion of the two extremes of the First Sermon, in relation to bodily deportment and social location, is that that so-famous text is precisely talking specifically about two kinds of asceticism, which are, each in its own way, opposed to the (future) Buddhist community of monks who are to live demurely, without either useless oversevere self-mortification out in the boonies or undignified, lazy hedonism (though not, at least not publicly, sexual) close to villages. Buddhist monastics are (or will be, if this is taken to be the First Sermon, given before the Saṅgha was founded) organized in disciplined groups, neither lazy and hedonistic nor overzealous in self-torment, and, one can assume, with a social performance carefully choreographed to signify this "Middle Way." In the myth of the founding of the Buddhist monastic order, its first dwelling place was a park given by King Bimbisāra, who reigned in the city of Rājagaha but had the idea of providing a place near to a village, but not too far away. Clearly not thinking of himself personally, he had thought: *Where might the Blessed One live, which would be not too far from a village and not too close, convenient to go to and come back from, approachable by people wanting this or that, with few people during the day and at night quiet and with no noise, with no one talking, where one can sleep apart from (other) people, and suitable for privacy [i.e., for personal practice]?* This idyll of accessibility and quietude had by Buddhaghosa's time, and no doubt long before it, if it ever existed, given place both to monasteries in remote regions with sometimes just one monk and to busy city monasteries with hundreds of monks. But the bodily and dress ideals remained the same: "he wears his inner robe properly, wears his upper robe properly, his manner inspires confidence."

2.4.3. Spiritual Direction: The Good Friend, Ways of Life, and Occasions for Practice

Central to Pierre Hadot's conception of ancient philosophy was the notion of philosophy as a way of life, as created and maintained through spiritual exercises. Such exercises were, in turn, dependent on the guidance of a spiritual director. Hadot often referred to a book and an article by his wife, Ilsetraut, the latter entitled "The Guide" (in antiquity). She wrote, "according to ancient thought [the guide's] work is considerably aided by two factors: authority and friendship."[36]

Likewise Foucault, in distinguishing *spiritualité* from *philosophie*, emphasized in relation to the former the importance of the spiritual director, and the friendship, affection, and freedom of speech (parrhēsia) that should exist between them. As I said in 1.3.4, however, it should be remembered here that in ancient, as, I think, in many premodern and still some modern vocabularies, friendship refers not immediately or only to an affective bond between equals but to two people in a hierarchical relation, sometimes though by no means always, and certainly not necessarily infused with affection: that is, the relation of patron and client, often expressed explicitly in political and economic terms, that is, one might say, senior to junior friend.

There is a direct parallel to this in the Buddhist concept of the kalyāṇamitta (the good friend), who is also one's ovādaka-bhikkhu (advisor/admonisher monk). This was an elder monk with whom a younger monk would enter into a formal relationship, which one may see as that of a client to patron, junior to senior friend, who, crucially important here, would choose for his junior friend a kammaṭṭhāna, literally "a place for work," but usually translated "meditation subject." This translation is loose. These "meditation subjects" are usually seen as the very heterogeneous list of forty classified as such by the *Path of Purification* (which drew on an earlier list of thirty-eight given in a similar text called *Vimutti-magga*, the *Path to Liberation*). But linguistic and semantic analysis of the term makes the word, I think, more complex and more interesting.

The familiar word kamma, from √ kṛ, to make or do, means all manner of things: action, deed, work, practice, and so on; ṭṭhāna, from √ sthā, to stand, has as many meanings as the English "thing." Here it is best taken as "location" or "occasion." The compound thus means place or occasion for action, and can mean simply "occupation," "métier": examples given in Pali texts are that of farmer (both arable and pastoral), merchant, carpenter, scribe, etc. So "meditation subjects" is not a good translation: "occasions for practice" seems to me better for a number of reasons, one of which is that the occasions for practice given in the lists are very heterogeneous: they do not conform at all to the usual binary distinction between samatha (calming) or samādhi (concentration) versus sati (mindfulness) or vipassanā (insight), promulgated by modernist Buddhists and secondary sources alike. As will be seen, many such occasions for practice conform to one or other of the many quite different meanings given for the English "meditation."

It is one of the good friend's tasks to choose an "occasion for practice" from the list of thirty-eight or forty for his junior friend. This is done according to the junior friend's cariyā, translated by Ñāṇamoli and hence everyone else as "temperaments." I have no great objection to this translation, as long as it is remembered that "temperament" involves behavior, physical action as well as mental disposition. The *OED* gives for "temperament," in one of its many heterogeneous senses, "constitution or habit of mind, esp. as depending upon or connected with physical constitution." The word cariyā is from √ car, whose most basic meaning is "to move (around)," "to live one's life"; thus the *Dictionary of Pali* gives for cariyā, among other closely similar senses: "action, performance, deeds, character, disposition." Cariyā is one's way of being, one's way of life. These "ways of life" are given, of course, in a list: those whose cariyā is predominantly characterized by passion (rāga), hatred (dosa), delusion (moha), faith (or confidence, saddhā), intelligence (buddhi), and reasoning (or conjecture, vitakka). I find it rather charming that Buddhaghosa says that out of his list of forty occasions for practice the only two that are "generally useful" are those on friendliness and death, but somewhat less charming that he has to add: "some say also the perception of foulness" (in corpses). A nod to his more ascetic fellows, no doubt.

2.4.4. How to Get Started: Ten Restrictions; Eighteen Faults of a Monastery; "Living Alone"

As with so many lists in Pali texts, one is sometimes moved to ask: Why just these? This seems to me to be a good question with the "ten restrictions," which one must be rid of even before approaching a good friend. They are: the (kind of) dwelling place; one's family; receiving (alms); (one's) group; (building) work; (thoughts about making) a journey; relatives; illness; (responsibility for) texts; supernormal powers. It is impossible and pointless here to go through all ten. "Receiving alms," for instance, is when a monk is well behaved and gets a good reputation; he is then pestered by people wanting to give him gifts. "He should leave his group and go alone to a place where he is not known." "One's group" means a group of students to whom he is teaching discourses (sutta-s) or "further doctrine" (Abhidhamma). They can (like modern students) present various problems, for which the text offers solutions. If, though, he can't find a solution, he should just up and go and (literally) do his own work, or as we might say, do his own thing. Supernormal powers are attainable through concentration, but they are a restriction for those who are aiming at insight. And so on.[37]

The "eighteen faults of a monastery" are: largeness, smallness; oldness; closeness to a road, a rock pool, leaves, flowers, or fruits; desirability (= fame); closeness to a town, a timber yard, fields, or (the) presence of uncongenial people; closeness to a port (or turnpike); location in a borderland; closeness to a kingdom's boundary; unsuitability. These seem fairly self-explanatory, but here are three of Buddhaghosa's elaborations. Famous means highly regarded by people. Esteeming someone who lives in a monastery . . . because people think he is enlightened (note, not that he is or claims to be), they come from everywhere to revere him. He is uncomfortable. If it's good for him, he can live there at night and go somewhere else during the day. Location in a borderland means that the people who live there are not well disposed toward the Buddha (and dhamma and saṅgha). Closeness to a kingdom's boundary means that there is danger from kings (or: fear of kings). The king on one side attacks the other because his territory does not fall within his power; the other attacks (the former) because his territory does not fall within his power. "There a monk lives at one time in the territory of one, and at another in that of the other. [The kings] bring him distress and misfortune, thinking he is a spy." Both of these last two faults show that monasteries are better built close to towns where kings, and their soldiers, live.[38]

These restrictions and faults of a monastery seem realistic enough, although the lists seem somewhat arbitrary. And their realism shows that many other texts are not to be taken literally but metaphorically, referring to psychology rather than positivist-historiographical sociology. Such are two that are well known in secondary sources: the introduction to many texts dealing with development, and a poem from the *Sutta Nipāta*—"The One Horn of the Rhinoceros." The introduction to many practices of bhāvanā is "a monk, in the forest or at the root of a tree, or in an empty house, sits down with legs crossed, keeping his body straight." This can no doubt in some cases be taken literally, although in a busy city monastery there is no forest and there are not likely to be enough trees or empty houses to go round. The forest and the roots of trees are places to be in the imagination more than in actual, lived space (and none the worse for that).[39]

The "One Horn of the Rhinoceros" poem certainly seems to recommend in many verses that "he [the monk] should live his life alone, like the one horn of a rhinoceros." The verb is carati, which almost all translators take, literally and naïvely, as "wander," which is only one of its meanings. I discussed this verb in the previous section: cariyā is one's way of being, one's way of life. "Wander" suggests that the idea is that the monk moves around, but in fact it refers to a monk's psychological way of life, his inner mode of being, not his behavior in the outer world. Thus, in verses 45–47:

> If one can find an intelligent companion, a friend who lives virtuously and resolutely, (then) mastering all risks one should live with him, willingly and mindfully. But if one cannot find [such a friend] then one should live single like a rhinoceros horn, like a king who has abandoned his kingdom. Assuredly let us praise the good fortune of having [such] a companion; one should associate with companions who are better than or equal to one. Not obtaining [such as] these one should live single like a rhinoceros horn, enjoying [only] what is blameless.[40]

So the poem is addressed to monks who live in busy, bustling city monasteries as much as to, in fact much more to, those very rare monks who do actually wander alone (and who don't read texts). Commentaries often gloss the word eka, which is also the number one, with the word adutiya, "without a second," and take the "second" to be craving. So if one is without craving one lives single, alone, whatever one's physical circumstances.

2.4.5. Inner Liturgy and Rumination; Textual Instrumentalism: The Recollection of the Buddha

Of the thirty-eight/forty occasions for practice, ten are called anussatis. This term is from √ smṛ, to remember, with the prefix anu (which has no significant meaning here). The standard and perfectly acceptable translation for this is "recollections" (the word sati, mindfulness, is also from √ smṛ). I shall argue later that in that form of practice it might often best be understood, though perhaps not translated, as "not forgetting"). Here one occasion for practice, called "recollection of the Buddha," is calling (back) to mind his good qualities, in a specific, fixed form. One may certainly call it liturgical, not in the Christian sense but in the expanded ideology-free sense of a fixed text used in public and private rituals. Recollecting in sequence the Buddha, the Dhamma (his teaching), and the Saṅgha (the monastic order) is very common in chanting, known by heart by most laity as well as monks. Moreover, the syllables contained within all three (108, a standard South Asian auspicious number) are used together in what I will presently call imaginative and instrumentalist ways. Buddhaghosa deals with the "Recollection of the Buddha" chant at far greater length than the others, and for the sake of brevity I will summarize him here. The text referring to the Buddha by itself is known as the "itipiso" verse, for reasons that will soon be obvious. Because of the importance of the Pali syllables in themselves, I must give the Pali as well as the translation of the "Recollection of the Buddha":

> itipiso bhagavā: arahaṃ sammāsambuddho vijjācaraṇa-sampanno sugato lokavidū anuttaro purisadamma-sārathi satthā devamanussānaṃ Buddho Bhagavā ti (The Blessed One is like this: he is a worthy one, completely enlightened one, endowed with [excellence in] knowledge and [good] behavior, the happy one, the knower of [all] worlds, the unsurpassed trainer of people to be trained [the metaphor here is elephant- or horse-training], the teacher of gods and men, the enlightened one, the blessed one).[41]

Buddhaghosa elaborates and explains the nine epithets in a manner entirely reminiscent of a commentarial text rather than one giving specific and detailed instructions for a mental practice. He often offers what are called in Sanskrit and Pali exegesis niruttis (Sanskrit niruktis). These are nongrammatical analyses of words, often called "folk etymologies," although there is nothing folklike about them. They are often very inventive, both sophisticated and playful. The people (like Buddhaghosa) who made them up were perfectly well aware of what we call the science of grammar (veyyākaraṇa, Sankrit vyākaraṇa). A well-known example: the first epithet, arahaṃ, is a nominative singular of arhat (also arahat or arahant)—these latter are used in English works as technical terms for an enlightened person—which is a present participle from √ arh → arahati, to be worthy of, to deserve. Buddhaghosa knew this. But he also chose to offer five nirutti analyses of the word. One, which became very influential in Sanskrit and Tibetan, is ari-han, "enemy killer," where the enemy is the mental defilements to be got rid of. I prefer to see such analyses as creative or imaginative etymologies.[42]

The sequence of epithets is so familiar as a chant that I cannot imagine a monk just saying it to himself rather than mentally chanting it. And clearly the idea is that a practitioner is to ruminate on these internally chanted epithets each in his own way, perhaps guided by Buddhaghosa's exegeses if he is familiar with them, depending on his knowledge and the time available to him. Perhaps he too might make up his own exegeses and niruttis. This is "meditation" in the *Webster's* sense of "a spoken or written discourse treated in a contemplative manner"; or the *OED*'s "the continuous application of the mind to the contemplation of a particular religious text." Buddhaghosa says that the successful practitioner "has the idea that he is living with the Teacher (and) his body, inhabited by the recollection of the qualities of the Blessed One, is worthy of worship, as if it were a shrine room." That is, his body is the room, and the mental spiritual exercise, the "Recollection of the Buddha," is a Buddha image inside it.

The epithets are appreciated in other ways also, using the syllables of the three recollections of Buddha, Dhamma, and Saṅgha. This usage occurs elsewhere: the first syllables of the four truths: suffering (dukkha), the arising (samudaya) of suffering, the ending of suffering in nirvana (Pali nibbāna), and the path to that end (magga) are "du, sa, ni, ma," which are then manipulated in various ways and in various orders. Similarly, the first syllables of a ubiquitous common phrase of respect for the Buddha, namo Buddhāya, "Honor to the Buddha," become the pentad na-mo-bu-(d)dhā-ya. This pentad could be chanted by itself, aligned with other pentads, etc. The "Recollection of the Buddha" has fifty-six syllables, itipiso bhagavā, etc.

The first syllables of each of the nine epithets are: a-saṃ-vi-su-lo-pu-sa-bu-bha. All these are put together in various orders and various patterns, orally, in written and other forms, to achieve ends different from the semantic values of the words from which they are taken. These permutations and uses are often called "magical," but that word is, as I have said, far too vague, and always potentially too pejorative to be of any use academically, in an existentialist, ideology-free discourse. Such uses seem better characterized as creative, and their value instrumental rather than semantic. They can be spoken or written as mantras, drawn on cloth (called yantras), and used in many ways, for example, woven into shirts and worn as protection in war. They can be installed in specific places in images of the Buddha, and in the human body. It is for this kind of reason that some people used to call these practices "Theravāda Tantra," which I suppose had and maybe still has some useful shock value for those who still see Theravāda as conservative, rationalist, etc. No one, to my knowledge, has yet found a good word for them, though I personally find the phrase "instrumental rather than semantic uses" helpful.

A quite extraordinary use of these syllables is found in a Pali text from Cambodia published by François Bizot and Oskar von Hinüber, to whom we owe our knowledge of much in the preceding paragraph. This is to form an acrostic, each verse of which has four lines, each of which begins with the appropriate syllable. This is not a specialist book, so I will merely give a brief example. Using just the first four, itipso, i-ti-pi-so, the text has: "iṭṭ ho sabbaññutaññāṇaṃ . . . ti ṇṇ o yo va ṭṭ adukkhamhā . . . piyo devamanussānaṃ . . . sokā viratacitto yo." Bizot and von Hinüber say that the text is learned, memorized, and passed on orally.[43] It seems to me, although they do not go into this, that the text, the installation of syllables in the body and Buddha images, and the like, could just as easily been a matter of inner imagination as external ritual instrumentalism. In any case, the practice is a discursive liturgy and not a nonverbal form of "meditation."

2.4.6. Heavenly Life: The Brahma-vihāras

"Heaven" here, though evocative I hope for nonspecialist readers in English, is strictly speaking a mistake, according to Buddhist cosmology. In that, the universe is made up of three parts In all of these realm beings are gendered, and, apart from the hells, are capable of enjoying sense pleasures except for the two subrealmsof form and formlessness (the details of which, fortunately, need not concern us here). In these two realms live celibate Brahmas, who are ungendered (but who are, alas, misogynistically said to have bodies shaped like those of men). These Brahmas "remain (there) for a long time, made of mind, feeding on rapture (pīti), providing their own light, moving about in the air, glorious."

The word vihāra is derived from √ vi-hṛ, among whose meanings is that relevant here, to spend or pass time. What I have been calling a monastery is a vihāra, a place where monks or nuns spend most of their time. The verb viharati is ubiquitously used for spending time in a meditative state, usually translated in that context (for reasons I don't know) "dwells." The word Brahmavihāras is standardly translated (again, for reasons I don't know) as "Divine Abidings," an ugly phrase. I will use the longer but more accurate "Living (Like) Brahmas."

There are four ways of Living (Like) Brahmas, which are constituted by the virtues of friendliness, compassion, (sympathetic) joy, and equanimity. First, some linguistic notes:

1. "Friendliness" is mettā, from mitta (Sanskrit mitra), "friend." The usual translation is "loving-kindness," which I suppose we are stuck with (see the discussion of pāramitā in 1.2). Someone, sometime in the nineteenth century no doubt, thought that this was a good translation for mettā (Sanskrit maitrī), and since then almost everyone has simply followed suit. The English compound "loving-kindness" was invented by Myles Coverdale in his 1535 translation of the Old Testament Hebrew word *chesed*, which refers, in the first instance, to God's love for Israel. How appropriate for Buddhism.
2. "Compassion" is karuṇā (in Pali and Sanskrit), of uncertain derivation. There is no reason to object to the translation. There are other words translatable as "compassion," such as anukampā and dayā, but they are very much less common.
3. "Joy" is muditā, from √ mud, to be happy, glad, rejoice, etc. There could be many translations of muditā, but "joy" has become standard and is unobjectionable. Its Buddhist use is specifically to rejoice in the happiness or success of others, and so the word is usually accurately rendered as "sympathetic joy."
4. "Equanimity" is usual, and unobjectionable, for upekkhā (Sanskrit upekṣā). The linguistic derivation of upekkhā is, I think, helpful to know. It is from the verb √ upa-īkṣ, which means simply to look at or toward. There is a synonymous verb, ajjhupekkati (from √ adhi-upa-īkṣ), though there is no commonly

used noun derived from it. In Buddhist Hybrid Sanskrit the meanings given for adhyupekṣati are "ignores, disregards, is indifferent to," which are far from the spirit of Pali upekkhā. The Pali verb upekkhati does indeed mean to look at detachedly, but this is not the quality of a psychopath. The four ways of Living (Like) Brahmas are a sequence, and equanimity is not separate from—indeed it is the culmination of—the virtues and experiences that precede it.

Buddhaghosa's treatment of these four virtues in the ninth chapter of the *Path of Purification* is very insightful psychologically, and I cannot hope to do it justice here. I will just choose a few examples from his treatment of friendliness.

First, one should start by showing friendliness to oneself. If this seems egocentric, even narcissistic, perhaps one might gloss it in contemporary therapeutic terms as getting over self-hatred, not an easy thing to do. Then one should "break down the barriers" by developing friendliness toward a very dearly beloved friend, next toward a person to whom one feels indifferent as if he were a very dearly beloved friend, next toward an enemy as if he were a person to whom he feels indifferent. Eventually, naturally, he is to show friendliness toward the whole world. When he does, he gains eleven benefits:

> He sleeps well, is happy when he wakes, he has no bad dreams, he is dear to human beings, dear to nonhuman beings, deities look after him, fire, poison and weapons do not affect him, he is able to concentrate his mind quickly, his expression is serene, he dies unconfused, and although he does not understand further [i.e., he does not attain nirvana] (nonetheless) he will be reborn in a Brahma-world.[44]

Friendliness, like the other three kinds of "heavenly life," has both near and far enemies, who must be guarded against. A near enemy is a state of mind close to the state in question, a far enemy is its opposite. The near enemy of friendliness is (sexual) passion, since both alike see good qualities in someone. This is why friendliness should not be practiced toward someone of the opposite sex. Its far enemy is ill will. Whereas passion stays close and can get an opportunity (to take over) easily, ill will is like someone hiding in a place like a mountain grove (and who, presumably, can suddenly ambush one).

2.4.7. Aggressivity Against Oneself: Mindfulness of the Body and the Foulness of Corpses

It is a commonly held perception, and one with which I agree, that although asceticism generally—but by no means always—promotes or seems to promote the popular value of what is called "nonviolence" (ahiṃsā), it can be seen as in fact (or at least also) violence directed against oneself. In many people's eyes, the fact of living a chaste life in homosocial institutions, relying on the generosity of others for one's food, not eating after midday, and all the other aspects of a monk's or nun's life is intrinsically a violence against natural human tendencies. But then, abstaining from natural human tendencies is precisely what monks and nuns intend to do.

Buddhism is often seen as a "peaceful religion." How can it be violent? Well, for external military violence ask, for example, Tamils in Sri Lanka in recent decades; Muslims in contemporary Burma, Sri Lanka, and southern Thailand; and Thais in 1767 when Burmese armies conquered and ransacked the city of

Ayutthaya, destroying in a general devastation countless manuscripts almost certainly containing valuable texts now lost forever. But that is not my concern here, which is practices of self. How can they be violent?

First, as so often in this book, let us stop to look at the word, its etymology, and thus the possibilities for accuracy in translation. Hiṃsā is a desiderative noun from √ han, to strike or kill, and so the word refers in the first instance not to external acts of violence but the internal, psychological fact of desiring or imagining performing them. So better renderings would be "desiring to kill" or "aggressivity" (seen as a state of mind). Aggressivity can be seen most egregiously in "Mindfulness Concerning of the Body and the Foulness of Corpses" in *The Path of Purification*.

> "Mindfulness Concerning the Body": the body is not always viewed as something necessarily to be deconstructed into its constituent parts and seen negatively: "when he reflects wisely, [a monk] uses alms food not for enjoyment, not excessively, not for (self-)decoration or adornment [bodybuilders of the world: take note!], but only for the continuing and keeping going of this body, so that it does not come to harm (vihiṃsā) and for the practice of the celibate life."[45]

In the meditation on the body, by contrast, a monk is to regard "this filthy body" as containing many kinds of "filth" (asuci): "(1) head-hairs; (2) body-hairs; (3) nails; (4) teeth; (5) skin; (6) flesh; (7) sinews; (8) bones; (9) bone marrow; (10) kidneys; (11) heart; (12) liver; (13) midriff; (14) spleen; (15) lungs; (16) bowels; (17) entrails; (18) gorge; (19) dung; (20) bile; (21) phlegm; (22) pus; (23) blood; (24) sweat; (25) fat; (26) tears; (27) grease; (28) spittle; (29) snot; (30) oil of the joints; and (31) urine." A thirty-second can be added, the brain. This is called the "perception of repulsiveness."[46]

The *Path of Purification* spares nothing in going into the repulsiveness of all this in detail. In a remarkable passage Buddhaghosa explains why the Buddha said that birth is suffering. One has to live in a mother's absolutely disgusting womb, just above her stomach and above her bowels, between her belly and her backbone, like a worm in rotting fish, rotting dough, or a cesspit, (in a place) that is very cramped, completely dark, pervaded by all manner of putrid smells and really bad-smelling winds.[47] But as well as the negative evaluation there is in this practice a certain recitational skill, whether this is done mentally or verbally. One first recites the first five parts, called the skin pentad (novices must learn this as part of their ordination ritual) in the order one to five, then backward five to one; then the kidney pentad in the order six to ten and backward to the beginning ten to one; then the lungs pentad, eleven to fifteen and backward to the beginning fifteen to one; and so on. This recitation seems more akin to the deconstructive rather than evaluative aspects of the practice. Its performative elegance balances the inelegance of the subject matter.

"The foulness of corpses": the ten kinds of foulness are probably close to impossible to see in the modern world, where corpses are no longer left visible in public, at the side of roads, in forests, in charnel grounds, on biers and funeral pyres, etc., but are carefully hidden from view in hospitals, mortuaries, and coffins. Some monks nowadays do, however, when given permission, visit mortuaries and hospitals to perform this practice. The ten kinds, which may, I imagine, now also function (as perhaps they did in the past) as forms of imagination, are: the bloated, livid, festering, cut up, gnawed, scattered, hacked and scattered, bleeding, worm-infested, and the skeleton. Dwelling on the details of corpses would no doubt be classified nowadays as a form of pathology, but the general moral point is still valid: "as these corpses are, so I (this body) will be also."[48]

2.4.8. Concentration Exercises: Meditation Levels; Mythic Cosmology

There are many different practices of concentration. I will describe just one, one of the easiest to understand, in a simplified manner. These are the ten kasiṇa exercises. The word kasiṇa seems to mean "whole" or "entire," and the idea is that one's mind becomes wholly immersed in one object. To take one example: one sets up a blue disk and concentrates one's mind on it until one's consciousness is completely filled with the perception of blueness. Then one closes one's eyes and concentrates on a mental counterpart of that perception. Then one can move into the first of four meditation levels (jhānas). These are characterized by gradually decreasing levels of mental activity, or perhaps better, increasing levels of mental concentration.

> The first, characterized by fixing one's mind on the object, thinking about it with two difficult terms standardly translated as "applied thought" and "sustained thought" (vitakka and vicāra), [experiencing] joy and happiness arising from seclusion [both physical and mental: seclusion from desires and their objects]. One suffuses one's entire body with joy and happiness, like soap-powder kneaded into a ball and suffused by the water. The second is characterized by the calming down intrinsic to fixing one's mind on but not applying either applied thought and sustained thought to the object, by inner clarity (tranquility), by unification of the mind, and by the joy and happiness born of concentration.

> One suffuses one's entire body with the joy and happiness born of concentration, like a lake with cool water arising from underground springs. The third is characterized by the fading away of joy, where one lives with equanimity, mindful and aware, experiencing happiness with the body, one suffuses . . . like lotuses growing under water, suffused with cool water from their tips to their roots. The fourth is characterized by getting rid of pleasure and pain, by the going down [like the sun] of previous [mental] well-being and ill-being, [where one experiences] purity of equanimity and mindfulness which is characterized by neither pain nor pleasure. Like a man sitting completely covered by a white cloth there is no part of one's body or mind which is not characterized by purity and cleanliness.[49]

These meditation levels, along with four above them, are correlated with cosmological spheres above that of desire, in Brahma worlds above the human and divine worlds. Some of these are (to me at least) both incomprehensible and unimaginable, like the "sphere of infinite consciousness" and that of "nothingness." Dying in such a meditation level guarantees immediate rebirth in the corresponding Brahma world. Moreover, when one has attained the fourth level, one becomes capable of supernatural powers, such as producing a mind-made body, knowing the minds of others, remembering past lives, etc. These meditation levels, above the first, cannot be concerned with knowing the truth, since they are noncognitive: no applied or sustained thought.

2.4.9. Thinking About Death

There can surely be no civilization, no culture, no person, at whatever level of education or sophistication, without thoughts about death. As children we used to sing: "Your eyes fall in, your teeth fall out, your brains come trickling down your snout, oo-oo-oo-oo, where will you be in a hundred years from now?" Apparently there are versions of this that expand on the first two lines and replace the last with "Be Merry!" which I suppose is either a grim irony or some version of Horace's carpe diem idea: "seize the day" (for tomorrow you may die!). More sublime than our children's song is the tradition of vanitas art, which flourished in the sixteenth and seventeenth centuries in Flanders and the Netherlands, with later versions in the work of Van Gogh and Cézanne, among others. These are still-life paintings, often of flowers on a table with a human skull next to them.

The ancient Greek and Roman Stoicism and Epicureanism so dear to Hadot and Foucault are notable for their "meditations on death": as Hadot put it, "for various and almost opposite reasons [they] advised their disciples to live always aware of the imminence of death, and to concentrate their attention on the present moment, freeing themselves from worry about the future and from the weight of the past.'[50] And so on.

The subject is so ubiquitous, emphasized throughout Buddhist texts, that it hardly needs elaboration. There are, though, some interesting aspects of the Buddhist practice of mindfulness of death (maraṇa-sati, not forgetting death), as summarized in the *Path of Purification*. There are, it says, four kinds of death: "(i) the cutting off of the life faculty in one lifetime (ii) the (final) death of the enlightened person (iii) the momentary death of formations [i.e.,conditioned events] (iv) everyday expressions such as 'a dead tree.'"[51]

It is only (i) that is the subject of mindfulness of death. Someone who wants to practice it should go into seclusion and repeat the formula "there will be death, the life faculty will be cut off," or simply the mantra "death, death." In passing one might compare the modern mantra "Buddho, Buddho" (the nominative singular of Buddha) used by Thai Forest monks, or the modern Thai Dhammakāya movement's sammā arahaṃ ("the rightly Enlightened One"). Perhaps there is some neurophysiological effect of such constant repetition of syllables and phrases. Unlike the practice of friendship, mindfulness of death should not start with oneself. One among various ways of being mindful of death unwisely is to think of it in relation to oneself: "distress arises in someone reflecting on his own death, like someone with a fearful nature on seeing a murderer with upraised sword."[52] He should, rather, think of the inevitable death of others. Various verses follow, which are less childlike than "your eyes fall in" but are nonetheless bromides: "the days and nights pass away, life comes to an end; the life of mortals wastes away, like water in small streams."[53]

Although one is not to start with oneself, Buddhaghosa offers some striking images to reflect on death in general:

> [The monk] should reflect in this way: "in the presence of a murderer" means as if in the presence of a murderer. He is to be aware that death is present as if a murderer were present, holding a sword at his neck in order to kill him. Why? Because it [death] comes with birth, taking life away. Just as the spore of a mushroom arises with dust on its top, so beings come into existence with old age and death [on their heads]. . . . There are eight ways of recollecting death, among which is comparing oneself with successful and famous others, all of whom had to die. These include Enlightened persons, and the Buddha himself: even the peerless Blessed One "was extinguished in a moment by the falling rain of death, like a great fire [extinguished] by a shower of rain."[54]

Less universal than such reflections are sentiments such as the fact that the body "is shared with many." These are worms and other small creatures who live in the body, where they are born and die, urinate and defecate. The body is their maternity home, hospital, cemetery, toilet, and urinal.[55] How uninviting to stay there! In most Indian texts from the ancient Vedic period, a full life is figured as one of a hundred years. At first this may seem strange: surely in premodern times everywhere life expectancy was considerably lower? But I suppose what is meant is that, now as then, the most one can hope for is a life of a hundred years. These hundred years, for Buddhaghosa, are divided into ten decades:

> The first is the tender decade: a person is then tender and unsteady; the second is the sport decade: he takes great pleasure in sports; the third (the 20s) is the beauty decade: he attains the full extent of beauty then; the fourth (30s) is the strength decade: he attains the full extent of strength and power then; the fifth (40s) is the wisdom decade: his wisdom is very firmly established then—it seems that, even in someone who is naturally weak in wisdom, to a small extent wisdom arises then; the sixth (50s) is the decade of decrease: his pleasure in sporting, his beauty, strength and wisdom (all) decrease then; the seventh (60s) is the leaning decade: his body (starts to) lean forward then; the eighth (70s) is the bent decade: his body is bent like the end of a plough then; the ninth (80s) is the bewildered decade: he forgets everything he has done; the tenth (90s) is the lying-down decade: a centenarian lies down a lot.[56]

In the *Path of Purification* it is said that

> A monk who is devoted to Mindfulness of Death is constantly diligent . . . becomes well-versed in the perception of impermanence, and as a consequence of that perception of suffering and

> not-self arise (also) . . . People who have not developed (Mindfulness of) Death at the moment of death are fearful, distressed and confused, as if overpowered by a beast of prey, a malevolent spirit, a snake, a bandit or a murderer; he (who has) does not fall prey to these states but dies without fear and unconfused. If he has not in this life attained the Deathless, then after the break-up of the body he is bound for a Good Destiny. [There follows the verse:] Therefore an intelligent man should diligently work at Mindfulness of Death, which has (such) great power![57]

2.4.10. A Practice Rediscovered: Borān Kammaṭṭhāna

So far in dealing with Buddhist practices of self I have been content to draw on Buddhaghosa's *Path of Purification*, which—according to many modern Buddhists and Buddhist scholars alike—has come both to symbolize and to embody what they see as "orthodox" or "mainstream" Theravāda. Given the present state of our knowledge of Pali texts and their (more or less accurate) translations, there has been until recently nothing to counterpose with this as, in an unfortunate choice of words, "unorthodox" Theravāda.

The existence of such traditions was first revealed from Cambodia by François Bizot in 1975, before the débacle of the Khmer Rouge. Since their removal, from 1979 onward, study of this tradition, or these traditions, has been continued by Bizot, Catherine Becchetti, and Olivier de Bernon in France; and latterly Kate Crosby, Andrew Skilton, and their associates in England. It has always been and still is a problem to know what to call it. At first some people used to say "Tantric Theravāda," which is accurate in some respects but wildly misleading in others. Kate

Crosby, in what is the only book-length study of this in English, prefers borān kammaṭṭhāna. Borān is the Cambodian way of saying and spelling Sanskrit and Pali purāṇa, "old"; kammaṭṭhāna has already been discussed, "occasions for practice," or loosely "subjects for meditation." What Crosby and others describe is much more than meditation practice, though it includes that.

Some might be tempted to call this "Esoteric Buddhism" rather than the exoteric works of Buddhaghosa and the canon he (they) constructed. This too is unfortunate, for reasons I will come to presently.[58] But what is this borān kammaṭṭhāna? Here I can only offer a brief guide, using a few examples. I refer the reader to Crosby's book for deeper description and analysis. First, there is an extensive elaboration of what I described in 2.4.5 as the textual instrumentalist uses of syllables, combined with a very sophisticated understanding of Sanskrit and Pali grammar. At its most simple, syllables of phrases can be homologized with other lists: thus namo Buddhāya, "honor to the Buddha," is resolved into na-mo-bu-(d)-dhā-ya, and then these five syllables, in various orders, can be set alongside, or superimposed on, other lists of five things or ideas. I am intentionally avoiding the word "symbolize," which I don't find helpful. In ancient (and still modern) study of the Vedas in India, the hymns are not only learned in a semantically standard order of words: they are also learned, in a process designed to help exact memorization, in other orders. Thus where a Vedic text may read comprehensibly with syllables in the order A-B-C-D, it is also learned in other ways: A-C-B-D, D-A-C-B, etc. In addition to this kind of practice in borān kammaṭṭhāna, there is the borrowing (and direct use) of the Sanskrit and Pali grammatical practice where one syllable can to refer to a known list that follows or more usually precedes it. Crosby refers to this as the "principle of substitution," a principle that is then used in other ways.[59] There is use of group theory in mathematics, alchemy, as well as much overlap with and use of ayurvedic medicine, particularly its obstetrics, both directly and in homologization. The creation of an embryo within a womb is a transformation homologized with the creation of a Buddha within. If this seems odd, "unorthodox," remember the idea that the successful practitioner of the "Recollection of the Buddha" comes to feel his body as a shrine room with the "Recollection of the Buddha as a Buddha image" within it. Ah, one says, this is metaphorical. But where does literal language end and metaphorical start?

There is much more fascinating detail than I can even begin to go into here. The title of Crosby's book is *Traditional Theravada Meditation and Its Modern-Era Suppression*, by which she means the unconscious and conscious suppression of this kind of thought and practice by the ideas and practices of modern science, imported from the West, and the promulgation within modernist Theravāda of sati and, especially, vipassanā practices as rational processes compatible with those of science.

I will end this brief sketch by looking at the word "esoteric," often used of this kind of thought and practice. We are often told that Buddhist and Hindu tantra is "esoteric," and there will be the temptation to use this word about borān kammaṭṭhāna also. But the texts so called, or at least so far some of them, are here in our libraries, available to us for study. How then are they "esoteric"? The answer is that there are sociological and interpretive meanings of the word. To take a modern Western example: if one wants to read James Joyce's *Finnegan's Wake*, all one has to do is to go to a bookstore, amazon.com or somewhere, and there it is, in one's hands, with no trouble in gaining access to it. Nothing "esoteric" about that. But open the book, start reading it and trying to understand it: this is not so easy. Without some sort of reader's guide it is impossible, for most of us anyway, to follow at all, or at least in any depth. *Finnegan's Wake* is not sociologically esoteric, but it certainly is so interpretively.

Some of the written texts in which borān kammaṭṭhāna has been entextualized have now become available to Western scholarship, and one hopes more will. But the practices of understanding them may—though one certainly hopes not—be dying out in Cambodia and Thailand with the last generations of those who could understand and interpret them.

2.4.11. Premodern Vipassanā?

It is often assumed by Buddhist modernists that "Buddhist meditation," or even "Buddhism," is constituted by, or at least has as its central practice, a form of "meditation" [*sic*] called "insight" (vipassanā). Thus, although they often say that they are not Buddhist but nonsectarian (even "scientific"), S. N. Goenka's Vipassanā Research Institute, the Insight Meditation Society at Barre, MA, and Spirit Rock, CA, and many others are in fact for the most part closely associated, in one way or another, with traditional Buddhist ideas, metaphors, and modes of exposition. It is further assumed that insight practice has ancient roots. It does, but not in the central place they accord it with.

Modernists also often assume that insight is autonomous, unconnected with calming (samatha) or concentration (samādhi). In fact texts most often put calming and insight together as a pair, an interconnected dyad. There are no specific practices, in the sense of the many separate ones I have described with Foucault's title of practices of self, called insight or calming. Samādhi is often connected with the attainment of meditative levels (jhānas, treated in 2.4.8). The word (vi)passanā is from √ dṛś, to see, and is used either for particular kinds or stages of understanding on the Path (the *Path of Purification* lists eighteen) or as a synonym for enlightenment, "seeing things as they really are" (yathābhūta-dassanā, dassanā also being derived from √ dṛś). Words for "seeing" and "understanding" are used synonymously or as closely related in many languages.

Here are two contrasting statements of the relation between calming/concentration and insight in premodern Pali texts. The first is from Walpola Rahula, a Sri Lankan modernist and political activist, whose book *What the Buddha Taught* must have been used in thousands of university and college Introduction to Buddhism courses (including my own). It is lucidly written, in such a way that students can readily get to grips with Buddhist ideas, as Rahula sees them, whether or not they are persuaded of their truth or not. In it he says:

> There are two forms of meditation. One is the development of mental concentration (samatha or samadhi), of one-pointedness of mind . . . by various methods prescribed in the texts, leading up to the highest mystic states such as "the Sphere of Nothingness" or "the Sphere of Neither-Perception-nor-Non-Perception." All these mystic states, according to the Buddha, are mind-created, mind-produced, conditioned (saṃkhata). They have nothing to do with Reality, Truth, Nirvana. This form of meditation existed before the Buddha. Hence it is not purely Buddhist, but it is not excluded from the field of Buddhist meditation. However it is not essential for the realization of Nirvana. The Buddha himself, before his Enlightenment, studied these yogic practices under different teachers and attained to the highest mystic states; but he was not satisfied with them, because they did not give complete liberation, they did not give insight into the Ultimate Reality. He therefore discovered the other form of "meditation" known as vipassanā . . . , "Insight" into the nature of things, leading to the complete liberation of mind, to the realization of the Ultimate Truth, Nirvana. This is essentially Buddhist

> "meditation," Buddhist mental culture. It is an analytical method based on mindfulness, awareness, vigilance, observation. (Quotation marks in the original.)[60]

The American monk Thanissaro (Geoffrey DeGraff), a distinguished translator of Pali texts and a meditation teacher, says on the contrary (I happen to agree with this):

> Almost any book on early Buddhist meditation will tell you that the Buddha taught two types of meditation: samatha and vipassanā. . . . These two methods are quite separate, we're told, and of the two, vipassanā is the distinctive Buddhist contribution to meditative science. Other systems of practice pre-dating the Buddha also taught samatha, but the Buddha was the first to discover and teach vipassanā. Although some Buddhist meditators may practice samatha meditation before turning to vipassanā, samatha practice is not really necessary for the pursuit of Awakening. As a meditative tool, the vipassanā method is sufficient for attaining the goal. Or so we're told. But if you look directly at the Pali discourses . . . you'll find that although they do use the word samatha to mean tranquility, and vipassanā to mean clearseeing, they otherwise confirm none of the received wisdom about these terms. Only rarely do they make use of the word vipassanā—a sharp contrast to their frequent use of the word jhāna [that is, the practice of meditative levels discussed in 2.4.8]. When they depict the Buddha telling his disciples to go meditate, they never quote him as saying "go do vipassanā," but always "go do jhāna." And they never equate the word vipassanā with any mindfulness techniques. In the few instances where they do mention vipassanā, they almost always pair it with samatha—not as two alternative methods, but as two qualities of mind that

a person may "gain" or "be endowed with," and that should be developed together.[61]

*2.4.12. The Large(r) Discourse on Establishing Mindfulness (*Mahā-satipaṭṭhāna Sutta*)*

A term very much more frequently encountered in Pali texts than vipassanā is sati (mindfulness). Nowadays the English word "mindfulness" is extremely common, in all manner of contexts, most often partly or completely disconnected from any genealogy in Buddhism. Commercial companies, for example, often now send their employees on courses of mindfulness training to increase their awareness, perhaps also reduce their stress, and so increase their productivity.[62] Even when the genealogy in Pali texts is not entirely forgotten or occluded, there are innumerable places to find out about it, in books, on websites (accesstoinsight.org, pariyatti.org), on YouTube, and elsewhere. Because of this plethora of existing sources I shall keep my remarks short. There are two well-known texts that include the word sati in their title, the *Satipaṭṭhāna Sutta* and the *Mahā-satipaṭṭhāna Sutta*, the latter the longer, thus Mahā, the great (or longer). It is longer because it has more kinds of doctrinal lists in the fourth and last form of mindfulness, which is significant: this is mindfulness of dhammas, a word very difficult to understand and translate in this context (and many others). Despite its popularity, this text has problematic issues in the fourth section, to my knowledge largely glossed over, specifically about the relation between phenomenology and conceptualization ("experience" and "doctrine") in Buddhist spiritual exercises, practices of self. Hadot has already prefigured this in his discussions of the relations between dogma and philosophy in Hellenistic and especially Epicurean exercises.

The text is also important in the modern history of Theravāda practice, for (at least) two reasons. It played a significant and newly emphasized role in the teaching of two influential Burmese monks, Ledi Sayadaw in the nineteenth century, one of the most influential figures in the early development of Buddhist modernism, and Mahasi Sayadaw in the twentieth, who popularized in the 1950s the technique of "labeling" or "noting" passing thoughts and emotions in the mind during meditation, a practice now (as usual) thought to be ancient. The labeling is usually done in the local vernacular but sometimes in Pali, the language of power, here over oneself, and truth, here, again, about oneself. This form of mindfulness has become very widespread in Asia, where it is often known as the Burmese method. The sutta also formed the basis of one of the most influential books in modern Buddhist practice in the West, Nyanaponika's *The Heart of Buddhist Meditation*, first published in 1962 (although with sections written as early as 1954) and then in a revised edition in 1969.[63] Jon Kabat-Zinn, the central figure in making mindfulness part of scientific therapy in the West, says that "[It] is the book that started it all—the book that, with great clarity and ardor, introduced Vipassana and mindfulness to the West."[64] Maurice Walshe, who updated T. W. Rhys Davids's translation of the *Dīgha Nikāya* in 1987 as *Thus Have I Heard*, says that the *Mahā-satipaṭṭhāna Sutta* "is generally regarded as the most important Sutta in the entire Pali canon."[65]

The four foundations are body, feelings, (states of) mind, and dhammas. Contemplating the body (kāya) involves both experiential-phenomenological perceptions and ideological-evaluative descriptions. It starts with "mindfulness of breathing"; continues with "awareness of bodily posture"; then "reflection on this filthy body" and the "foulness of corpses" as described in "aggressivity toward oneself" above. The first two are matters of everyday reflection, albeit in a special meditative context; the latter two are clearly descriptive in an ideological-evaluative manner. Next is "mindfulness of feelings" (vedanā), which is the easiest to comprehend, being entirely experiential-phenomenological, albeit in the text articulated in a Buddhist manner. One contemplates feelings of different kinds: the pleasant, painful, and neither-pleasant-nor unpleasant, of both material and nonmaterial kinds, both "internally" and "externally" (this means in oneself and in others). One sees how feelings arise and pass away. This could, of course, be heavily inflected by Buddhist ideological-evaluative understanding. States of mind (citta) are contemplated in a way that connects the experiential-phenomenological with the ideological-evaluative. For example, the first is a state of mind characterized by rāga, which one can translate simply as (from Monier-Williams) "any feeling or passion (esp.) love, affection, or sympathy for." But in a Buddhist ideological-evaluative context it must be translated as "passion" in a bad sense, "lust," and the like. It forms the first of a common triad, rāga, dosa, moha, "lust, hatred, and delusion," all of them bad or "unskillful."

The fourth is where the trouble starts. In the compound dhammānupassī, he/she contemplates dhamma(s), dhamma could, being in the stem form dhamma-, be either singular or plural. But other passages in the sutta, in its commentary and in texts such as *The Path of Purification*, show that it must be plural. The most common usage of dhammā in the plural is to refer to objects of mind: the eye sees material things, the ear hears sounds, etc., and the mind (the sixth sense, manas) knows its objects, its thoughts. (These senses and their objects are the twelve "sense-bases," āyatanas.) If this were the case, one would expect something familiar from modern mindfulness, in either its ideological-evaluative Buddhist or its experiential-phenomenological non-Buddhist form: the attempt simply to watch and note thoughts arise and pass away in the mind, without either becoming attached to them or identifying with them. But in fact what the text gives is a long series of the numbered lists so familiar from Buddhist doctrinal texts: the "five hindrances," the "five aggregates," the "seven factors of enlightenment," the "four truths," the "eightfold path," and others of that kind. This has, naturally, puzzled translators: one finds for dhammā here "mental qualities" or "qualities" simpliciter, "elements of the Buddhist teachings," "mental objects," "phenomena," "principles," "mind-objects," or (from T. W. Rhys Davids) "ideas, cognoscible objects."[66]

One might, perhaps, understand this as the contemplator coming to learn directly, "realize" (understand and make real) the truth(s) of Buddhism as a matter of experience. But the text says nothing like this. The quandary, in this "most important Sutta in the entire Pali canon," remains, for me anyway, a quandary. Or one might say that the four foundations contain "meditation" of a number of different kinds, in the fourth as expressed in some dictionary definitions: "pondering, continuous thought or musing upon one subject or series of subjects," and, in mindfulness of the body, aggressivity toward oneself, "brown study."

2.4.13. A New Subjectivity? New Forms of Truth?

In 2.1 I quoted some rather extravagant and obscure remarks by Foucault on Buddhism: "the principles of Buddhist spirituality must tend towards a disindividualization, to a desubjectification, to pushing individuality truly to its limits or beyond its limits, with the aim of an emancipation from the subject." I suspect here that, since the interview was taking place in Japan, and Foucault had had a very short experience of a Zen monastery, that he, like so many authors, conflating what he has picked up about various traditions of Buddhism and making them into a single rather impressionistic whole. But there is, of course, some genuine understanding of the idea of non-self, anattā, here, and a typically interesting and productive way of seeing it. Here as always he leaves out the civilizational and institutional context, taking the ideas of systematic thought directly as constituting "the principles of Buddhist spirituality." I have been at pains to point out not only that the consensual truth of narrative thought plays an extensive part in Buddhist spiritual exercises but also that even an experienced practitioner, whether real or a textual-aspirational ideal, must use it in the commerce of everyday life. This hardly needs exemplification: the Buddha always addressed "monks," even though anattā analyzes them out of existence.

Consensual truth is, as I have said many times, a truth. But remember Buddhaghosa's advice to his audience: "There is no elimination of view for someone who thinks, 'I see with insight, insight is mine.'" "Mental formations see mental formations with insight, think, determine, comprehend, define [them]." The practice of vipassanā, in both its premodern and modern forms, is supposed to lead not to an experiential dissolution of self—which would, again, be schizophrenia, not enlightenment—but to a reflective, evaluative stance on one's experience, on anything in it that one might be disposed to regard with pride and attachment as "oneself." It is a mistake to say, of any physical or mental event, "this is mine, this I am, this is myself."

There are so many expressions of this attitude to experience and to oneself in Pali texts that it is unnecessary, indeed would be tedious for any reader familiar with Buddhism, to continue to exemplify them. But I do want to give two more excerpts from the *Path of Purification*, one an extension of the theoretical attitude to be taken toward oneself, one a practical example from walking meditation. Buddhaghosa says: "In one who understands, . . . sixteen obsessive thoughts are got rid of":

> Did I exist on the road of past time? Did I not exist? What was I? How was I? Having been what (first) what (then) did I become? Will I exist on the road of future time? Will I not exist? What will I be? How will I be? Having been what (first) what (then) will I become? Am I (now)? Am I not? What am I? How am I? Where does this being (that I am) come from? Where will it go? In all lives, wombs, destinies, stations (of consciousness), dwellings, it is only mind-and-body which appears, occurring because of the coming together of cause and fruit. [The practitioner] sees no agent beyond the action; no one to experience the result beyond the occurrence of the result. It is rightly seen with right wisdom that wise people say conventionally "when there is action there is an agent, and when there is the occurrence of the result there is someone to experience the result" merely as a matter of common designation. So the Ancients said: There is no agent of action, no experiencer of the result: pure Existents occur, this is rightly seeing." Thus action and its result occur through causality, and no first point is seen, as with seeds and trees.[67]

Here is how to see, "with clear comprehension," one step in the practice of walking meditation:

> [The practitioner] divides a single footstep into six parts as "lifting up," "shifting forward," "shifting sideways," "lowering down," "placing down," and "fixing down." Herein, lifting up is raising the foot from the ground. Shifting forward is shifting it to the

> front. Shifting sideways is moving the foot to one side or the other in seeing a thorn, stump, snake, and so on. Lowering down is letting the foot down. Placing down is putting the foot on the ground. Fixing down is pressing the foot on the ground while the other foot is being lifted up. . . . The elements [earth, water, fire, air, which in each stage of a step are more or less predominant] and the kinds of derived materiality [a total of twenty-four, the details of which are not relevant here] occurring in the lifting up all cease there without reaching the shifting forward: therefore they are impermanent, painful, not-self. Likewise those occurring in the shifting forward . . . the shifting sideways; those occurring in the shifting sideways . . . the lowering down; those occurring in the lowering down . . . the placing down; those occurring in the placing down cease there without reaching the fixing down; thus formations keep breaking up, like crackling sesame seeds put into a hot pan; wherever they arise, there they cease stage by stage, section by section, term by term, each without reaching the next part: therefore they are impermanent, unsatisfactory, not-self.[68]

I find it implausible to think that any Buddhist monk or nun, or indeed anyone else, could maintain this attitude throughout all the hours of day and night, through months, years, or a lifetime. Modern ethnography shows that this can indeed be done, by individuals in meditative retreat, for a limited number of days. In ordinary, nonretreat communal life a monk or nun, even so-called Enlightened Ones, might say to another, in the familiar terms of consensual truth, "What are you doing this afternoon?" and receive the reply, "I'm going for a walk. I like walking."

It is problematic (though both Hadot and Foucault do it) to derive phenomenology from textual descriptions and prescriptions, but here it seems quite clear that the practitioner is supposed to regard his or her experience directly while practicing the "mindfulness of walking," and to remember the descriptions and prescriptions (not forget them) when not so engaged but living in commerce with others. And this is surely, in two senses, a "new subjectivity." First, directly in the act of walking "with clear comprehension" and in other exercises, the practitioner (or at least the textual-aspirational model of one) is consciously inculcating and experiencing a new kind of subjectivity, one that does not identify with any physical or psychological states. This new subjectivity is (or is supposed to be) a matter of immediate experience during the exercise. Second, attitudes consciously inculcated within exercises are obviously intended to spill over, as it were, into the rest of life, as an attitude toward and (potential) experience of oneself, potentially available on any occasion when living within the commerce of consensual truth (that is, almost all of the time). It is not a description of schizophrenia but of (an alleged) wisdom. But what could it possibly mean to say that an enlightened person is perfect in all this variety of lists of dhammas, simultaneously and continuously? Indeed, even further, how could she or he be simultaneously adept at all the kinds of practice of self described in this section, and how could anyone understand them deeply, and necessarily in most cases discursively, at one and the same time? To be deeply immersed in the foulness of corpses while radiating friendliness to all beings and reflecting on death? If one wants to read texts mythologically, of course, such (as is often said) unthinkable celebrities like the Buddha are capable of anything. But obviously these attainments can only be rationally understood to be dispositional: that is, an enlightened person would be capable of excellence in all these ways if and when he or she wanted to be.

And so, I would argue, these practices of self do not, cannot be imagined to result in a single, continuous, new, more-than-dispositional type of subjectivity—not, I think, in what

Foucault was looking for specifically as "formative of [Buddhist] individuality and subjectivity" in the way he saw Christianity as being formative in the West.

2.4.14. The Loss of Regimen(s) of Transcendental Truth and Modernist Changes in the Aims of "Meditation"

Ascetics are a tiny minority, which everyone else pays for. Why? Durkheim famously saw, as I have mentioned already, a certain level of asceticism as a necessary condition of any social life, as did Freud: civilization requires the renunciation of both individualistic and animal impulses, thus its "discontents." As Durkheim put it,

> Precisely because society lifts us above ourselves, it does constant violence to our natural appetites. . . . The contempt [great ascetics] profess for all that ordinarily impassions men strikes us as bizarre. But those extremes are necessary to maintain among the faithful an adequate level of distaste for easy living and mundane pleasure. An elite must set the goal too high such that the mass does not set it too low. Some must go to extremes so that the average may remain high enough.[69]

There is much to comment on and criticize here, but I will restrict myself to one point. If asceticism is a universal requirement for social life, and if "an elite must set the goal too high such that the mass does not set it too low," it would follow that all civilizations should have produced such elite ascetics, which they have not. I have argued, however, that all civilizations have produced institutionalized regimens of (transcendentalist) truth. That's part of what makes them civilizations. And it is indeed only a tiny minority, a subset of the ideological elite, who have concerned themselves with the creation and maintenance of such truth. How far, then, do the practices of self described in 2.4 go toward constituting an elite regimen of truth? One immediate, tedious, and unhelpful answer its that the descriptions of them in Buddhist texts all do constitute such a regimen, in the sense that they are all, or mostly, entextualized in terms deriving from Buddhist ideology, and hence the practice of them supports and reinforces that ideology. But let us define truth here in two more specific ways: in the Buddhist terms of consensual and ultimately referential truth, and as universal truth, intended to be accessible to anyone, from within or outside of Buddhist ideology.

In these practices there are a very great deal of Buddhist consensual truths (how could there not be?): the good friend, mindfulness of death, indeed any sentence with a verb. It is important to say, though, that much or most of this consensual truth is shared by many other, non-Buddhist traditions. Mindfulness of death expressed as maraṇa-sati is certainly articulated in Pali Buddhist words, but they say nothing substantively different from much of what is said by any other tradition. It is, moreover, offensive to suggest that Buddhism owns friendliness, compassion, sympathetic joy, and equanimity. These are pan-human values, however much they may be expressed in Buddhist texts in a specifically Buddhist style. The "Recollection of the Buddha" is no doubt a consensual truth specific to Buddhism, but the practice of hagiographical liturgy, outer and inner, is hardly unique to it. And so on. But what of ultimately referential truth? Well, as specific practices set alongside others, nowadays almost nothing of what non-Buddhists (or at least nonmodernist Buddhists) might regard as truth is left. "Mindfulness of the body" deconstructs it into thirty-two parts, but the choice of which parts to refer to is not much use in a modern hospital, and in any case seems arbitrary. Aren't there, even within a Buddhist perspective, others? Vaginas and ovaries, penises and testicles, and so many others?

It is certainly a pressing desideratum of research to investigate what might be made, especially in modern terms of emotional intelligence, of the many terms for emotions, kinds of intentionality, and so on, referred to in ultimately referential truth. Our current translations and understandings of these are woefully inadequate, following blindly the likes of early twentieth-century pioneers such as Caroline Rhys Davids. It seems to me that there would be much to learn from the kinds of wise understanding of oneself and others that might be learned from such research. But something vital has been lost in modernist Buddhism's appropriation of these traditional exercises: the anchoring of all these exercises and analyses in Buddhist transcendental truth. The ultimate aim of modernist Buddhist spiritual exercises is no longer enlightenment, release from rebirth, but advances in here-and-now experiences of lessened stress, increased happiness, and so on. Here are two descriptions of insight practice, one from the website of Goenka's Vipassanā Research Institute and the other from the International Meditation Center in Wat Rampoeng in northern Thailand, where Joanna Cook did her ethnographic research.[70] First, the VRI: despite holding classes in Pali, producing the (extremely useful) *The Chaṭṭha Saṅgāyana Tipitaka* CD of Pali texts, and possessing the huge Global Vipassanā Pagoda, which "is a monument of peace which aims to spread teachings of compassion and nonviolence propagated by the Buddha and to promote the practice of Vipassanā," the VRI states:

> The technique of Vipassanā is a simple, practical way to achieve real peace of mind and to lead a happy, useful life. Vipassanā

> means "to see things as they really are"; it is a logical process of mental purification through self-observation. From time to time, we all experience agitation, frustration and disharmony. When we suffer, we do not keep our misery limited to ourselves; instead, we keep distributing it to others. Certainly this is not a proper way to live. We all want to live at peace within ourselves, and with those around us. After all, human beings are social beings: we have to live and interact with others. How, then, can we live peacefully? How can we remain harmonious ourselves, and maintain peace and harmony around us? Vipassanā enables us to experience peace and harmony: it purifies the mind, freeing it from suffering and the deep-seated causes of suffering. The practice leads step-by-step to the highest spiritual goal of full liberation from all mental defilements.[71]

And the site of Wat Rampoeng, before going on to describe the "Foundations of Mindfulness" in traditional style, says:

> Mental Development is a personal experience. It does not matter if you are Buddhist, Christian, Jewish or Moslem [*sic*]. Nor is it important what nationality or color you are, since each person in the world is longing for a better life. The Insight Meditation technique taught here is a way to prepare a path to a better, peaceful life through clear understanding about oneself. "Meditation" is the best word in English for the concept of Mental Development.[72]

There are Insight teachers such as Sylvia Boorstein, who regards herself as a practicing Orthodox Jew as well as a vipassanā teacher, and who writes books with such arresting titles as *That's Funny, You Don't Look Buddhist* and *Don't Just Do Something, Sit There!*[73] It is well known that many of the earliest and contemporary Vipassanā teachers have been Jewish, and there are a much greater proportion of Jews in their congregations than the percentage of Jews in the United States. I don't know anyone who knows why this is, but I doubt that many of them abandon Judaism.

Achieving real peace of mind, living at peace within ourselves, experiencing peace and harmony, a better life, a clear understanding about oneself: who could quarrel with these as the aims of any practice? And who could deny that, if these aims are achieved, then in a certain nonphilosophical sense, these practices are spiritual exercises and regimen(s) of truth (about oneself)? But they are not Buddhist aims in any specific, historical, or genealogical sense.

2.4.15. Global Salvation?

Nyanaponika, clearly thinking of the incipient Cold War and the possibility of nuclear disaster, begins *The Heart of Buddhist Meditation* with a "Message of Help":

> In the present era after two world wars [history repeats its lessons but they are not heeded] . . . To a thoughtful mind, more gripping and heart-rending than all the numerous single facts of suffering produced by recent history, is the uncanny and tragic monotony of behaviour that prompts mankind to prepare again for a new bout of that raving madness called war. . . . To this sick and truly demented world of ours, there comes an ancient teaching of eternal wisdom and unfailing guidance, the Buddha-Dhamma.[74]

In 2018, now, as we are worrying about, I assume, overpopulation, climate change, global warming, and other joys of contemporary life, Jon Kabat-Zinn introduces *Coming to Our Senses: Healing Ourselves and the World Through Mindfulness* by writing: "I don't know about you, but for myself it feels like we are at a critical juncture of life on this planet. It could go in a number of ways. . . . The challenge is one of coming to our senses, both individually and as a species. . . . Where the adventure is taking us as a species, and in our individual lives, even from one day to the next, is unknown."[75] Mindfulness, it seems, can do great things.

CONCLUSION

I stated at the start of part two that the work of Pierre Hadot and Michel Foucault, with their slogans of "spiritual exercises" and "philosophy as a way of life," "practices/technologies of self," and "subjectivity and truth," was a major influence not only on that part but also on the book project as a whole. I do not think it necessary to repeat here what I have said on many occasions in that part to show what I see as the usefulness, in both directions, of the comparison. I hope there to have provided enough detailed material from the Pali tradition to enrich the comparison between their work and Buddhism, a project they explicitly wanted, which has been started by other scholars in relation to other forms of Buddhism than what is now called "Theravāda."

But in another way this book is in contradiction or addition to theirs, rather than a comparison with them. That is to say, while I find their discussions of Hellenistic and early Imperial Roman forms of Stoicism, Epicureanism, and other traditions immensely stimulating and informative, I find two things lacking. First, as a scholar interested in the sociological (macro- and micro-) dimensions of systematic thought as a human civilizational activity, as well as the institutional contexts—homosocial institutions—in which it was done, I would like to see more work in those areas, in all traditions, than Foucault or Hadot, or the scholars of Buddhism who have so far essayed the comparison, have been inclined to do, apart from Hadot's very occasional and brief mentions of educational institutions, the existence or at least extent of which in the periods they were interested in are debatable. Second, as a textualist and intellectual historian I think, as I have said many times, that narrative thought is just as important as, if not more important than, systematic thought, especially in the abbreviated form in which the latter is presented in the usual introductory books. The kind of unitizing project in either "spiritual" (so-called, not in Foucault's sense) or "philosophical" "wisdom" and "sagehood" forms—which I called, perhaps too irreverently, "high-falutin'"—needs to be supplemented and complicated by the diverse forms in which these two concepts, and others related to them, are dealt with in narratives.

Such stories are not "simpler." This is especially true in their ethical dimensions. In the collection of *Birth Stories* the ethical issues and moral dilemmas involved in living a human social life are not solved but stated, and the precariousness and complicatedness of everyday life is not subsumed in a unifying systematic project but preserved, with all its variety of values and value conflicts intact.

I have not attempted, in this book, to write an "introduction to Buddhism" that could be used in the standard pedagogical ritual of lecturing and discussing, writing papers, assigning grades, and so on. But perhaps it could be, at least in the hands of a teacher prepared to jettison the old ways of doing things. I do, however, hope to have introduced Theravāda Buddhism in a new way, to anyone who is interested. Classifying Buddhism as a "religion," immediately makes one think, *Ah, a religion: it will then have a life of the founder, an early history, basic doctrines, later developments, and so on*. And this, indeed, is the model for most of the surprisingly many "introduction to Buddhism" books on the market. I have chosen otherwise. I don't know in what institutions, if any, the book will be read. I just wrote it as I see it. Evincing complete skepticism with regard to any knowledge of the life of the Buddha (if there was one), and of its "early history" and "doctrines," I have chosen to see Theravāda intellectual history.

The novelty of the book, if such there is, lies in my view, or at least in my aspiration, in two things. First, eschewing a chronological narrative, histoire événementielle, I have tried to situate Theravāda's intellectual, cultural, and practical history, embodied at least as much in its narratives as in its systematic thought, in the longue durée context of civilization, of its institutions, its various elites, supported by tribute-producing, taxpaying peasants, and surrounded by hill tribes and nomads who were not interested in, or had escaped from, that kind of enclosed existence. I have tried to deal with the aspirations as well as the ideas, the conceptions and stories of wisdom, the many and various practices of self and regimens of truth and the positioning of those mini-elites who could be concerned, as a way of life, with what is now called "Buddhist meditation," of which I have provided quite a few examples, to try to rid ourselves of modern preconceptions about it.

Second, I have tried to shake free of the idea that texts produced and/or circulated by such traditions always have something to sell, always some moral or spiritual advice offered and to be taken with humorless, monolithic seriousness as "soteriological." I tried to show in the first part that Pali stories are often deliberately funny, in sophisticated or vulgar ways, try to entertain (though often in thoughtful ways) rather than simplistically to edify, and even satirize what Buddhist systematic thought would regard as its most cherished ideals. Buddhist wisdom is a many-splendored thing.

AFTERWORD

Reading Collins Today, and Tomorrow

CHARLES HALLISEY

To take flight every day! At least for a moment, which may be brief, as long as it is intense. Every day a "spiritual exercise," alone or in the company of someone who wishes also to better himself.

—Georges Friedmann[1]

Steven Collins died at the age of sixty-six in February 2018 in New Zealand.[2] His was "an untimely death," an *akāla māraṇa*, to use a familiar Buddhist idiom. His death was as unexpected as it was sudden and in its wake, conversations were left unfinished, plans unrealized, amends unmade, and dreams unfulfilled.

Left too was a manuscript of a book.

Long before his death, Steven Collins's family, friends, colleagues, and students knew about the book project that the manuscript carried. The project came up in conversations and correspondence with him; aspects of it were part of his university courses and academic presentations. At the time of his death, in fact, the manuscript was among the materials being read and discussed in seminars organized by Benjamin Schonthal, his student, at the University of Otago; these seminars were the reason that Steven Collins was in New Zealand when he died. He had already announced that this was to be his last academic work in Buddhist studies, and he seemed to envision it as something of a capstone to his life of research. It was also clear that, for him, it was to be an attempt to articulate a new way of seeing and understanding Theravāda Buddhism, and this was explicit in the subtitle that he gave to the work in the manuscript: "Theravāda Buddhism Seen Anew."

Those of us who had heard about the work in progress expected that the completed book would be like Steven Collins's earlier monographs, *Selfless Persons: Imagery and Thought in* Theravāda *Buddhism* (1982) and *Nirvana and Other Buddhist Felicities: Utopias of the Pali Imaginaire* (1998)—that is to say, it would be filled with lasting lessons and big surprises, all seasoned with an abundance of redolent details that even on their own could be savored and relished. Above all, it would help us to see familiar things differently.

The manuscript, however, was unfinished, even if close to completion. Close enough, in fact, that before leaving for New Zealand, Steven Collins had circulated it to others, asking for comments and suggestions. After his death, a decision was quickly taken by his wife, Claude Grangier, that this manuscript had to be brought to publication as a book. Claude Grangier knew more than anyone else how important this project was to Collins and how much of himself he had given over to it. Once the question of publication was settled, a host of other questions presented themselves, about what needed to be done to the manuscript before it could be published. It fell to Justin McDaniel to address most of these questions. He took on the necessary task of editing the manuscript, and this he followed in the exemplary footsteps of Steven Collins, who had himself brought to posthumous publication the work of his Concordia University colleague Lynn Teskey Denton, *Female Ascetics in Hinduism*.[3] Justin McDaniel is an able editor, but like any editor, he inevitably had to make choices, and he draws attention to the most important of these in his "Editor's Introduction." His editing is judicious and skillful, even if what Collins says in his foreword to Lynn Teskey Denton's book about his own editorial work equally applies to this book: "Since we cannot know what the final drafts of Lynn's work would have looked like, we cannot know whether she would have approved of their being published in this form. There is, however, a clear consistency in a number of themes running through this book which suggests that the main ideas are presented here in something like the way she might have wanted them."[4]

HOW TO READ *WISDOM AS A WAY OF LIFE*?

After the question about whether to publish the manuscript was settled, after it was edited, and after it is acknowledged that we cannot know whether Steven Collins would have approved of it being published in this form, another kind of question must be addressed: How are we to read it?

Every book is inevitably read in conjunction with other books. Collins is perhaps more self-conscious than many other authors in anticipating a particular kind of future reception, insofar as he articulates a hope that all of his work would be read in conjunction with works by other authors with programs and purposes very different from his own. This hope is clearly seen, for example, in *Nirvana and Other Buddhist Felicities* when he suggests

> that the best way of exploring the interplay between imaginaire and history is not by any one author—and certainly not myself—attempting to write a comprehensive, or somehow uniquely privileged history, but for historians of different stripes to write in the knowledge, or at least in the hope that their work will be read in conjunction with other forms of historiography. . . .
>
> It seems to me this problem [of the question of authorial voice in history writing, and the problem of necessary partiality and prejudice] is itself individualist in conception, and too focused on the writing side of the communication process: However strong and controlling a single authorial voice might be (as in the present work), any single book forms part of a community of works and scholars. If a reader has only one book to read on any given topic, he or she is indeed at the mercy of the single author's voice, and his or her prejudgements [*sic*] and choices. But when any single reader has multiple books, and therefore voices, to consult, there is necessarily a plurality of voice: and that is reception situation envisaged in and for this book.[5]

I have no doubt that the same "reception situation" is "envisaged in and for" *Wisdom as a Way of Life*. It is visible, for example, at the end of part one in Collins's commendation of recent work by Sarah Shaw that compares "the Vessantara story to *The Merchant of Venice*, and to what she refers to as 'Shakespearean dramas, mediaeval Western mystery plays and ancient Greek tragedies and comedies.'"[6] His final comment at the end of part one, following right after this commendation of Shaw, is arresting. "This, I think, is the direction the study of Pali Literature ought to go." We should pause and consider Collins's orientation to the future here, as it conjures before our eyes scholarly interpretations of Pali stories and narratives that will assume that they have to be read with "all the respect and acknowledgment of the unending possibility for interpretation that Western literature has"[7] and that will continue what Collins lays out in *Wisdom as a Way of Life*. Steven Collins may have seen this book as something of an end to his research life, but at the same time, the "reception situation envisaged in and for this book" defines *Wisdom as a Way of Life* as ever a beginning for its future readers.

Given that this book is based on an unfinished manuscript, as part of the reading side of the communication process, we may have to engage this work more deliberately and more self-consciously than we might otherwise. What is needed is a more abstemious way of reading *Wisdom as a Way of Life* that will make the single authorial voice more pronounced, a way of reading it that encounters it fully as a work by *Collins*, only after which can it go on to have its anticipated and proper "reception situation," which will have "necessarily a plurality of voice" when read and re-read in combination with multiple books of very different stripes.

The more abstemious reading practice that I have in mind is not unusual. It is, quite simply, let Collins interpret Collins. To the degree that we are able to do so, *Wisdom as a Way of Life* can be made fuller, in the sense that its single authorial voice can be made clearer and stronger by being read as a part—and I would emphasize, a *key* part—of the whole, the *oeuvre*, that is Collins. Toward this end, I will include some very long quotations from his other works in this afterword. Once Collins's authorial voice is made stronger and clearer by the manner in which *Wisdom as a Way of Life* is read, some readers may come, as I have, to appreciate this book as truly what the subtitle of the manuscript promised, "Theravāda Buddhism Seen Anew." What Steven Collins left us here is indeed something that we have not clearly heard yet in the study of Theravāda Buddhism, in particular, and in the study of Buddhism, more generally.

In his insistence that "the external, etic analyst should see Buddhists as human beings first and Buddhists second" and that "not everything [Buddhists] write is religious,"[8] Collins gestures toward contours of Theravāda Buddhism that have barely been named, let alone explored and mapped. *Wisdom as a Way of Life*'s achievements are such that even with all of the rough and schematic qualities the text may still have, the continuing traces of the state that the manuscript was in at Steven Collins's death, it is a great book, the potential of which is to be realized in its reception "by other living beings who have their own time," that is, by us.[9]

To say that *Wisdom as a Way of Life* needs to be read in an abstemious way is not to say that it should be read in a penurious way. We might say, to employ a distinction first made by Roland Barthes, that we should expect ourselves to be *writerly* readers of *Wisdom as a Way of Life*, in contrast to a conventional assumption that academic works are best read by *readerly* readers,[10] who purportedly desire to let a text "speak for itself." We can get a better sense, a tactile sense, of what we should expect of ourselves as abstemious and disciplined readers of Collins with an analogy from music. Eric Siblin has spoken of Bach's Cello Suites as works in which "the listener is forced to imagine what is going on." Siblin says that "there are hints, gaps, half-uttered statements, and fragmented lines in the Cello Suites," and much the same thing could be said about some sections of *Wisdom as a Way of Life*: hints, gaps, half-uttered statements, and fragmented lines are to be found throughout. Siblin further suggests that some of the character of Bach's Cello Suites

> stems from the cello itself, which is a melodic instrument, melodic because no more than two strings can generally be bowed at the

> same time. That limits how much harmony—the simultaneous playing of different notes—can be achieved. . . .
>
> Harmony was Bach's specialty. At the summit of his harmony was polyphony, the braiding of two or musical lines that create a greater whole while at the same time retaining their separateness. So how does Bach accomplish harmony with just one cello? How does he compose for a situation in which he cannot stack the notes vertically and pull off his trademark polyphony? He does it by creating "implied harmony." . . .
>
> I once sat in on a master class given by Anner Bylsma, the Dutch cellist, who spoke about how "thrifty" Bach had to be in the Cello Suites, as he was working with only four fingers and four strings. "It's funny," said Bylsma, "how much you can leave out in music and still make the picture complete in the mind of the listener."[11]

Those familiar with Collins's earlier essays and monographs know that he has his own "trademark polyphony," achieved by especially braiding together "detailed accuracy in philological and textual specifics" with discussions of "wider (and difficult) philosophical and sociological issues."[12] *Wisdom as a Way of Life* may seem quite unlike his earlier monographs and essays in its "frugality." This frugality seems to have been intentional. As Justin McDaniel puts it in his "Editor's Introduction," "Not only did Steve want to write a short and direct book about ideas, but he also insisted that there be no footnotes to clutter the argument and distract the reader."[13] At the very least, *Wisdom as a Way of Life* seems put together differently than Collins's other works, in a way that seems analogous to how Bach's Cello Suites are unlike Bach's other compositions. This suggests that a good way of reading *Wisdom as a Way of Life* is not to try to add to it, out of an assumption that its form is only because its author did not live to finish it, but rather to read it with an attentive ear to the implied harmonies and resulting polyphony in interpretation that are to be found throughout, attentive to how a "complete picture" gradually comes into view in our minds as we read and re-read this book.

There is no doubt that we can prepare ourselves to attend to these implied harmonies in any number of ways. I will take up two ways in the remainder of this afterword. First is to trace the tacit presence of some elemental forms in Collins's overall approach to the study of Buddhism and highlight their presence in this book. Second is to address four probitive questions, formulated by Steven Collins himself, to this book, as a way of highlighting a horizon against which *Wisdom as a Way of Life* might be read.

To try to read *Wisdom as a Way of Life* guided by a few elemental forms that become visible in the course of reading Collins's other works is obviously to read it intertextually. There are, of course, some "nearer" ways of reading *Wisdom as a Way of Life* intertextually. These are valuable in themselves and should not be overlooked. Most notable is Collins's lucid essay "Hadot, Foucault and Comparisons with Buddhism," which should be read in conjunction with part two of *Wisdom as a Way of Life*, "Practices of the Self." A striking element in that essay is Collins's astute reminder of the necessity of placing intellectual discourses and practices within their institutional context, and this is just as true for us today as it was for any intellectual in the past.[14] The essay "Hadot, Foucault and Comparisons with Buddhism" can be grouped together with his earlier essays on Mauss and Dumont, both of which are usefully read when trying to discern the intellectual project that informed *Selfless Persons*;[15] one could wish that there were also analogous essays by Collins on

Jacques Le Goff, Georges Duby, and Cornelius Castoradis that would aid readers trying to discern the intellectual horizons towards which Collins turns in *Nirvana and Other Buddhist Felicities*, especially in regard to his first deployment in that book of the notion of the imaginaire, a notion also found here in *Wisdom as a Way of Life*.[16]

IMPLIED HARMONIES: FOUR ELEMENTAL FORMS IN COLLINS

By elemental forms in Collins, I mean the basic components of his approach to the study of Theravāda Buddhism. I have already referred to his dual insistence that "the external, etic analyst should see Buddhists as human beings first and Buddhists second" and that "not everything [Buddhists] write is religious,"[17] and in these two clauses, we see what may well be the two most elemental forms of Collins's study of Theravāda Buddhism: Buddhists are humans first, and not everything they do is religious.

Buddhists Are Human First: "Categories" of Thought, Ways of Thinking

Wisdom as a Way of Life rightly has a place alongside Collins's earlier monographs, *Selfless Persons: Imagery and Thought in* Theravāda *Buddhism* (1982) and *Nirvana and Other Buddhist Felicities: Utopias of the Pali Imaginaire* (1998); taken together, they form a major trilogy, comparable in ambition and accomplishment to Stanley Tambiah's very different trilogy.[18] Each of Collins's monographs takes up for exploration a centrally visible idea in the intellectual history of Theravāda Buddhism, with *Selfless*

Persons focusing on *anattā* ("no-self"), *Nirvana* considering, in part, the soteriological goal of *nibbana*,[19] and *Wisdom as a Way of Life* focusing on *paññā* ("understanding," "discernment," "wisdom"). The reason for grouping them together as a trilogy, however, is not only their chosen foci, even though that may be attractive in and of itself. There is no doubt that their respective foci are emically significant in Theravāda Buddhism across time and space, but as the second part of the title of *Nirvana and Other Buddhist Felicities* makes clear, Collins's approach to these central Buddhist notions is ever as an "etic analyst." That is to say, he chooses to privilege non-Buddhist terms of analysis as guides for his efforts at understanding and explaining Theravāda Buddhism. As Marshall Hodgson says in his *The Venture of Islam: Conscience and History in a World Civilization*, a work the imprint of which can be seen in Collins first in *Nirvana and Other Buddhist Felicities* and then in subsequent publications, "Terms are the units by which one constructs one's propositions":

> The terms one uses determine the categories by which one orders a field—or at least all those categories that are not the immediate focus of one's inquiry. The categories one presupposes, then, necessarily delimit the questions one can ask—at least all the constants implied in the questions, apart (again) from the special point of focus. The questions posed, in turn, determine what answers will ultimately be reached when the questions, as posed, are pursued. The story of scholarly error is largely one of questions wrongly put because their presuppositions were wrong; correspondingly, the story of scholarly achievement can almost be summed up in successive refinements of terminology.[20]

In the essay "Categories, Concepts or Predicaments? Remarks on Mauss's Use of Philosophical Terminology," Collins begins by noting that

> it is common to find anthropologists, sociologists, intellectual historians and others, as well as philosophers, using the philosophical terminology of *categories of thought* to refer to the more or less fundamental ideas, concepts or simply patterns of thinking which are found in different cultures and different historical periods. When these "categories" are viewed as organized (more or less) into a system, we are often said to be confronted with different frameworks, perspectives, world-views, or more drastically—different worlds.[21]

In the course of this insightful essay, Collins poses and returns to a set of questions that seem more generative in their being asked than in their being answered:

> *Are categories of thought empirical or* a priori *in origin?*
>
> *Are categories of thought different in different societies, or is there a single, fundamental and universal set?*
>
> *Are categories of thought capable of historical change and development?*[22]

A striking feature of Collins's approach to the study of Theravāda Buddhism is his apparent refusal to choose between the binary options inherent in these questions; thus the Pali vocabulary of *anattā*, *nibbāna*, and *paññā* is deployed right next to general notions of "person," "felicity," and "the search for wisdom." Collins suggests that we might preserve the dialectical tension that results from this heuristic proximity by speaking of "human predicaments," which need to be seen as somehow not varying cross-culturally and not developing historically while simultaneously somehow also varying cross-culturally and developing historically. That is, human predicaments need to be seen in two ways simultaneously, just as light needs to be seen as both a wave and a particle. "If personhood consists in the (universal) fact of a body needing psychological and social 'completion,' it will be necessarily the case, as Hegel saw, that any completed realization of personhood will be particular, dependent on the—contingent—conditions of a specific time and place."[23] This astute comment is from a relatively early essay by Collins, but it is in harmony with what he later finds in Hadot, so important in *Wisdom as a Way of Life*, as can be seen when he quotes Hadot as follows:

> I think, indeed, that these [Hellenistic and early Imperial Roman] models correspond to permanent, fundamental attitudes which all human beings find necessary when they set about searching for wisdom. . . . Perhaps we should say that the choices of life we have described—those of Socrates, etc.—correspond to constant, universal models which are found in various forms specific to every civilization, throughout the various cultural forms of humanity.[24]

A distinctive part of Collins's approach to the "constant, universal models which are found in various forms specific to" Theravāda Buddhism is his attention to the distinction (and interrelation) between doctrinal or systematic thought and other ways of thinking. In *Selfless Persons*, his attention is on imagery as a way of thinking distinct from doctrine, while in *Nirvana and Other Buddhist Felicities* and *Wisdom as a Way of Life*, his attention is on narrative thought. Collins's modes of analysis of imagery and of narrative thought are quite different from each other, but the interpretive horizon against which both are explored is quite similar, as is evident when we compare a passage from *Selfless Persons* with one from *Nirvana and Other Buddhist Felicities* and one from *Wisdom as a Way of Life*. Midway through *Selfless Persons*, Collins says that he will "introduce a kind of analysis which will recur throughout the rest of this study":

> That is, I will try to depict a certain pattern of imagery contained in the texts. I will argue that such patterns of imagery give us access to fundamental and unconscious structures of the imagination in Buddhist culture; and that these structures unite all Buddhists, from the mediators and scholastics to the ordinary peasant, into one cultural world. They do this by providing the possibility of shared patterns of self-perception, and by placing this self-perception in a single social and psychological universe.[25]

Narrative thought comes to the fore in *Nirvana and Other Buddhist Felicities*, but as a focus of analysis, it is initially deployed in that book largely in contradistinction to systematic thinking. However, the work ends on a note giving considerably more primacy to narratives for the study of Theravāda Buddhism on their own:

> The categories of Buddhist systematic thought are very thickly descriptive, and it is easy to despair of ever fully translating texts of that kind. I think Hayden White is right to say, however, . . . that "narrative 'is *translatable* without fundamental damage'" in a way that a lyric poem or a philosophical text is not. . . . [There is a] capacity of narrative to render intelligible and imaginable certain aspirations to felicity—life in heaven, for instance—which in systematic thought remain abstract possibilities, positions on a chart. But if [White's point, taken from Roland Barthes] about translatability is correct, it is entirely suitable that the wider eu-/ou-topia discourse of felicity within which I have tried both to decenter and to recenter nirvana, and the

> alternative pre-modernity to which that discourse gives access, only become fully visible when one admits narratives, in all their protean diversity, fully into one's understanding of the civilizational history of the Pali imaginaire. At least, that is one of the things that this book has tried to propose.[26]

Part one of *Wisdom as a Way of Life* seems to pick up just where *Nirvana and Other Buddhist Felicities* left off, engaging both the "protean diversity" of Buddhist narratives and their "translatability":

> This chapter explores Pali narratives, taking as an example the collection of *Jātakas*, *Birth Stories*. This is a collection in which the stories are told in a standard form but have very heterogeneous content. I want to explore them as a world of the Pali imagination [*sic*] in general. . . .
>
> I am making a large claim: it is that narratives rather than texts of systematic thought ("doctrine") are the heart and humanity of the Pali tradition, and what is standardly presented nowadays as the "Theravāda." . . . Pali systematic thought attempts to resolve value conflicts, by hierarchization and by the use of a very large number of interconnected lists. Narrative thought states them. . . . Human life, apart from systems of specialist askēsis, contains irresolvable value conflicts. *The Birth Stories* can be enjoyed and admired by everyone, for many different reasons, without being subjected to the classificatory categories of, for example, "the eightfold path," "conditioned co-origination," and still less—since in *The Birth Stories* it does not occur—nibbāna (nirvana). They express many of the aspirations of Theravāda civilization, and thence of its intellectual history.[27]

With its gestures to "humanity" and "irresolvable value conflicts," this passage encourages us to extend Collins's comment on "human predicaments," quoted above, with a paraphrase of our own that joins that insight with what he says about narratives in *Wisdom as a Way of Life* in something like the following:

> If personhood consists in the (universal) fact of a body needing psychological and social "completion," it will be necessarily the case that any completed realization of personhood will be particular to specific times and places, dependent on the contingent range of ideals and aspirations, all promising some kind of psychological and social "completion," that are on offer to and made available to humans, in all their individual variety, at those times and places. Narratives seem to be especially effective in helping individuals to imagine particular modes of desired "completion" for themselves, as persons, because of the manner in which narratives acknowledge and state some of the irresolvable value conflicts (universally) found in human life. In so far as they do this, narratives translate "humanity."

Not Everything Buddhist Is Religious: Studying Theravāda Buddhism Civilizationally

In the manuscript left at Steven Collins's death, the importance of "civilization" to the overall project was signaled by its inclusion in a provisional title: "Civilization, Wisdom, Practices of the Self: Theravāda Buddhism Seen Anew." "Civilization" was also the name given to what was called "chapter one" in the manuscript. As Justin McDaniel's introduction explains, that chapter asks us to consider "What does it mean to study the tradition of Pali texts civilizationally?" Keeping this question in mind while reading *Wisdom as a Way of Life* turns our attention to another of the implied harmonies in Collins.

Significant portions of part one of the manuscript are quoted in the introduction, and readers are encouraged to read and reread those portions, and take to heart especially Collins's comment that "'Civilization' is . . . a descriptive and analytical tool which, though like all such tools not perfect, helps to understand certain social formations, certain domains of textuality and also—though this is all-too-often not emphasized enough—certain entextualized aspirations, of which the realization, ideal or actual, may be held to be accessible to everyone or just to one or more kinds of elite."[28] In this passage the term "civilization" gestures in three different directions: toward "certain social formations"; toward "certain domains of textuality"; and toward "certain aspirations." All of these are relevant for reading *Wisdom as a Way of Life*, for attending to its implied harmonies, as will become apparent if we look at each in turn.

Collins's crucial choice to study Theravāda Buddhism civilizationally is first articulated in *Nirvana and Other Buddhist Felicities*, and considering carefully what he says there will help readers to flesh out more of what he is doing in *Wisdom as a Way of Life.* A reference to Marshal Hodgson's *The Venture of Islam: Conscience and History in a World Civilization* (a major work that itself was published posthumously) in the general introduction ("Buddhism and Civilizational History I: Structures and Processes") to *Nirvana and Other Buddhist Felicities*[29] suggests that a consideration of Hodgson's ground-breaking work is also germane to understanding more of what Collins is doing in a civilizational study of Theravāda Buddhism. Collins quotes Hodgson in the course of arguing that cities "are implied in the very idea of civilization":

> Violence, exploitation and inequality entered into the very constitution of the agrarian states in which Buddhist felicities were

> produced as objects of human aspiration, including the utopian discourse that wished such things away. That is to say, this is a theme of importance for understanding not only some particular products of the work of Buddhist culture, but also the conditions under which the work of Buddhist culture could take place at all. . . . [T]he word agrarian does not exclude cities—on the contrary they were central, in more ways than one and increasingly so, in the agrarian stage, and are implied in the very idea of civilization. Marshal Hodgson's terminology is useful if rather ungainly: he saw civilization as a product of "agrarianate citied society" or "citied agrarianate communities."[30]

Much of what Hodgson has to say about civilization as a kind of social formation resonates with the way that Collins approaches Theravāda Buddhism. For example, it is easy to imagine that Steven Collins would have seconded, in 1998 and also in 2018, Hodgson's comment made in 1974 that "we have yet to develop an adequate analysis of cultural forms for studying the pre-Modern citied societies," as well as Hodgson's observation that the "lack of a proper world-historical framework [for the study of premodern societies and civilizations] has probably arisen at least in part for want of a proper framework for scholarly cooperation."[31] Above all, Hodgson's insightful suggestion about what distinguishes civilizations from other kinds of social formations and cultural continuities could be transposed exactly to Theravāda Buddhism as a civilization:

> On the wider and more rarefied level of what may be called a "civilization," cultural identity is even more problematic and what will make for continuity is even less predictably formulable. We may indeed describe the most likely situations in general terms which may seem to settle the matter. If we may call a

> "civilization" any wider grouping of cultures in so far as they share consciously in interdependent cumulative traditions (presumably on the level of "high culture"—of thc widely shared cultural forms at the urban, literate level of complexity and sophistication), then the shared traditions will likely to centre in some range of "high" cultural experience to which the cultures are committed in common.[32]

Hodgson articulates here one way of demarcating what Collins means by premodern Theravāda civilization as an object of study: it is that wider grouping of cultures stretching from Sri Lanka and south India to mainland Southeast Asia that shared consciously in interdependent cumulative and discursive traditions preserved and transmitted at the urban, literate level of complexity and sophistication, which was marked by the choice of the Pali language as vehicle of expression.[33] In this sense, to study Theravāda Buddhism civilizationally is to acknowledge that the notion of culture alone is not sufficient for studying any wider grouping of cultures, and also, as Collins himself says, that "Identity language doesn't have much use here"; when studying Theravāda Buddhism civilizationally, the accent must always be on both the Buddhist and the civilizational, the former separating Theravāda civilization from others, the latter connecting Theravāda civilization to others in a complementary way.[34]

There is another way Collins's approach to the study of Theravāda Buddhism civilizationally approximates Hodgson's approach to the study of Islam as a world civilization, and that is in their respective efforts to see Theravāda Buddhism and Islam as more than religions. Hodgson coined his "unwonted term" "Islamicate" to "refer not directly to the religion, Islam, itself, but to the social and cultural complex associated with Islam and the Muslims, both among Muslims themselves and even when found among non-Muslims."[35] It may be simultaneously fortunate and unfortunate that the academic community of Buddhist studies has not invented a term analogous to Hodgson's ungainly, but extremely useful one. Collins, however, seems to have something on the model of "Islamicate" in mind when he names eight criteria that he suggests can be used heuristically to differentiate civilizations from cultures. The full list of eight criteria is found in Justin McDaniel's introduction; it is sufficient to say here that the criteria range from issues of the transfer of wealth (taxes and tribute) and bureaucratized jurisprudential institutions to court culture and the production of elite Literature in prestige languages. As with Hodgson's notion of Islamicate and Islam, none of Collins's criteria point directly to Theravāda Buddhism as a religion; rather, taken together, they point to the existence of social and cultural complexes associated with the *Buddhasāsana* and with Buddhists in southern and Southeastern Asia. In this sense, to study Theravāda Buddhism civilizationally is to insist that not everything Buddhist is religious.

To see Theravāda Buddhism comparatively and complementarily as a civilization is to see it in a broader frame than as either a religious tradition or an inchoate assemblage of distinct but historically connected cultures. We do not find a general theory of civilizations articulated in *Wisdom as a Way of Life* or elsewhere in Collins. His own critical self-consciousness, however, seems to hold him back from trying to conceptualize what a civilization is within any broader social theory, on the grounds that his own background in textual studies may not be adequate to such a task. In *Nirvana and Other Buddhist Felicities*, he quotes "Hodgson's sensible remarks, on Arabic and Islam, about the difficulties [that we inherit with received notions of civilizations] deriving from the fact that 'it has largely been philologians [*sic*] who have—by default—determined our category of 'civilizations': a civilization is what is carried in the literature of a single language, or a group of culturally related languages."[36] Expanding on

Hodgson in part two of *Wisdom as a Way of Life*, Collins says to similar effect:

> Nineteenth-century scholars, as well as many now, have not only thought and think that their expertise in the language(s) necessary—difficult as this is to attain, requiring many years of study—gives them, as it obviously does, authority in linguistics matters, but also have thought that that kind of expertise made and makes it possible for them to write about philosophy, sociology (of both the macro -and micro- kinds), historiography of more than the positivist-empirical kind, and other things with some kind of intellectual authority. Sometimes their attempts to do so seem, to me anyway, of spectacular naïveté.[37]

In not giving his own definition or general theory of "civilization," *tout court*, Collins clearly takes his own counsel to heart, being content to say, "In this book I claim no such authority [to be able to write about philosophy, sociology, or historiography], although I have tried over the years to familiarize myself to some extent with those disciplines, and I have tried in this book to enter into those fields of study in an exploratory way."[38]

This is all to say that there is much still to be done before we are able to understand and explain Theravāda Buddhism civilizationally, not only conceptually and theoretically but also empirically. We need detailed studies of examples of the individual criteria of civilizations as well as historical studies of the movements of persons and goods across premodern southern and Southeastern Asia that provided some of the material and institutional conditions for Theravāda civilization to exist.[39]

Let us return to three directions toward which, for Collins, the notion of civilization inevitably gestures: social formations, domains of textuality, and entextualized aspirations.[40] All three of these interpretive directions illuminate *Wisdom as a Way of Life*, but entextualized aspirations have a pride of place and are a key to hearing some of *Wisdom as a Way of Life*'s most important implied harmonies.

Theravāda civilization, as an ideal type in the singular, offers many aspirations through its narratives, and these may be distinguished, in turn, as themselves being of two ideal types: quotidian and supererogatory. Collins explains: "The quotidian is a simple idea: matters of fact and aspiration (along with their opposites) that are part of everyday, ordinary, normal, usual life and thought. . . .'Supererogatory' is probably a word many readers will find unusual and initially difficult. It is actually also quite simple. . . . An act of supererogation . . . is the doing of something that is morally praiseworthy, but the not doing of which is not blameworthy."[41]

It is easy to point to examples of the supererogatory characteristic of Buddhist lifeworlds, including some especially visible ones, such as the living of a celibate monastic life, and it is also easy to make accurate sociological generalizations about the supererogatory, as Collins does when he says that the supererogatory "are ideals and aspirations that will be matters of practice in actual life only for a minuscule proportion of any population in Theravāda civilization, quite irrelevant demographically but very important aspirationally."[42] To study Theravāda Buddhism civilizationally, then, is to study supererogatory aspirations in particular.

More challenging are the conceptual implications of what Collins introduces as "the civilizational enigma of asceticism" in *Civilisation et femmes célibataires dans le bouddhism en Asie du Sud et du Sud-Est*,[43] and his explorations in that small volume are very germane to appreciating the role of supererogatory aspirations in Theravāda civilization. A passage from the unfinished manuscript is also very helpful for attending to implied harmonies of supererogatory aspirations in *Wisdom as a Way of Life*:

> In many, but not of course all civilizations, the search for Truth—not just any truth or truths, but an overarching and universal Truth with ontological as well as epistemological dimensions—is pursued by a tiny minority of the population, specifically in very many though not all cases by celibate professionals (usually males) living in homosocial institutions. This is a sufficiently widespread phenomenon, in a sufficiently large number of civilizations, as to warrant attention and comparative analysis. It is not, in my view, an issue to be approached individualistically. Individuals may want to live a life of chastity and behavioral restriction, to wear always a particular uniform, and so on. What I like to call the civilizational enigma of asceticism is not why some individuals do this kind of thing but why other people pay for it. Why do some civilizations cherish and support materially as the embodiment of their highest values (at least rhetorically) a way of life which, if followed by everyone, would lead to the extinction of humanity after a generation?

What is especially noteworthy here is that attention to the role of supererogatory aspirations in Theravāda civilization requires a narrowing of focus, even as the turn to the civilizational effected a broadening of the frame of relevance for the description, understanding, and explanation of Theravāda Buddhism.

The Imaginaire and Buddhist Becoming[44]

In part one of *Wisdom as a Way of Life*, Collins alerts his readers that he will use two distinctions in his exploration of "Pali

Buddhist wisdom in *The Birth Stories*." We have already taken note of one of these, the distinction between the quotidian and the supererogatory. We turn now to the second, the distinction between "forms of wisdom and wisdom-seeking that are matters of practice, or might be, or "are textual tropes" as found in narratives. This distinction grounds the division of *Wisdom as a Way of Life* into two parts. The latter are much more common than the former, and they have "a wider audience even among the small educated elite within civilization than does 'systematic thought.'"[45]

This distinction suggests two further elemental forms in Collins's approach to the study of Theravāda Buddhism, both of which he names with "unwonted terms," á la Hodgson: *imaginaire* for the textual tropes and *askēsis* for the matters of practice.

Imaginaire is one of the most challenging terms in Collins's analytic toolbox, largely because it overlaps with another key term for him, "the Pali imaginaire," which will be considered below. It is also challenging because it remains, I think, underconceptualized by Collins even though it is frequently deployed in all of his work, beginning with *Nirvana and Other Buddhist Felicities*. Collins himself sometimes explicitly acknowledges this, as when, in a reference to Jacques Le Goff's attempt to delineate separate meanings for "imaginaire," "representation," "symbolism," and "ideology," he observes that such "distinctions are difficult to retain in practice. Unambiguous terminological precision is not possible; but this is not to abandon the hope of achieving clarity in these matters."[46]

Achieving clarity in what Collins means by the imaginaire is, however, made more complicated by the emergence of the notion of "the imaginary" as a term of art in recent scholarship, and will be enriched by reading his work in conjunction with more recent works by others; once again, we see the necessity of providing a "reception situation" with a plurality of voice when reading Collins.[47]

For reading *Wisdom as a Way of Life*, it is critical to note that Collins's notion of the imaginaire is bidirectional. On the one hand, it explicitly directs our attention to what had been called *mentalités* in the Annales school of French historiography, as part of a collective effort by historians to apply the lessons of anthropology to historical research and also to enlarge the field of sources for historical research to include works of literature and art. As Collins says,

> The word "imaginaire" can have various meanings, broad and narrow, and sometimes seems to be used to mean more or less the same thing as "culture." My usage is in particular influenced by the work of the historian Jacques Le Goff, where it has the slightly more precise sense of a non-material, imaginative world constituted by texts, especially works of art and literature. Such worlds are by definition not the same as the material world, but in so far as the material world is thought and experienced in part through them, they are not imaginary in the sense of being false, entirely made up.[48]

As Matthew Kapstein has suggested, it would be profitable to read Collins with the intellectual history of the Annales school in mind.[49] This allow one to see that many contours of Collins's approach to the study of Theravāda civilization are hardly unique, especially his suspicions of "event history" (*histoire événementielle*) as a suitable goal for a civilizational history of Theravāda Buddhism and his willingness to regard more than a thousand years as an acceptable period for research.[50]

On the other hand, Collins's notion of the imaginaire also turns our attention in quite another direction, but in a manner very much less explicit than the turn to the Annales school. That is to say, Collins's discussion of the imaginaire can at times seem to owe more to Cornelius Castoradis's notion of the *imaginaire radical* than to Le Goff's notion of a "non-material imaginative world constituted by texts," even though Collins does nothing more than make a passing reference to the "arresting incongruity" of the title of Castoriadis's book, *Institution imaginaire de la societé*.[51] In Castoriadis, the *imaginaire radical* becomes a register for both the collective and the individual capacity to become other than one is, to better oneself, in an indeterminate and properly creative manner.[52] Arnason, commenting on Castoriadis, suggests an important possibility for how we should engage Collins's understanding of civilization, as a social formation, when he asks whether there is in the realm of the social-historical a particular dimension in which the radical imagination becomes more markedly creative than in other contexts:

> The concept of the radical imagination and the specific questions linked to it should be set against [this] background: they relate to human sources of social creativity and the need for an anthropological perspective that would complement the ontology of the social-historical. But there is another side to the issue. If the radical imagination feeds into significations on the socio-historical level, it does not seem far-fetched to ask whether there is—within the social-historical domain—a particular dimension where it becomes more markedly creative than in other contexts.[53]

With Arnason's question in mind, I suggest that what Collins marks off as "civilization" is just such a particular dimension within the sociohistorical domain, one in which the radical imagination becomes more markedly creative than in other contexts, and this is especially visible in the Pali narratives of Theravāda civilization. In the light of Castoriadis's notion of the *imaginaire radical*, Collins's comment that Pali narratives must be read "with all the respect and acknowledgment of the unending possibility for interpretation" gains a special force. What we should look for in the narratives are not representations of normative Buddhist goals, representations of *transcendence*; rather, we should see such representations as occasions for human *transcendingness*, humans *becoming* other or better than they are. If we revisit Collins's observations about human predicaments, quoted above, we can see that giving flesh to his notion of the imaginaire by considering it intertextually with Castoriadis's notion of the *imaginaire radical* reveals quite another, albeit very significant contour to personhood: "If personhood consists in the (universal) fact of a body needing psychological and social 'completion,' it will be necessarily the case, as Hegel saw, that any completed realization of personhood will be particular, dependent on the—contingent—conditions of a specific time and place. These conditions may be of a determinant type, as cultures often provide, or of an indeterminate type, as sometimes found in civilizations." The psychological and social "completion" afforded by the imaginaire, and especially the *imaginaire radical*, in contingent conditions specific to different times and places is defined not by this or that pattern of ideals and norms, but by the human tendency to aspire and by the actions that persons take to sustain themselves as they make efforts to become other than they presently are. It should come as no surprise then that Collins shows that "Pali stories are often deliberately funny, in sophisticated or vulgar ways, try to entertain (though often in thoughtful ways) rather than simplistically to edify, and even satirize what Buddhist systematic thought would regard as its cherished ideals."[54] In short, the imaginaire in Theravāda civilization provides resources—conceptual, practical, and institutional—for making aspirations, to make the choice to become other than what one is and then to set about doing so. Above all, the imaginaire provides resources for radical self-creation on the part of persons because its resources problematize and call into question established ideas and visions as well as social norms and conventions. In "Buddhist 'Nuns' (*Mae Chi*) and the Teaching of Pali in Contemporary Thailand," an extraordinary essay written with Justin McDaniel, Collins provides an empirical study of the results of the work of the radical imaginaire, focusing on "the lives and aspirations of [some educated Thai] women, [and] the hopes and aspirations they have for themselves," concluding:

> The idea of a *mae chi*'s life as "beautiful," with meticulous and inspiring pedagogy, sophisticated learning, and meditative expertise as goals and values *per se*, with intrinsic virtue as well as instrumental value in reducing suffering and leading to nirvana, has not been emphasized enough in the existing literature, which tends too often to concentrate on the issue of *bhikkhuni* ordination, and more generally to focus on *mae chi*'s hardships (which are often many), and on discrimination in the Thai ecclesia.[55]

Askēsis, *Practices of Self, and Buddhist Becoming*

What does someone do to make her life "beautiful"? What does someone do to become "a better person"?

"Terms are the units by which one constructs one's propositions," as Marshall Hodgson said. "The terms one uses determines the categories by which one orders a field—or at least all those categories that are not the immediate focus of one's inquiry." One of the most distinctive things about Collins's approach to the study of Theravāda Buddhism is the kind of terms he consistently deploys, terms that are bidirectional, Janus-faced, as it were. As we have already seen, Collins characteristically prefers and privileges "categories, concepts, predicaments" that both "refer to the more or less fundamental ideas, concepts or simply patterns of thinking which are found in different cultures and different historical periods" and can also be viewed "as organized (more or less) into a system, [and to such a degree that] we are often said to be confronted with different frameworks, perspectives, world-views, or more drastically—different worlds."[56]

Wisdom seeking can be a bidirectional category, in Collins's sense, as in his use of the quotation from Hadot cited above, but wisdom is not. Collins's explorations of "wisdom" in the Pali narratives found in the *Birth Stories* show just how minimally *paññā* is organized into a coherent system; it is not at all clear what Buddhists have in mind when they speak of seeking *paññā* or becoming someone who has *paññā*. Collins shows instead how radically plural and even indeterminate the notion of *paññā* is in just a single collection of stories. As I have already suggested, this plurality and indeterminateness may actually be part of its intrinsic value for the imaginaire, and especially for the radical imaginaire.

But what do persons actually do when "they set about searching for wisdom"?[57] What do Buddhists do when they set about searching for *paññā*? "Imaginaire" is one of the terms that Collins uses to order a relevant field of inquiry that will help us to answer questions of this sort. As a category, imaginaire turns our attention to hopes and aspirations, to fields of possibility. The other key category that Collins uses in *Wisdom as a Way of Life* is *askēsis*, variously called "practice of the self" and *bhāvanā* as well.

Askēsis is more prominent in *Wisdom as a Way of Life* than in any of Collins's earlier writings, but it is not completely new. His awareness of the significance of *askēsis* for intellectual historians like himself is visible in the title of his 1994 essay "What Are Buddhists *Doing* When They Deny the Self?"[58] This is the first time he acknowledges the impact that reading Foucault was beginning to have on him; the presence of Foucault's later thought is, of course, centrally visible throughout part two of *Wisdom as a Way of Life*.[59] Collins's answer to the question of his title is given in one long, very generative paragraph, the points of which he describes as "inspired by Foucault." It is worth quoting in full, since it is quite prescient to what is found in this book.

> One may juxtapose the deconstruction and rejection of the body in meditative analysis with the construction of it in social behavior as a unified and valued public object. This strategy, this form of "socio-religious theater," has a number of results. First, I suggest, the Monastic Rules, the meditations on the body, and the effort to eradicate all desire for material and sexual existence serve to create in the Buddhist monastic practitioner the space for an individualized, privatized or "subjectivized" analysis. In so far as salvation is conceived as a spiritual state manifested in both mind and body, the attempt wholly to inhibit all sexual drives and thoughts, and not merely to avoid overt sexual activity, necessarily induces psychic conflict, a conflict which opens up the interior terrain for which texts and doctrines provide the map. In the private zone of operations the desexualized, and thus in one sense de-socialized individual can embody in imagination the immateriality posited in the doctrines of Buddhism, and in this way, as the Buddhist phrase has it, "touch the deathless with the body."

> Second, the social position and image of the Monastic Order, both in theory and as played out in behavior and in prescribed social interactions with laity, facilitate monks' being construed, by themselves and others, as independent, autonomous, and individual agents; the orientation towards a purely personal and immaterial goal both differentiates them from the laity, bound up in networks of material concern, and creates the actual behavioral space in which the "subjectivized" interiority inculcated by meditative practices can take place.[60]

Part two of *Wisdom as a Way of Life* uses the categories of *askēsis* and practices of self to bring together in a very dense survey a dizzying range of diverse behaviors found among Buddhists, from the expected monastic and meditative practices to the unexpected practices of chanting, paying respects, devotional ritual, bodily deportment, and more. Collins shows that all of these different kinds of behaviors are to be connected in a way that they have not been before:

> Like any and every form of performance art, chanting, paying respects and devotional ritual require training, askēsis, and concentration, whether the devotion and respect by given by monastics or laity. They are certainly spiritual exercises and practices of self in Hadot's and Foucault's senses: in each and every repetition, done with concentration, they change the knowing subject, which is more important than changing what is known, which stays the same. Buddha images and the forms of paying respect to them remain the same. In Foucault's words,. . .
>
> > We could call "spirituality" the pursuit, practice and experience through which the subject carries out the necessary transformations on himself in order to have access to truth. We will call this

> "spirituality" the set of these pursuits, practices, and experiences, which may be purifications, ascetic exercises, renunciations, conversions off looking, modifications of existence, etcetera, which are not for knowledge but for the subject, for the subject's very being, the price to be paid for access to the truth.[61]

Toward the end of "What Are Buddhists *Doing* When They Deny the Self?," Collins uses the distinction between knowing *how* and knowing *that* to bring into greater focus what the "knowledge" that results from Buddhist practice is. This applies equally well to what the "wisdom" that results from Buddhist askēsis is:

> The former kind of knowledge [knowing *how*] refers not only to non-propositional skills such as knowing how to swim or ride a bicycle; many features of this kind of knowledge are required for even the most abstract and formal cognitive operations. These skills are also *forms of practice*, which have to be learned through trial-and-error training, and which can be performed more or less successfully, more or less intelligently, more or less wisely. It seems to me sensible to interpret the Pali words for "knowledge" [and also Pali words for "wisdom"] as denoting various forms of knowing how. . . . To practice for enlightenment is to train oneself in living selflessly, without suffering; the capacity to live and act thus, and the fact of doing so, are an essential part it means to *know* that there is no self. To adapt R. R. Marrett's well-known remark about religion, Buddhist enlightenment is not only thought out, but also "danced out."[62]

To adapt Collins's adaptation of R. R. Marrett a step further, *Wisdom as a Way of Life* shows us that Buddhist wisdom is danced out in an incalculable number of ways.

THE FOUR COLLINS QUESTIONS

Students, colleagues, and friends of Steven Collins remember, with considerable affection and appreciation, that there was always a moment in a collective review of a dissertation proposal, a grant proposal, or a project proposal when he would ask four questions directly. This became so routine for such occasions that they have been dubbed "The Collins Questions." They are:

1. What is your question?
2. What is your archive?
3. Is your archive adequate?
4. Why is your question important?

We can take up the task of reading *Wisdom as a Way of Life* by addressing these four questions to Collins himself. It was the rule on the occasions when he asked "The Collins Questions" that "brevity is the soul of wit," to use a worn cliché, and the answers I will provide will be brief themselves. The formulation here is based on what I think is a clear consistency in a number of themes and interpretive choices running throughout Collins's work.

What Is Your Question?

Adapting the title of Collins's essay "What Are Buddhists *Doing* When They Deny the Self?," *Wisdom as a Way of Life* asks—and answers—the question, "What are Buddhists *doing* when they set out to search for wisdom?"

In the background to this question is another, related question: How is the search for wisdom inflected by being pursued in civilizational contexts?

What Is Your Archive?

The archive that Collins resorts to in *Wisdom as a Way of Life* is actually a very restricted one. In part one, it is only the Pali *Jātakas or Birth Stories*. It is slightly more expansive in part two, but still relatively limited compared to the range of sources used in, for example, *Nirvana and Other Buddhist Felicities*.

The restricted archive in *Wisdom as a Way of Life* may not be significant in itself, beyond the point that sources were chosen because of the questions that were being asked and the adequacy of that archive for answering them. This is explained in section 1.3:

> I have chosen to discuss *The Birth Stories* (*Jātaka*s), that is, *Past Lives of Our Buddha Siddhattha Gotama*. . . . [It] is the largest single collected set of narratives one can use as an archive of Pali literature, and on many occasions of Pali Literature [n.b. the difference in capitalization here]. . . . It would have been possible to use any or all of these texts [which contain stories in Pali], but I have concentrated on the *Birth Stories* because they are the longest and most varied collection.[63]

Collins alludes in the above passage to a larger archive available to him. This is what he calls the Pali imaginaire and delineated in *Nirvana: Concept, Imagery, Narrative* as "any and every text written (or translated) into Pali."[64] He utilized different parts of that larger archive in all his other research projects.

Is Your Archive Adequate?

For the question that Collins is asking in *Wisdom as a Way of Life*, his restricted archive, a story collection in Pali and Pali handbooks for practices of self, is without question adequate. It could even be argued that the very fact that the texts are in this restricted archive makes them adequate. They are in what Collins, following A. K. Ramanujan, calls a "Father tongue," a language that no one has as their mother tongue but is only learned in some intentional way. This necessity of first learning Pali to read Pali texts makes those texts intrinsically adequate for questions about what Foucault—and Collins—call "spiritual practices," "the pursuit, practice and experience through which the subject carries out the necessary transformations on himself in order to have access to truth."[65] To choose to learn Pali is to carry out a transformation on oneself in order to have access to the truth and to become other than one is.

I noted above that Collins's "imaginaire" and "Pali imaginaire" are some of the most difficult tools in his interpretive toolbox, in part because of the overlapping ways he used the terms. In one sense, "imaginaire" is a resource for human life, providing a register of possibilities and potentials, found in all societies and civilizations. In that sense then, the Pali imaginaire is just one instance of the general category imaginaire, the one found among some Buddhists. Collins is very explicit that the Pali imaginaire is not coterminous with the imaginaire of Theravāda Buddhism: "The Pali imaginaire is not equal to the imaginaire (still less 'the culture') of premodern Southern Asian Buddhism, and obviously was only one element of civilization in Southern Asia."[66] Finally, he uses "Pali imaginaire" as a name for the archive of texts that is the vehicle for the Pali imaginaire in the second sense.

Collins's multiple uses of the terms "imaginaire" and "Pali imaginaire" have created room for both indiscriminate use of the terms to refer to things far beyond what he intended and for criticism of his very notion itself. A very learned critique has been given by Peter Skilling, and some readers of *Wisdom as a Way of Life* will want to consult it as a way of enhancing Collins's arguments in this book.[67] Collins accepts some of Skilling's insights, as we see in this book,[68] but it is not at all clear to me that Skilling understands what Collins means by the term, as he himself says.[69]

Why Is Your Question Important?

Collins's question, "What are Buddhists *doing* when they set out to search for wisdom?," is complex and multifaceted, and this is part of the challenge of reading *Wisdom as a Way of Life*. We can suggest one answer to this all-important question by turning to some distinctions that Foucault made in an interview in 1984:

> For a long time, I have been trying to see if it would be possible to describe the history of thought as distinct both from the history of ideas (by which I mean the analysis of systems of representation) and from the history of mentalities (by which I mean the analysis of attitudes and types of action [schémas de comportement]). It seemed to me there was one element that was capable of describing the history of thought—this was what one could call the problems or, more exactly, problematizations. What distinguishes thought is that it is something quite different from the set of representations that underlies a certain behavior; it is also quite different from the domain of attitudes that can determine this behavior. Thought is not what inhabits a certain conduct and gives it its meaning; rather, it is what allows one to step back from this way of acting or reacting, to present it to oneself as an object of thought and to question it as to its meaning, its conditions, and its goals. Thought is freedom in relation to what one

> does, the motion by which one detaches from it, establishes it as an object, and reflects on it as a problem.[70]

We might use Foucault's distinctions between the history of ideas, the history of mentalities, and the history of thought to map Collins's trilogy. *Selfless Persons* is largely a work in the history of ideas; *Nirvana and Other Buddhist Felicities* is largely a work in the history of mentalities, as informed by a history of ideas; and *Wisdom as a Way of Life* is largely a work in the history of thought, informed by histories of ideas and mentalities.

Wisdom as a Way of Life demonstrates that writing a history of thought in Buddhist contexts is possible, and it does so in an exemplary way. It realizes with specifically Buddhist evidence what Foucault anticipated a history of thought would achieve:

> Actually, for a domain of action, a behavior, to enter the field of thought, it is necessary for a certain number of factors to have made it uncertain, to have made it lose its familiarity, or to have provoked a certain number of difficulties around it. These elements result from social, economic, or political processes. But here, their only role is that of instigation. They can exist and perform their action for a very long time, before there is effective problematization by thought. And when thought intervenes, it doesn't assume a unique form that is the direct result or the necessary expression of these difficulties; it is an original or specific response—often taking many forms, sometimes even contradictory in its different aspects—to these difficulties, which are defined for it by a situation or a context, and which hold true as a possible question.[71]

It may well be that *Wisdom as a Way of Life* is the first history of thought in Buddhist studies. Whether it is or not, it is a remarkable achievement. The consistent focus on human aspiration and hopes, rather than the objects of aspiration and hope, highlights that there is a significant, a crucial, area of Buddhist lifeworlds and of human life that we know too little about.

Throughout *Wisdom as a Way of Life*, Collins worries about translations, their inevitable inadequacies and inevitable necessities. On one occasion when he is worrying about the inadequacy of a translation of Foucault, we can glimpse Collins in a moment of thought, in Foucault's sense, presenting *Wisdom as a Way of Life* to himself as an object of thought, to be questioned as to its meaning, its conditions, and its goals:

> In a short piece on academic work, *Dits et écrits*, Foucault writes, beautifully, that it is "ce qui est susceptible d'introduire une différence significative dans le champ du savoir, au prix d'une certain peine pour l'auteur et le lecteur, at avec l'eventuelle récompense d'une certain plaisir, c'est à dire d'un accès à une autre figure de la vérité." The English translation *Ethics, Subjectivity and Truth*, trying to give, I suppose, a literal and therefore, apparently, accurate translation has: "That which is susceptible of introducing a significant difference in the field of knowledge, at the cost of a certain difficulty for the author and the reader, with, however, the eventual recompense of a certain pleasure, that is to say of access to another figure of truth." There are three main problems here, though quite a few of the words could be better translated. The first two problems are perhaps minor: *peine* is stronger than "difficulty": it means "penalty, punishment, pain, suffering." The author and reader have to pay the price for their work; they must suffer in doing it. "Figure of truth" is, to me, entirely unclear in English. French *figure* (which can mean simply "face"), as well as English "figure," mean primarily (*OED*) "shape, appearance." That is, figure means here "shape, appearance, form." The work

> of author and reader might result in truth appearing differently to them than it did before their work. But the third is the worst. French *eventuel* and English "eventual" are seriously false friends: the French means only "possible" where the English means (*OED*) "that will arise or take place," "ultimately resulting." What Foucault means is that the suffering of author and reader might result in truth appearing in another way, not that it will be the (inevitable) result of the difficulty they (temporarily) experience. Foucault's French is much stronger: their suffering will not necessarily have the "eventual recompense" of a new appearance of truth: it might result in nothing.[72]

Steven Collins did his work as the author of *Wisdom as a Way of Life*. It is now up to us, Collins's readers, to do our part. He warns that we will have to pay a price: the book makes many demands on its readers. He looked hopefully toward his work being read in a reception situation with a plurality of voices, but here we see him fearful, that after all this, it might result in nothing. I am confident that Collins's fear here is misplaced. *Wisdom as a Way of Life* does offer us "a new appearance of truth," one in which Theravāda Buddhism is seen anew.

To the memory of Steven Collins, my friend

NOTES

PREFACE

1. All these (going back to previous paragraph's "my main interest is philosophical") from *Selfless Persons: Imagery and Thought in* Theravāda *Buddhism* (Cambridge: Cambridge University Press, 1982), 1.
2. LeGoff is here quoted in *Nirvana and Other Buddhist Felicities* (Cambridge: Cambridge University Press, 1998), 74, in the course of Steve's elaboration of the idea of an *imaginaire* as a unit of analysis for what he calls "civilizational history"; see 73–74 *et passim.*

EDITOR'S INTRODUCTION

1. Steve knew that Theravāda was a controversial rubric in Buddhist studies. In his original preface he included a long reflection justifying its use. It is worth reading a lengthy excerpt.

> The word "Theravāda," as a name for a socio-cultural ensemble of ideas, aspirations, practices, etc.—what is called a "religion"—is a modern European invention. Before the 19th century in Pali the word "Theravāda" referred to one or both of two things: a monastic lineage tradition and/or the collection of texts and ideas which that lineage preserved, in the Pali language. It would have been impossible, for example, for a king or any other layman to call himself a Theravādin, since he was neither a monastic lineage nor a textual

tradition. The first use of the term in the modern sense was, it seems, by a British civil servant in the 1830s in what was then Ceylon. . . . The turning point came as recently as 1950, when a conference of the World Fellowship of Buddhists took a resolution to use "Theravāda." Since then, but only since then, it has become standard, both in scholarship and among at least some Buddhists, notably outward-looking intellectuals: for example, Burma now has, since 1999, an International Theravāda Buddhist Missionary University. In South and South Asian countries where what we call "Theravāda Buddhism" exists, even now, if one were to ask an ordinary person what religion they follow it would be extremely unlikely that he or she would say "Theravāda Buddhism": they would just say "Buddhism." Nonetheless, it would be absurd, despite these historical and ethnographic facts, for scholars to attempt now to give up the term "Theravāda": we are stuck with it. . . . If the term "Theravāda" in its current descriptive sense is a modern invention, what can be the point of using it now? First, modern Buddhists (or at least some of them—it would be very useful to have contemporary ethnographic evidence on this) use the word, and it would be insulting for western scholars to fly in the face of that. Second, common sense suggests that it would be quixotic for any Westerner to attempt to prevent in scholarship the use of such a now standard term.

2. This paragraph is an excerpt taken from my comments read at his funeral ceremony.
3. https://www.psychologytoday.com/us/basics/emotional-intelligence.
4. Steve assumed that readers of this book would be familiar with Hadot's *Philosophy as a Way of Life* (New York: Wiley-Blackwell, 1995) and *What Is Ancient Philosophy?* (Cambridge, MA: Harvard University Press, 2004) as well as Foucault's *Technologies of the Self* (Amherst: University of Massachusetts Press, 1988) and *The Hermeneutics of the Subject* (New York: Picador Press, 2005). These were the editions he drew from throughout this book, and he often consulted the French as well.
5. One of the more controversial asides (of which there were several) in Steve's original draft of the preface and preliminary remarks was his criticism of what he called the "Religious Studies Industry." Although it has largely nothing to do with the two major arguments and

subjects of his book, I think it is worth listening to his warning to readers here:

> I need to make something clear immediately: I think the existence of Religious Studies departments in Universities is a very good thing, culturally and politically. What their adherents (not me) call religions have always and still do so often in the world cause conflict, oppression, violence and bloodshed, and it is of very great value, in my view, that there should be educational and other institutions in which such "religions" can be studied and discussed rationally and without conflict, either alongside or, sometimes, in comparison with each other. Would it not be a very good thing if in India, for example, which has not a single such University department, there were some, where Muslims, Hindus and others could study and discuss their traditions together peacefully? But this important cultural-political value does not mean that there is anything which can be, non-conversationally, usefully called "religion" cross-culturally, in which such departments could specialize. There isn't. Conversationally, if I am asked, for example, what is the majority religion in Thailand I will happily answer "Buddhism." I doubt that any such interlocutor would want a lengthy disquisition from me on the word "religion" and its uselessness. But in academic study the word is of no use: it has no descriptive or analytical value, coming, as it and so many other apparently normal words do, from Christian theology. Using it just serves to confuse things. Defining "religion" has become a sub-Industry of its own, providing no useful instruments to achieve anything outside itself. The concept of World Religions, a Christian theological term, has now been shown to have been a nineteenth century invention. (I particularly enjoy the notion, at that time apparently popular, that there are five World Religions: Judaism, Christianity, Islam, Hinduism and Idolatry). University departments of Religion or Religious Studies were originally outgrowths of liberal Christian Theology, which wanted to welcome some (what Robert Orsi has called "good" as against "bad religions"), though rarely many representative examples of the Other, as a means of justifying its own existence and in the end its own superiority. Nowadays the term "Religious

> Studies," when applied to University departments, is just an umbrella term for a lot of people doing a lot of different, hopefully useful, things. But it is not a discipline. I will use what may seem to be—but is not intended to be—the pejorative term Religious Studies Industry to refer to what I see as the majority of people in that endeavor who use categories derived from Christian theology unthinkingly, without explicit comparative exegesis. This is a heritage from the earlier pre-eminence of Christianity in such departments, a pre-eminence unfortunately still the case in many Universities, where departments are still often called Theology and Religious Studies.

6. Steve offered a lengthier explanation of what he meant by asceticism in an appendix:

> I have used the Greek word askēsis a number of times, as do Foucault, Hadot, and others. This is not obscurantism or an attempt at cleverness. "Asceticism" in modern English tends to be used with partial or complete reference to ideas and practices of self-mortification. Sometimes the kinds of askēsis being talked about here do mean or at least include this, but the more important sense is the original Greek one of "training," a special way of life, now as well as then, with both behavioral and mental aspects, devoted to the attainment of some specific end. A simple example, used often as a metaphor for monastic training in early Christianity, is that of athletes, who must follow a strict regime of training to achieve mastery in their particular sport. Not everyone, obviously, is expected to or able to follow that way of life. And not everyone in fact, I repeat, but only a tiny minority within a civilized community, is expected to practice the kinds of askēsis which lead to knowledge of the Truth, to that kind of Wisdom which allows, for example in the Stoic case, identification with God, or in the Buddhist case emancipation from rebirth and suffering. In the modern world where the fact or at least the aspiration to education is universal, it might seem strange, indeed undesirable, that this should be the case. But so it was. (This is not the place to talk about it, but in fact modern education is both hierarchical and elitist, the higher reaches

of which are only possible for a tiny minority.) There are Pali analogies to askēsis in this sense: sādhana, more common in fact in Hindu than Buddhist texts, from a root √ sādh, "to go straight"; sādhana, according to Monier Williams' Sanskrit-English Dictionary, means, amongst other things, "leading straight to a goal, effective, bringing about, accomplishing," etc, The more typical Buddhist word is bhāvanā, a causative noun from the root √ bhū, to be, so "making occur, bringing into being, developing," etc. This is a very common word, often translated as "meditation," but that is only one of the practices designated by the word, one amongst others.

7. The question whether Buddhism was a "religion" or a "philosophy" did not much concern Steve. He felt that Buddhist ways of approaching and solving humanistic and existential problems should be studied in history departments, religious studies departments, and departments of anthropology, philosophy, literature, art historical, political science, psychology, etc. He argued the same for Islamic, Christian, Jewish, Hindu, etc. responses to the human condition. This civilization wisdom should not be confined or dismissed as simply "religious." However, he did offer thoughts on how "religion" is understood in Theravāda Buddhism. He wrote:

> If one were to ask a Buddhist intellectual, and perhaps also a wider range of people, what it was in Theravāda Civilization that spread from India and Sri Lanka to Southeast Asia, they would reply "the sāsana." What is this emic concept, and how useful is it in external etic analysis? It is often said, with considerable justification, that before modern times Buddhism had no concept of "religion" and, indeed, no concept of "Buddhism" as a separate entity, a token, as philosophers say, of which "religion" is the type. In Sanskrit philosophy this is not true: the adjective Bauddha, "Buddhist," derived of course from Buddha, was standardly used by its opponents to designate a group of people holding specific views. They were also called kṣanikavādin-s, "those who hold the doctrine of Momentariness," which is a basic principle of developed Buddhist Systematic Thought. But in that purely intellectual context the words were

rather like modern "Kantianism" or "Wittgenteinianism." They had intellectual and doxographical but no social significance, and they did not aim to have one. It is also said, again with considerable justification, that the premodern, indeed ancient Pali concept of sāsana can be taken, effectively, as an analogy for both "religion" and "Buddhism" (although other teachers are said to have their own sāsana). The word sāsana is from the root √ śās, which has many meanings, of which the relevant here are "teach, instruct, inform," as well as "inform" or "order," and so in the latter sense in certain narrative contexts the word used for a straightforward, non-ideological "message," or "letter," sent from one person to another is "letter." Also relevant are the senses "order, decree, command." Thus in all these senses, one reads frequently of Buddha-sāsana, the Teaching and Instruction(s) of the Buddha, Satthu-sāsana (of the Teacher), jina-sāsana (of the Conqueror). . . . Sāsana as a historically-institutionalized "Teaching" can be usefully contrasted with the timeless dhamma. . . . This latter is universal Truth, true whether or not anyone knows it. . . . Hundreds of other examples of sāsana as a term of discourse can be found. But what is interesting, and what makes people say that the concept is at least analogous to the modern use of the word "religion," is the fact that sāsana can also refer to institutions, particularly of course the Monastic Order, which the Buddha founded. In the Jātaka-s, Birth Stories, for example, which avoid anachronism ubiquitously, with a very few exceptions, it is found often in Stories of the Present, but not in those of the Past. The most usual form there is pabbajitvā, an absolutive from the verb √ pra-vraj, to go forth, to renounce, regularly with imasmiṃ sāsane. The literal (and awful) translation of imasmiṃ sāsane pabbajitvā would be "having gone forth" (or "renounced") in this sāsana. "This sāsana" is obviously what we mean by "Theravāda" or the "'Theravāda' Buddhist religion": one cannot "go forth" in a collection of texts. As an historical institution, sāsana is often translated Dispensation, and in so far as people do not know the tangled history of this word in Christian theology, from which so much of Buddhist translationese comes from, that is not important. But alas, if one wants precise existential, ideology-free translation of a term which can refer both to discourse and to an institution, there seems no accurate English word to use. So I will take the coward's way out and leave it untranslated. . . . So the crucial emic defining concept in what we now call "Theravāda" has always been the sāsana. But we, writing necessarily and properly with etic concepts and wanting to know from a wider, external perspective, cannot say that what spread from India and Sri Lanka to Southeast Asia was, simply, the sāsana. "Theravāda Civilization" refers, for this book, as any large-scale, trans-local formation which looks to Pali as its most important (but rarely, its only) prestige language. "Trans-local" here does not mean "internationally," a concept which presupposes modern nation-states. It means any large-scale political/military formation (unified, to a greater or lesser extent) which looked to Pali as its most important prestige language, which must be used, inter alia, in rituals, in liturgies of instrumentalist efficacy, as well as in a voluminous collection of texts, including but not limited to those which constituted the tipiṭaka, the Three Baskets of what is now called the "Pali Canon," fetishized in the modern academy not only as equivalent to "Theravāda Buddhism" but as recording the early history of it, in the manner of a newspaper. Neither of these things are true, or useful. It seems that at first Buddhist monks, along with Brahmin priests, who traveled either by land, taking Sanskrit texts (perhaps most importantly the Rāmāyaṇa, but also grammatical works) and at least some in Pali, from Northeast India to the Southeast Asian mainland, or by sea (about which there are many Pali Birth Stories), first by cabotage—in the old sense of sailing close to the shore-line—until some time in the mid-1st millennium AD sailors learnt how to manage the monsoon winds in such a way as to enable them to sail directly across the Bay of Bengal in both directions during the monsoon season, between India and what are now Burma, Malaya or beyond. But if we are honest, we must say that we know little or nothing with certainty, or anywhere even approaching that, of the event history, histoire événementielle, either of early Buddhism or the spread of "Theravāda." There are, of course, Pali Buddhist "histories" of such things, which refer in the first case to a so-called mission sent out by the Emperor Aśoka.

But this is mythology and not history. There is an old positivist method of reading such texts: leave out the obviously mythological or supernaturalist content, and the rest is reliable history. Of course not. It is just as possible to make up events, kings' names, and what-not, as it is to make up stories about gods. It is often thought that inscriptions are more reliable historically. But it is just as easy to tell lies on stone as it is on palm-leaf, birch bark, etc. The dating of such inscriptions is guess-work. In secondary sources the passive voice is often used: "such-and-such an image or inscription is dated to the such-and-such century." What this means is that some influential scholar, usually from the 19th or early 20th century, made a guess and everyone follows him, faute de mieux. The first inscriptional evidence of Pali is, apparently, from the 4-5th centuries in Burma and Thailand (Siam). Thereafter in the following centuries a few inscriptions have been found, from, again apparently, in the second half of the 1st millennium AD. Inscriptions have been found in both mainland Southeast Asia, and in insular Southeast Asia, in what we know as Pali or a kind of semi-Pali, attesting—if such they do—to Theravāda there during these centuries. But we cannot know if the Pali inscriptions were from the main source we have now, the Mahāvihāra school in Sri Lanka, which only in the 12th century became Theravāda there, thanks to the suppression of other schools by King Parakkamabāhu I. Inscriptions have been found, equally numerously, in Sanskrit, everywhere in Southeast Asia. The dating of inscriptions in, or containing Pali, Sanskrit or other prestige languages is, as usual, a matter of guesswork. It would seem that, according to legends recorded—or perhaps more cautiously, created—in texts, kingdoms were created in Northern Burma in the 11th century and the 14th in Northern Thailand which used Theravāda as a state-consolidating ideology. Thereafter various kingdoms did so also. It would be wrong to call these ideological uses of Pali and "Buddhism" "Established Religions," this being a later Christian term meaning "officially supported by the state." We cannot know if this phrase is appropriate for what occurred in these Southeast Asian kingdoms. So, any narrative of histoire événementielle in the spread of Theravāda in Southeast Asia is an invented story, not empirical history. The story is found in many modern books. Believe it if you wish. More useful, in my view, than such an attempted histoire événementielle, taken from inscriptions and from texts, both unreliable, of the apparent history of what we now call state-systems, is the following incomplete and non-chronological list of what civilizational phenomena are likely to have spread, at whatever time they did. The list is not given in order of importance. Some or all of these things must have been present in what is now called the spread of Theravāda, but it is an empirical issue which were significant, and how far they were so, in any given time and place. We will almost certainly never know.

PART ONE: WISDOM

1. In the original draft, Steve almost never used italics for Pali terms and words in other non-English languages. He abhorred arbitrary formatting conventions in modern American English usage. I have generally followed his lead, except for his unconventional capitalization. I have italicized the titles of Pali, Sanskrit, and other texts that Steve did not.
2. In the original draft, Steve often capitalized the English words he was translating from Pali. Indeed, there are hundreds of examples of English words capitalized throughout the draft. I changed most of these to follow Columbia University Press style.
3. Charles Hallisey, "Ethical Particularism in Theravāda Buddhism," *Journal of Buddhist Ethics* 3 (1996): 35–37.
4. Steven Collins, *Nirvana and Other Buddhist Felicities* (Cambridge: Cambridge University Press, 1998).
5. F. H. Bradley, "My Station and Its Duties," in *Ethical Studies* (Oxford: Oxford University Press, 1896), chapter 5. Steve did not add any footnotes or endnotes at all to this draft. I relied on some notes, the books in his home office, the hints in the text, and investigative work to track down exact references, page numbers, etc.
6. Peter Brown, *Authority and the Sacred: Aspects of Christianization of the Ancient World* (Cambridge: Cambridge University Press, 1995), 53.
7. J. O. Urmson, "Saints and Heroes," in *Essays in Moral Philosophy*, ed. A. I. Melden (Seattle: University of Washington Press, 1958).

8. K. R. Norman, *A Philological Approach to Buddhism* (London: School of Oriental and African Studies, 1997), chapter 7.
9. T. W. Rhys-Davids, *The Buddhist Birth Stories* (1880; reprint, London: Routledge, 1925), lxxviii–lxxix.
10. John Garrett Jones, *Tales and Teachings of the Buddha: The Jātaka Stories in Relation to the Pāli Canon* (Sydney: Allen and Unwin Books, 1979), introduction.
11. K. R. Norman, "Pali Literature," in *The History of Indian Literature* vol. 7, ch. 2 (Wiesbaden: Otto Harrassowitz, 1983).
12. I removed unrelated comments on the "Religious Studies Industry" for reasons stated in the introduction.
13. Maurice Winternitz, *History of Indian Literature*, Vol. 1, trans. S. Ketar (Calcutta: University of Calcutta Press, 1927).
14. Maurice Winternitz, *History of Indian Literature*, Vol. 2, trans. S. Ketar (Calcutta: University of Calcutta, 1933), 113–156.
15. Winternitz, *History of Indian Literature*, 2: 125.
16. Such textual comparisons are also made extensively in Leslie Grey, in *A Concordance of Buddhist Birth Stories* (London: Pali Text Society, 1990), though without any exemplification of the stories.
17. Drawn from *Nirvana and Other Buddhist Felicities* (Cambridge: Cambridge University Press, 1998), 140.
18. Michael Hahn, "Ratnākaraśānti's Vidagdhavismāpana: An Old and Unpublished Work on Sanskrit Riddles," *Bulletin d'Études Indiennes* 20, no. 2 (2002): 22.
19. Peter Skilling, "King, Saṅgha, and Brahmans: Ideology, Ritual and Power in Pre-modern Siam," in *Buddhism, Power and Political Order*, ed. Ian Harris (London and New York: Routledge, 2007), 182–215.
20. *Rājanīti* 35.
21. *Dhammanīti* 34.
22. Steve added this intertextual note:

> A short note here, in passing, on the word bodhisatta. This was Sanskritized from Pali or some other form of Middle Indo-Aryan as bodhisattva, sometime spelled bodhisatva, which is the form in which the character is usually spoken of in English. This is, however, grammatically incoherent, the compound is Sanskrit being

as bizarre as the literal English translation "Enlightenment-Being." The Sanskrit sattva can indeed be equivalent to Pali satta, "being," but it must here be in fact one of two words satta, both past participles. One is from √ sañj, to be attached to or intent on: thus bodhisatta would mean "(someone) intent on Enlightenment." It could also be from √ śak / sak, to be able: bodhisatta would thus mean "(someone) capable of Enlightenment." There is no way of choosing between these two, so I use the interpretive phrase "Future Buddha."

23. Naomi Appleton and Sarah Shaw, *Ten Great Birth Stories of the Buddha* (Chiang Mai: Silkworm Books, 2015), introduction.
24. Lloyd Daly and Grace Muscarella, *Aesop Without Morals* (Philadelphia: Thomas Yoseloff, 1961).
25. *The Birth Story About Sirikālakaṇṇi* (#382, *Sirikālakaṇṇi Jātaka*). Collins looked at the Pali Text Society's seven-volume edition of the *Jātakas* in the original Pali, as his handwritten notes reveal (V. Fausboll, ed., *The Jātaka Together with its Commentary* [London: Pali Text Society, 1962]), as well as translations in the six-volume Pali Text Society edition edited by E. B. Cowell, *The Jātaka or the Stories of the Buddha's Former Births* (London: Pali Text Society, 1981) and various other translations like those by Appleton and Shaw (2015). He didn't cite these texts directly in his draft or notes. The reader of Pali can easily find the Pali passages in Fausboll's edition. I am including the page numbers for Cowell's English edition in the notes here when passages are directly quoted and simply listing the story's title when the text isn't quoted directly. This way the reader of English can compare Collins's translations with the most common English translation by the translators under Cowell's edition. Sometimes there are slight changes, sometimes significant, but as Collins himself notes in the main text, Cowell gets the stories straight. Collins often disagrees with the way certain words and phrases are translated, sometimes quite vociferously.
26. *The Birth Story About Sāma* (#54, *Sāma Jātaka*).
27. There is a belief throughout South Asia that if one says something significant that is true, some good practical result might follow.
28. *The Birth Story of the Cat* (#128, *Bilāra Jātaka*).

29. *Story About the Crane* (#38, *Baka Jātaka*).
30. Cowell, ed., *The Jātaka or the Stories of the Buddha's Former Births*, 95–98.
31. *The Birth Story About a Turtle* (#258, *Kacchapa Jātaka*), and the second, *The Birth Story About Temiya* (#538, *Temiya Jātaka*, also known as the *Mūgapakkha Jātaka*).
32. *Temiya/Mūgapakkha Jātaka* (*The Birth Story of the Dumb Cripple*).
33. Cowell, ed., *The Jātaka or the Stories of the Buddha's Former Births*, VI: 3.
34. Cowell, ed., *The Jātaka or the Stories of the Buddha's Former Births*, VI: 3.
35. Cowell, ed., *The Jātaka or the Stories of the Buddha's Former Births*, VI: 7.
36. Cowell, ed., *The Jātaka or the Stories of the Buddha's Former Births*, VI: 18.
37. *Udapānadūsaka Jātaka* (#271).
38. *The Story About Repetition* (#27, *Abhiṇha Jātaka*).
39. Westerners see a man in the moon; Asians see a hare. If you can't see this, look at the preface to Wendy Doniger's *The Hindus* (New York: Penguin, 2010).
40. *The Birth Story of the Pot* (*Kumbha-Jātaka*, #512).
41. Charles Keyes, *Karma: An Anthropological Inquiry* (Berkeley: University of California Press, 1983) 6.
42. Cowell, ed., *The Jātaka or the Stories of the Buddha's Former Births*.
43. Appleton and Shaw, *Ten Great Birth Stories of the Buddha*, 2: 98.
44. W. H. D. Rouse, trans., *The Jātaka*, in Cowell, ed., *The Jātaka or the Stories of the Buddha's Former Births*, IV: 171.
45. Lord Chalmers, trans., *The Jātaka*, in Cowell, ed., *The Jātaka or the Stories of the Buddha's Former Births*, I: 133.
46. Richard Gombrich and Margaret Cone, trans., *The Perfect Generosity of Prince Vessantara* (1977; reprint, Oxford: Clarendon Press, 2011), preface.
47. Gombrich and Cone, trans., *The Perfect Generosity of Prince Vessantara*, preface.
48. W. H. D. Rouse, in Cowell, ed., *The Jātaka or the Stories of the Buddha's Former Births*, VI: 282.
49. Melford Spiro, *Buddhism and Society: A Great Tradition and Its Burmese Vicissitudes* (New York: Harper and Row, 1971), 347.
50. Sarah Shaw, *The Jātakas* (New York: Penguin, 2007).
51. Appleton and Shaw, *Ten Great Birth Stories of the Buddha*. Naomi Appleton has also recently released a new online resource for research

on Buddhist birth stories: https://jatakastories.div.ed.ac.uk/. Steven Collins was a major influence on Appleton's work.

52. Patrick Olivelle, *Pañcatantra: The Book of India's Folk Wisdom* (Oxford: Oxford University Press, 1999); Saleh Sa'adeh Jallad, trans., *The Fables of Kalila and Dimnah* (London: Melisende, 2002); John Damascene, Barlaam and Ioasaph, trans. G. R. Woodward and Harold Mattingly (Cambridge: Loeb Classical Library 34, Harvard University Press, 1914).
53. Steve originally added this short note:

> Analogous Pali categories would be nīti, a word which means "advice" (especially to kings). In Sanskrit a closely related term is subhāṣita, things "well-said." These sometimes circulated as single verses in collections or as single or multiple verses within prose stories. One such collection of verses, the *Dhammapada*, which I would translate *Verses about What is Right*, has been translated (and mistranslated) into western languages probably more often than any other Pali text. These verses, sometimes profound but also sometimes bland and tedious, circulated in Pali by themselves, but also very frequently embedded in what are called in Pali (atthakathā) and in English "commentary," although they are certainly much more than that. Textual terms which can be translated, depending on context, as "stories" or "fable" are kathā, vatthu, or akkhāna (ākhyāna).

54. This paragraph in the original was unfinished and a bit convoluted. I reconstructed it following Steve's wording, but it is still awkward and must be read slowly.
55. Bhikkhu Bodhi, trans., A *Treatise on the Paramis: From the Commentary to the Cariyā-piṭaka* (Kandy: Buddhist Publication Society, 1978), 6.
56. *The Birth Story of the Tiṇḍuka Tree* (#177, *Tiṇḍuka Jātaka*).
57. *The Birth Story of the Full River* (#214, *Puṇṇanadī Jātaka*).
58. *The Birth Story About a Barley-Meal Bag* (#402, *Sattubhasta Jātaka*).
59. See Cowell, ed., *The Jātaka or the Stories of the Buddha's Former Births*, III: 210.
60. Cowell, ed., *The Jātaka or the Stories of the Buddha's Former Births*, III: 210.
61. *The Birth Story About a Needle* (#387, *Sūci Jātaka*).

62. *The Birth Story About Suppāraka* (#463, *Suppāraka Jātaka*).
63. Steve added this note:

> This sutta has usually been taken, in a positivist historiographical manner, as a straightforward record of the imagined "ideological ferment" which characterized the sudden growth of asceticism and ascetical sects at the time of the Second Urbanization of India. I disagree. The linguistic and conceptual clumsiness of these so-called "heretical" views is such that I think they are deliberately meant to be satirical: these so-called "teachers" are so stupid that they can't even speak or reason properly.

64. *The Birth Story About Wise Vidhura* (#545, *Vidhura-paṇḍita Jātaka*) and *The Birth Story about Mahosadha* (#546, *Mahā-Ummagga Jātaka*)
65. *The Birth Story About Mahosadha* (#546, *Mahā-Ummagga Jātaka*).
66. Shaw, *The Jātakas*, introduction.
67. *The Birth Story About Sulasā* (#419, *Sulasā Jātaka*).
68. Cowell, ed., *The Jātaka or the Stories of the Buddha's Former Births*, III: 261.
69. *Characterized by Being Weak Jātaka* (#66, *Mudulakkhaṇa Jātaka*). Mudulakkhaṇa is the ascetic's name.
70. See Collins, *Nirvana*, 108.
71. Fernand Braudel, *A History of Civilizations* (1963; reprint, New York: Penguin, 1995), 93:22, 27–28, italics and quotes in original).
72. Appleton and Shaw, *Ten Great Birth Stories of the Buddha*, 2: 515. I thank Sarah Shaw for her encouragement and support of this book's publication.

PART TWO: PRACTICES OF SELF

1. This was originally the third chapter. I have largely kept Steve's words and structure in this chapter intact. As in the first section, I added all the endnotes and scholarly references and removed his idiosyncratic use of capitalization and formatting in order to follow the Press's conventions. This does not take away from his argument or style. I refrained from adding any additional commentary.
2. Steve left no evidence in the draft of what editions or translations he was drawing on when discussing Hadot and Foucault. However, thanks

to his wife, Claude Grangier, I was able to see which books were in his office and found the passages he cited. I also was given some handwritten notes left on his desk that enabled me to track down citations. I also followed Collins's own previously published essay, "Some Remarks on Hadot, Foucault, and Comparisons with Buddhism," in *Buddhist Spiritual Practices: Thinking with Pierre Hadot on Buddhism, Philosophy, and the Path*, ed. David Fiordalis (Berkeley: Mangalam Press, 2018), see particularly p. 23, note 3.

3. Philip Mitsis, "The Institutions of Hellenistic Philosophy," in *Companion to the Hellenistic World*, ed. Andrew Erksine (Oxford: Blackwell, 2003), 464–476.
4. For a good summary of Martha Nussbaum's approach, from which Collins is drawing more broadly, see Rachel Aviv, "The Philosopher of Feelings," *The New Yorker* (July 25, 2016), https://www.newyorker.com/magazine/2016/07/25/martha-nussbaums-moral-philosophies.
5. Pierre Hadot, *What Is Ancient Philosophy?*, trans. Michael Chase (Cambridge, MA: Harvard University Press, 2002), 278. In French as *Qu'est-ce que la philosophie antique?* (Paris: Folio Essais, 1995).
6. Collins was drawing on two sources here in which Foucault published nearly the same quote. The quote comes directly from Foucault's "l'origine de l'herméneutique" (38) and the translation is his own. It also appeared in English (as the lectures were originally given in English) in "About the Beginnings of the Hermeneutics of the Self: Two Lectures at Dartmouth," *Political Theory* 21, no. 2 (1993): 198–227. See also Michel Foucault, "Technologies of the Self," lectures at the University of Vermont, October 1982, in *Technologies of the Self* (Amherst: University of Massachusetts Press, 1988), 16–49. I also thank Collins for a very enlightening conversation we had about Foucault's comparison of *exomologesis* and *exagoreusis* in the latter source, a subject he did not take up in this draft.
7. Michel Foucault, "Le scène de la philosophie," in *Dits et écrits*, vol. 2, 1970--1975 (Paris: Gallimard, 1994), 592–593.
8. Michel Foucault, *Le souci du soi* (Paris: Gallimard, 1984); translated by Robert Hurley into English as volume 3 of his *History of Sexuality: The Care of the Self* (New York: Vintage, 1986).
9. Hadot, *Qu'est-ce que la philosophie antique?*, 419; Hadot, *What Is Ancient Philosophy?*, 278.

10. Foucault, *Dits et écrits*, 2: 1186.
11. Michel Foucault, *Ethics: Subjectivity and Truth Essential Works of Foucault, 1954–1984* (New York: New Press, 1998), 1: vii.
12. The form *sammati* also occurs, showing immediately the derivation from √ man.
13. Gottlob Frege, "On Sense (Sinn) and Reference," *The Philosophical Review* 57, no. 3 (May 1948): 209–230.
14. I removed the original eighth point in Steve's litany, as it was an aside in regard to historical misuses in Buddhist studies scholarship that was incomplete and didn't contribute to the clear argument he was making about the two types of truth.
15. Buddhaghosa, *Manoratha-Purani* [Commentary on the *Aṅguttara Nikaya*], ed. Edmund Hardy et al. (London: Pali Text Society, 1956), I: 95.
16. Dhammapāla, *Itivuttaka-aṭṭhakathā* (from the *Paramattha-dīpanī*), ed. M. M. Bose in 1933–34 and reissued in two volumes in 1977 (London: Pali Text Society, 1977), I: 83.
17. G. Landsberg and C.A.F. Rhys-Davids, eds., "*Puggalapaññatti-aṭṭhakathā*," *Journal of the Pali Text Society* 7 (1914): 171–172.
18. There are exceptions, analogous to the English sentence "It is raining." How to build up the simplest kind of sentence (here a present indicative)?
19. Buddhaghosa, *Path of Purification*, trans. Bhikkhu Ñāṇamoli, 3rd ed. (Kandy: Buddhist Publication Society, 1979), XX: 83 (p. 654).
20. Horace, *Epistles of Horace*, trans. David Ferry (New York: Farrar, Straus and Giroux, 2002), book I, epistle x, line 24.
21. Which is anomalous only in that it contains reference to kind of person.
22. The word is from the verb √ sam-ā-dhā, which means to put together, to collect.
23. Buddhaghosa, *Path of Purification*, especially chapter 4.
24. Buddhaghosa, *Path of Purification*, I: 2 (p. 5).
25. Sarah Shaw, *Introduction to Buddhist Meditation* (London: Routledge, 2008), introduction.
26. I often accompanied Steve in Thailand to these chanting sessions and served as his translator. He was intensely interested, although it is not explained in this book, in the order of the chants, the choice of texts/passages, and the like.

27. Michel Foucault, *The Hermeneutics of the Subject: Lectures at the College de France 1981–1982* (New York: Palgrave, 2005), 15; French original: *Herméneutique du sujet* (Paris: Gallimard, 2001), 16–17.
28. I considered the title of this book "Training in Reverence," because this meant so much to Steve and I believe he taught me reverence. However, it did not do justice to the overall structure and content of the work.
29. See this passage quoted and a broader discussion of the body of the monk in Steven Collins, "The Body in Theravāda Buddhist Monasticism," in *Religion and the Body*, ed. Sarah Coakley (Cambridge: Cambridge University Press, 1997), 199.
30. Michael Carrithers, *Forest Monks of Sri Lanka: An Historiographical and Anthropological Study* (Oxford: Oxford University Press, 1983), 56–57.
31. R. L. Birdwhistell, *Introduction to Kinesics: An Annotation System for Analysis of Body Motion and Gesture* (Washington, DC: Department of State, Foreign Service Institute, 1952). See also R. L. Birdwhistell, *Kinesics and Context: Essays on Body Motion Communication* (Philadelphia: University of Pennsylvania Press, 1970).
32. This is a major subject in Jeffrey Samuels, *Attracting the Heart: Social Relations and the Aesthetics of Emotion in Sri Lankan Monastic Culture* (Honolulu: University of Hawaii Press, 2010).
33. Oliver Freiberger, "Early Buddhism, Asceticism, and the Politics of the Middle Way," in *Asceticism and Its Critics: Historical Accounts and Comparative Perspectives,* ed. Oliver Freiberger (New York: Oxford University Press, 2006), 235–258.
34. For readers of English, there are numerous translations. Collins consulted several. See *Dhammacakkappavattana Sutta: Setting Rolling the Wheel of Truth*, translated from the Pali by Ñanamoli Thera (from SN 56.11). See https://www.accesstoinsight.org/tipitaka/sn/sn56/sn56.011.nymo.html; the Pali is found in the Pali Text Society's edition of the Dhammacakkappavattana Sutta (S v 420), https://www.accesstoinsight.org/tipitaka/sltp/SN_V_utf8.html#pts.420.
35. The editor attempted to contact Prof. Gary Tubb numerous times and never received a response as to the source of Collins's citation here.
36. Ilsetraut Hadot, *Sénèque: direction spirituelle et pratique de la philosophie. Philosophie du présent* (Paris: Librairie Philosophique J. Vrin, 2014), introduction.
37. Buddhaghosa, *Path of Purification*, chapter 3 (p. 87).

38. Buddhaghosa, *Path of Purification*, chapter 4 (p. 113).
39. See Thanissaro Bhikkhu, trans., *Khaggavisana Sutta: A Rhinoceros* (in the third section of chapter 1 of the *Sutta Nipāta*, in the Pali Text Society Edition as Sn 35-75), www.accesstoinsight.org/tipitaka/kn/snp/snp.1.03.than.html.
40. Thanissaro Bhikkhu, trans., *Khaggavisana Sutta*, verses 45–47.
41. Buddhaghosa, *Path of Purification*, chapter 7 (p. 188).
42. Buddhaghosa, *Path of Purification*, chapter 7 (p. 188).
43. François Bizot and Oskar von Hinüber, *La Guirlande de joyaux* (Paris: L'Asiathèque, 1994), 54–67. See also Justin McDaniel, *The Lovelorn Ghost and the Magical Monk* (New York: Columbia University Press, 2011), 254n79.
44. Buddhaghosa, *Path of Purification*, chapter 9.
45. There seemed to be a little confusion in the original text. This section is actually drawn from *Path of Purification*, chapter 8 (pp. 237–245), not chapter 6 on "foulness of corpses."
46. Buddhaghosa, *Path of Purification*, chapter 6.
47. Buddhaghosa, *Path of Purification*, chapter 16 (p. 510).
48. Buddhaghosa, *Path of Purification*, chapter 16 (p. 510), section on foulness of corpses. I provide a lengthy description of these practices in *The Lovelorn Ghost and the Magical Monk*. See also Liz Wilson, *Charming Cadavers* (Chicago: University of Chicago Press, 1996).
49. Buddhaghosa, *Path of Purification*, chapters 4 and 5.
50. Hadot, *Qu'est-ce que la philosophie antique?*, 415 (translated by Collins).
51. Buddhaghosa, *Path of Purification*, chapter 8 (pp. 225–236).
52. Buddhaghosa, *Path of Purification*, chapter 8 (p. 227).
53. Buddhaghosa, *Path of Purification*, chapter 8 (p. 231).
54. Buddhaghosa, *Path of Purification*, chapter 8 (p. 231).
55. Buddhaghosa, *Path of Purification*, chapter 8 (p. 231).
56. Buddhaghosa, *Path of Purification*, chapter 20 (p. 646).
57. Buddhaghosa, *Path of Purification*, chapter 8 (p. 236).
58. For anoverview of the early study of "Esoteric Southern Buddhism" or the "Tantric Theravāda," see McDaniel, *The Lovelorn Ghost and the Magical Monk*, 101.
59. See Kate Crosby, "Tantric Theravāda: A Bibliographic Essay on the Writings of François Bizot and Others on the Yogāvacara Tradition,"

Contemporary Buddhism 1, no. 2 (2000). See also her book on the *borān kammaṭṭhāna*: *Traditional Theravāda Meditation and Its Modern-era Suppression* (Hong Kong: Buddha-dharma Centre, 2013).

60. Walpola Rahula, *What the Buddha Taught*, rev. ed. (1959; New York: Grove Press, 1974), 67.
61. Thanissaro Bhikkhu, "One Tool Among Many," online sermon, https://www.dhammatalks.org/books/NobleStrategy/Section0012.html.
62. The last time I saw Steve casually in Chicago was when I was speaking at the Chicago Humanities Festival on the topic of "mindfulness" and its uses in large corporations and in public school classrooms in the United States. I enjoyed conversing with him often on the ways Buddhist notions of mindfulness were being creatively used and often misunderstood in modern secular cultures.
63. Nyanaponika Thera, *The Heart of Buddhist Meditation* (London: Rider and Co, 1962).
64. This quote from Jon Kabat-Zinn appears on the back cover of the 2014 edition of Nyanaponika Thera, *The Heart of Buddhist Meditation*.
65. Maurice Walshe, trans., *Thus Have I Heard* (London: Wisdom, 1987).
66. *Mahā-satipaṭṭhāna Sutta* (found in the *Dīgha Nikāya* (#22) and at https://www.accesstoinsight.org/tipitaka/dn/dn.22.0.than.html.
67. Buddhaghosa, *Path of Purification*, multiple chapters.
68. Buddhaghosa, *Path of Purification*, multiple chapters.
69. Émile Durkheim, *Elementary Forms of the Religious Life*, trans. Karen E. Fields (New York: Free Press, 1995), 320–321 (original French edition published in 1912).
70. Steve was a champion of Joanna Cook's work in this book. See her *Meditation in Modern Buddhism: Renunciation and Change in Thai Monastic Life* (Cambridge: Cambridge University Press, 2010).
71. See https://www.vridhamma.org/What-is-Vipassana.
72. I did not find this source in Steve's notes. I believe it comes from a brochure at the temple of Wat Rampoeng.
73. Sylvia Boorstein, *That's Funny, You Don't Look Buddhist* (New York: Harper One, 1998) and *Don't Just Do Something, Sit There!* (New York: Harper One, 1996).
74. Nyanaponika Thera, *The Heart of Buddhist Meditation*, introduction.

75. Jon Kabat-Zinn, *Coming to Our Senses: Healing Ourselves and the World Through Mindfulness* (New York: Hachette, 2006), introduction.

AFTERWORD

1. Steven Collins, "Hadot, Foucault and Comparisons with Buddhism," in *Buddhist Spiritual Practices: Thinking with Pierre Hadot on Buddhism, Philosophy, and the Path*, ed. David V. Fiordalis (Berkeley: Mangalam Press, 2018), 67. There, Collins is quoting Pierre Hadot who is quoting Georges Friedmann, and Collins signals how important this passage was for Hadot: "Hadot refers to Friedmann often, and twice quotes a two-paragraph section from *La Puissance et la Sagesse* about Spiritual Exercises, . . . both times in significant places" (67).
2. Throughout this afterword, I will use the name Steven Collins to refer to the person and the name Collins to refer to the body of work, the scholarly oeuvre, produced by that person. The distinction is one made by Paul Ricoeur in his posthumously published book, *Living Up to Death*, in which he says in a fragment entitled "Time of work, Time of life":

> I read on an art book cover: Watteau (1684–1721). . . .
>
> The proper name Watteau thus designates two distinct referents: the name of the work (one says of a picture: it's a Watteau): an immortal name in the sense that it did not perish along with the painter, and the name of the existing being who once upon a time painted and who died in 1721.
>
> What does it mean for this existing being to die? It means dissociating the immortal from the mortal in his proper name by removing the work accomplished by him.
>
> The two times, that of the work, and that of the life, which until then were superimposed, get disjoined: the existing painter deserts the immortal time of the work and withdraws into the mortal time of life (immortal does not mean eternal, but unmarked by the mortality of a living being). (Paul Ricoeur, *Living Up to Death* [Chicago: University of Chicago Press, 2009], 59–60)

3. Lynn Teskey Denton, *Female Ascetics in Hinduism* (Albany: State University of New York Press, 2004).

4. Steven Collins, "Foreword," in Denton, *Female Ascetics in Hinduism*, viii.
5. Steven Collins, *Nirvana and Other Buddhist Felicities: Utopias of the Pali Imaginaire* (Cambridge: Cambridge University Press, 1998), 81.
6. Collins, *Wisdom as a Way of Life*, 83.
7. Collins, *Wisdom as a Way of Life*, 83.
8. Collins, *Wisdom as a Way of Life*, 16.
9. Ricoeur, *Living Up to Death*, 61.
10. Roland Barthes, *S/Z* (New York: Hill and Wang, 1974).
11. Eric Siblin, *The Cello Suites: J. S. Bach, Pablo Casals, and the Search for a Baroque Masterpiece* (New York: Grove Press, 2009), 55–56.
12. Quoting the publisher's description on the back of Steven Collins, *Self and Society: Essays on Pali Literature and Social Theory 1988–2010* (1989; reprint, Chiang Mai: Silkworm Books, 2013).
13. Justin McDaniel, "Editor's Introduction," xxiv.
14. "Intellectuals today . . . need institutions, and it is difficult to see what alternative to Universities there might be. Both Hadot and Foucault spent almost all of their lives in academic institutions. An intellectual nowadays who wishes to practice one or another philosophy (or a mixture) as a Way of Life is almost certain to need the physical and financial context of a University" (Collins, "Hadot, Foucault and Comparisons with Buddhism," 55).
15. Steven Collins, "Categories, Concepts or Predicaments? Remarks on Mauss' use of Philosophical Terminology," in *The Category of the Person: Anthropology, Philosophy, History*, ed. Michael Carrithers, Steven Collins, and Steven Lukes (Cambridge: Cambridge University Press, 1985), 46–82; Steven Collins, "Louis Dumont and the Study of Religions," in Collins, *Self and Society*, 227–246.
16. See Collins, *Nirvana and Other Buddhist Felicities*, 72–78.
17. Collins, *Wisdom as a Way of Life*, 16.
18. Stanley J. Tambiah, *Buddhism and the Spirits of Northeast Thailand* (Cambridge: Cambridge University Press, 1970); *World Conqueror and World Renouncer* (Cambridge: Cambridge University Press, 1976); *The Buddhist Saints of the Forest: A Study in Charisma, Hagiography, Sectarianism, and Millennial Buddhism* (Cambridge: Cambridge University Press, 1984).
19. Which is highlighted in the shortened and rewritten version of *Nirvana and Other Buddhist Felicities*, part I; see Steven Collins, *Nirvana:*

Concept, Imagery, Narrative (Cambridge: Cambridge University Press, 2010).

20. Marshall Hodgson, *The Venture of Islam: Conscience and History in a World Civilization*, Volume I (Chicago: University of Chicago Press, 1974), 45–46.
21. Collins, "Categories, Concepts or Predicaments?" 46.
22. Collins, "Categories, Concepts or Predicaments?" 51–53 and 71.
23. Collins, "Categories, Concepts or Predicaments?" 74.
24. Collins, "Hadot, Foucault and Comparisons with Buddhism," 29; page number will need to be supplied for *Wisdom as a Way of Life.*
25. Collins, *Selfless Persons*, 166. Note especially how the reference to "the possibility of shared patterns of self-perception [within] a single *social* and *psychological* universe" is echoed in the passage quoted above from Collins's essay on Mauss in a reference to "*psychological* and *social* 'completion'" (emphasis added).
26. Collins, *Nirvana*, 574.
27. Collins, *Wisdom as a Way of Life*, 3.
28. McDaniel, "Editor's Introduction," xlvii.
29. Collins, *Nirvana and Other Buddhist Felicities,* 10.
30. Collins, *Nirvana and Other Buddhist Felicities,* 9–10.
31. Hodgson, *The Venture of Islam,* 31.
32. Hodgson, *The Venture of Islam,* 33.
33. The notion of discursive tradition added here to Hodgson's statement is that of Tala Asad; see Talal Asad, "The Idea of an Anthropology of Islam," *Qui Parle* 17 (2009): 1–30. The presence of something like a discursive tradition as a social process, in Asad's sense, in Theravāda civilizations may help us to explain what Collins highlights as the perduring "coherence and stability of the Pali imaginaire in the traditional period" (*Nirvana and Other Buddhist Felicities* 76). The notion of cumulative tradition in Hodgson's own statement may be, of course, that of Wilfred Cantwell Smith; see Wildred Cantwell Smith, *The Meaning and End of Religion* (New York: Macmillan, 1962).
34. McDaniel, "Editor's Introduction," xliii–xlix.
35. Hodgson, *The Venture of Islam,* 59.
36. Collins, *Nirvana and Other Buddhist Felicities*, 76.
37. Collins, *Wisdom as a Way of Life*, 86.
38. Collins, *Wisdom as a Way of Life*, 86.

39. For an example of the former, see the work of D. Christian Lammerts on "the existence of bureaucratized, *jurisprudential* institutions"; *Buddhist Law in Burma: A History of* Dhammasattha *Texts and Jurisprudence, 1250–1850* (Honolulu: University of Hawai`i Press, 2018). For another example, see the work of Alastair Gornall on grammar as a vocation in Theravāda civilization; Alastair Gornall, *Rewriting Buddhism in Sri Lanka, 1153–1270* (forthcoming). For examples of the needed empirical studies of the connected history of the Theravādin world, see especially the work of Steven Collins's student, Anne Blackburn, including the essays "Buddhist Networks in the Indian Ocean: Trans-regional Strategies and Affiliations," in *Belonging Across the Bay of Bengal: Religious Rites, Colonial Migrations, National Rights*, ed. Michael Laffan (London: Bloomsbury, 2017), and "Buddhist Connections in the Indian Ocean: Changes in Monastic Mobility 1000–1500," *Journal of the Economic and Social History of the Orient* 58 (2015).
40. McDaniel, "Editor's Introduction," xliii–xlix.
41. Collins, *Wisdom as a Way of Life*, 9.
42. Collins, *Wisdom as a Way of Life*, 2.
43. Steven Collins, *Civilisation et femmes célibataires dans le bouddhism en Asie du Sud et du Sud-est* (Paris: Les Éditions du Cerf, 2011), 12.
44. The term "becoming" here and in the subtitle of the next section can be taken in two ways. First, as a reference to the Pali word *bhāvanā*, which Collins explores in Section 2.4; "Bhāvanā means 'development,' and is used for the whole ensemble of things one might include under the heading Practices of Self. Bhāvanā is an overall process, not a specific activity" (Page number will need to be supplied). "Becoming" in this subtitle is also an allusion to Naveeda Khan's important book, *Muslim Becoming: Aspiration and Skepticism in Pakistan* (Durham, NC: Duke University Press, 2012). Reading *Wisdom as a Way of Life* intertextually with Khan's *Muslim Becoming* will accentuate the implied harmony of aspiration, hope, and becoming in Collins, especially in the attention he gives to the nextness of aspiration and skepticism.
45. Collins, *Wisdom as a Way of Life*, 2.
46. Collins, *Nirvana and Other Buddhist Felicities*, 74.
47. For the recent emergence of "imaginary" as a term of art in scholarship, see Tony Stewart, *Witness to Marvels Sufism and Literary Imagination* (Berkeley: University of California Press, 2019), especially

chapter 4, "Mapping the *Imaginaire*: The Conditions of Possibility"; and Michael P. Cronin, *Osaka Modern: The City in Japanese Imaginary* (Cambridge, MA: Harvard University Press, 2017).

48. Collins, *Nirvana*, 4.
49. Matthew Kapstein, "Avant-propos," in Collins, *Civilisation et femmes célibataires*, 6.
50. For intellectual histories of the *Annales* school, see Francois Dosse, *New History in France: The Triumph of the* Annales (Urbana: University of Illinois Press, 1994), and André Burguiere, *The Annales School: An Intellectual History* (Ithaca, NY: Cornell University Press, 2009).
51. Collins, *Nirvana and Other Buddhist Felicities*, 73.
52. See Johann P. Arnason, "Creative Imagination," in *Cornelius Castoriadis: Key Concepts*, ed. Suzi Adams (London: Bloomsbury, 2014), 43–52.
53. Arnason, "Creative Imagination," 49.
54. Quoted from Collins's original ms.; not in the final edited version.
55. Steven Collins, "Buddhist 'Nuns' (*Mae Chi*) and the Teaching of Pali in Contemporary Thailand" (with Justin McDaniel) in *Self and Society*, 266–267.
56. Collins, "Categories, Concepts or Predicaments?" 46.
57. Collins, "Hadot, Foucault and Comparisons with Buddhism," 29; Collins, *Wisdom as a Way of Life*, 88.
58. Steven Collins, "What Are Buddhists *Doing* When They Deny the Self?" in *Self and Society*, 97–118.
59. Collins, "What Are Buddhists *Doing* When They Deny the Self?," 118, note 22.
60. Collins, "What Are Buddhists *Doing* When They Deny the Self?," 112.
61. McDaniel, "Editor's Introduction," xxxii.
62. Collins, "What Are Buddhists *Doing* When They Deny the Self?," 116.
63. Collins, *Wisdom as a Way of Life*, 13.
64. Collins, *Nirvana*, 4.
65. McDaniel, "Editor's Introduction," xxxii.
66. Collins, *Nirvana and Other Buddhist Felicities*, 76.
67. Peter Skilling, "King Rāma I and Wat Phra Chetuphon: the Buddhaśāsanā in Early Bangkok," in *How Theravāda is Theravāda: Exploring Buddhist Identities*, ed. Peter Skilling, Jason A. Carbine, Claudio

Cicuzza, and Santi Pakdeekham (Chiang Mai: Silkworm Books, 2012), 336–347.

68. Collins, *Wisdom as a Way of Life*, 20.
69. Skilling, "King Rāma I and Wat Phra Chetuphon," 336.
70. Michel Foucault, "Polemics, Politics and Problematizations," interview by P. Rabinow, May 1984, in *Essential Works of Foucault,* vol. 1 (New York: New Press, 1998).
71. Foucault, "Polemics, Politics and Problematizations."
72. Collins, *Wisdom as a Way of Life*, 94.

INDEX

Abhidhamma, 56, 106–7, 110
Aesop's Fables, 26–28, 36, 56
aggressivity, 132
ahiṃsā, 131
anattā (no-self), 95–97, 149, 172
animal stories, 41–45. *See also* specific *Birth Stories*
Annales school, 186
Anthony, Saint, xxxvii
Appleton, Naomi, 14, 24, 52, 54–55, 212–13*n*51
Aristotle, xxviii
Arnason, Johann P., 187
Asad, Tala, 222*n*33
asceticism: in *The Birth Stories*, 77–80; comparative study of, xxxi; defined, 204–5*n*6; and dress, 112–15; and living alone, 123–24; and Middle Way, 115–19; occasions for practice, 120–21, 124; and pacceka buddhas, 79–80; and philosophy, xxxvi; as requirement for social life, 153; and spiritual direction, 119–21; ten restrictions, 121–22; as violence against oneself, 131. *See also* askēsis; monasticism; practices of self
askēsis: and acculturation, xxxiv; in *The Birth Stories*, 8, 10; and civilizational study, xlix; comparative study of, lix; defined, 204–5*n*6; and devotional ritual, 111, 112; and Middle Way, 116; as minority practice, 204–5*n*6; and monasticism, xxxvi, xxxix; and philosophy, xxxii; as supererogatory, 8, 10, 11, 12; transformation as goal of, xxxiv; and translation issues, lvii; and wisdom, 57, 193. *See also* asceticism; practices of self
Aśoka, 10–11, 114
attha, 100

Bach, Johann Sebastian, 168–69
Barthes, Roland, 168, 175

reading *Wisdom as a Way of Life*, 165–71; and archive, 195–97; and authorial voice, 167; and civilizational study, 177, 183–84; and Collins Questions, 194–200; and entextualized aspirations, 182–84; and future orientation, 165, 166–67; and history of thought, 197–200; and imaginaire, 185–89, 196–97; intertextual approach, 170–71; and polyphony, 168–70. *See also* Collins's work

recollection of the Buddha, 124–28, 154

religion, concept of, xlv–xlvi, 160–61, 205–9*n*7

"Religious Rejections of the World and their Directions" (Weber), xxxix–xl

religious studies: Collins on, xxxii, xlv–xlvi, xlviii, 202–4*n*5; and narrative, 82

renunciant/renunciation, 32, 77–80. *See also* asceticism

reverence, 112, 217*n*28

Rhys Davids, Caroline, 155

Rhys Davids, T. W., 14, 15, 146, 148

Ricoeur, Paul, 220

riddles, 18, 61–62

Rouse, W. H. D., 52, 53

sādhana, 205*n*6

Sāmaññaphala (*The Fruits of Asceticism*), 66–67, 214*n*63

samatha/samādhi meditation, 87, 107–8, 142, 143–45, 216*n*22

saṃkhata, 80–81, 143

sammuti-sacca, 97–98, 99, 216*n*12. *See also* consensual truth

sati. *See* mindfulness

Satipaṭṭhāna Sutta, 145

Sayadaw, Ledi, 146

Sayadaw, Mahasi, 107, 146

Schober, Juliane, xvii, xlii

Schonthal, Benjamin, 163–64

self: denial of (anattā), 95–97, 149, 172; terms for, 91–92. *See also* subjectivity

Selfless Persons: Imagery and Thought in Theravada *Buddhism* (Collins), 164, 170, 171–72, 174–75

Senakapaṇḍita, 5, 83

Shaw, Sarah, 24, 54–55, 73–74, 75, 83, 109, 166

Siblin, Eric, 168–69

sikkhāpadas, 11–12

Skilling, Peter, 19–20, 197

Skilton, Andrew, 139

Smith, Wilfred Cantwell, 222*n*33

spiritual direction, 30–31, 119–21

spiritual exercises. *See* practices of self

Spiro, Melford, 53–54

Stoicism, 136, 159

Story About Repetition, The (*Abhiṇha Jātaka*), 43–44

subjectivity, 148–53

supererogatory dhamma (dhamma 2), 2, 7–12, 17, 183–84

Sutta Nipāta, 123

systematic thought: vs. narrative, xxvi–xxviii, xlix, 2, 19, 81, 174;

CPSIA information can be obtained
at www.ICGtesting.com
Printed in the USA
LVHW010957080820
662411LV00003B/5

9 780231 197212